BIG IDEAS MATH®
Modeling Real Life

Grade 4

Volume 1

Resources by Chapter

- Family Letter
- Warm-Ups
- Extra Practice
- Reteach
- Enrichment and Extension
- Chapter Self-Assessment

Big Ideas Learning™

Erie, Pennsylvania

Printed in the United States

ISBN 13: 978-1-63736-705-6

23456789—25 24 23 22 21

Contents

*Chapters 8–14 are in Volume 2.

About the Resources by Chapter

Family Letter (English and Spanish)

The Family Letters provide a way to quickly communicate to family members how they can help their student with the material of the chapter. They make the mathematics less intimidating and provide suggestions for helping students see mathematical concepts in common activities. A chart with the Learning Target and Success Criteria for each lesson is also provided.

Warm-Ups

Each lesson has three options for getting the class started. The Daily Skills Practice questions review previously-learned concepts. The Vocabulary Practice questions review previously-learned vocabulary words. The Prerequisite Skills Practice questions review prerequisite skills needed for the lesson.

Extra Practice

The Extra Practice exercises provide additional practice on the key concepts taught in the lesson.

Reteach

Each Reteach provides additional examples with more support for students who are struggling to understand the concepts. Exercises for these examples are also provided.

Enrichment and Extension

Each Enrichment and Extension extends the lesson and provides a challenging application of the key concepts.

Chapter Self-Assessment

Students can use the Chapter Self-Assessment to rate their understanding of the Learning Target and Success Criteria in each lesson.

Chapter 1

Name_____

Dear Family,

In this chapter, your student is learning place value concepts. The lessons address how to identify the values of the digits in multi-digit numbers, read and write multi-digit numbers in different forms, and use place value to compare and round multi-digit numbers. The vocabulary words associated with this chapter are: period, ones period, thousands period, and place value chart.

Your student can practice place value concepts by playing a number game. Write the digits 0–9 on two sets of index cards, with one digit on each card.

- Have your student select four index cards and arrange them to create a four-digit number. Then, have your student identify which digit is in each place value. Ask, "Which is the hundreds digit? The thousands?" Repeat using the cards to create five- and six-digit numbers.

- Give your student one set of the number cards and keep one for yourself. Each of you selects cards to create a four-digit number. Take turns identifying each other's number and writing it in standard form, word form, and expanded form. Repeat with five- and six-digit numbers.

- Select cards to create a four-digit number and have your student do the same. Take turns identifying the greater number and explaining your reasoning. Repeat with five- and six-digit numbers. Then, round the numbers to the nearest ten, hundred, thousand, ten thousand, and hundred thousand.

- State a rounded number, such as 500,000. Have your student use the cards to create two numbers that round to the given number. For example, say, "What is one number that rounds to 500,000 when rounded to the nearest hundred thousand? What is another number that rounds to 500,000?" Repeat using various rounded numbers and place values.

By the end of this chapter, your student should feel confident with the learning targets and success criteria on the next page. Encourage your student to look for numbers to round and compare, such as prices, page numbers in books, and numbers on license plates.

Have a great time practicing place value!

Lesson	Learning Target	Success Criteria
1.1 Understand Place Value	Identify the values of digits in multi-digit numbers.	• I can identify the first six place value names. • I can identify the value of each digit in a number. • I can compare the values of two of the same digits in a number.
1.2 Read and Write Multi-Digit Numbers	Read and write multi-digit numbers in different forms.	• I can write a number in standard form. • I can read and write a number in word form. • I can write a number in expanded form.
1.3 Compare Multi-Digit Numbers	Use place value to compare two multi-digit numbers.	• I can explain how to compare two numbers with the same number of digits. • I can use the symbols <, >, and = to compare two numbers.
1.4 Round Multi-Digit Numbers	Use place value to round multi-digit numbers.	• I can explain which digit I use to round and why. • I can round a multi-digit number to any place.

Nombre _____

Conceptos de valor posicional

Querida familia:

En este capítulo, su estudiante está aprendiendo conceptos de valor posicional. Las lecciones son para identificar los valores de los dígitos en números de varias cifras, leer y escribir números de varias cifras en diferentes formas, y usar el valor posicional para comparar y redondear números de varias cifras. Algunas palabras de vocabulario asociadas con este capítulo son: posición, posición de las unidades, posición de los miles, y tabla de valor posicional.

Su estudiante puede practicar conceptos de valor posicional jugando con los números. Escriba los dígitos del 0 al 9 para dos grupos de fichas, con un dígito por cada ficha.

- Haga que su estudiante seleccione cuatro fichas y las ordene para crear un número de cuatro cifras. Luego, haga que su estudiante identifique cual dígito está en cada valor posicional. Pregúntele, "¿Cuál es el dígito en la posición de las centenas? ¿Cuál en la posición de los miles?". Repita usando las fichas para crear números de cinco y seis cifras.

- Dele a su estudiante un grupo de las fichas de números y tome una para usted. Cada uno seleccione fichas para crear un número de cuatro cifras. Tomen turnos para identificar el número del otro y escríbanlo en su forma estandar, forma de palabra, y forma expandida. Repitan con números de cinco y seis cifras.

- Seleccione fichas para crear un número de cuatro cifras y que su estudiante haga lo mismo. Tomen turnos para identificar el número más grande y expliquen su razonamiento. Repitan con números de cinco y seis cifras. Luego, redondear los números a la decena más cercana, centena, miles, diez miles, y centenas de miles.

- De un número redondeado, por ejemplo 500,000. Haga que su estudiante use las fichas para crear dos números que redondeen al número dado. Por ejemplo, "¿Qué número redondea a 500,000 con respecto a la centena de miles más cercana? ¿Qué otro número redondea a 500,000?". Repita usando varios números redondeados y diferentes valores posicionales.

Al final de este capítulo, su estudiante debe sentirse seguro sobre los objetivos de aprendizaje y criterios de éxito que se indican en la siguiente página. Anime a su estudiante a observar números de cifras para redondear y comparar, como precios, números de página en libros, y números de placas de licencia.

¡Diviértanse practicando el valor posicional!

Lección	Objetivo de aprendizaje	Criterios de éxito
1.1 Entendiendo el valor posicional	Identificar los valores de los dígitos en un número de varias cifras.	• Sé identificar el nombre del valor de las seis primeras posiciones. • Sé identificar el valor de cada dígito en un número. • Sé comparar dos valores de un mismo dígito en un número.
1.2 Leer y escribir números de varias cifras	Leer y escribir números de varias cifras en diferentes formas.	• Sé escribir un número en forma estandar. • Sé leer y escribir un número en forma de palabra. • Sé escribir un número en forma expandida.
1.3 Comparar números de varias cifras	Usar el valor posicional para comparar dos números de varias cifras.	• Sé explicar cómo comparar dos cifras con la misma cantidad de dígitos. • Sé usar los símbolos <, >, y = para comparar dos números.
1.4 Redondear números de varias cifras	Usar el valor posicional para redondear dos números de varias cifras.	• Sé explicar cuál dígito uso para redondear y por qué. • Sé redondear un número de varias cifras a cualquier valor posicional.

Lesson 1.1 Daily Skills Practice
For use before Lesson 1.1

1. You have 6 baskets of apples. Each basket has 2 apples. How many apples do you have in all? Use the number line to help.

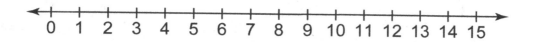

There are _____ apples in all.

Lesson 1.1 Vocabulary Practice
For use before Lesson 1.1

1. Write what you know about this phrase. Give an example.

standard form

Prerequisite Skills Practice

For use before Lesson 1.1

Circle the value of the underlined digit.

1. 40<u>7</u>   7   70   700

2. <u>5</u>36   5   500   50

Name _____

Write the value of the underlined digit.

1. 45,<u>7</u>18	**2.** 82,<u>0</u>15	**3.** 14,78<u>9</u>	**4.** <u>6</u>2,397
5. 248,3<u>1</u>1	**6.** <u>9</u>25,583	**7.** 7<u>2</u>3,610	**8.** 19<u>4</u>,762
9. 403,<u>2</u>27	**10.** <u>5</u>61,284	**11.** 315,6<u>7</u>5	**12.** 67<u>6</u>,219

Compare the values of the underlined digits.

13. <u>4</u>25 and <u>4</u>,037	**14.** <u>3</u>,715 and <u>3</u>41,095
15. 9<u>7</u>0 and 1<u>7</u>,525	**16.** 8,<u>3</u>25 and 6,54<u>2</u>

17. A member of the track team runs 6 miles per hour. A car can drive 60 miles per hour. The car is how many times faster than the runner?

_____

18. A CD is on sale for $9. A computer is on sale for $900. The computer costs how many times more money than the CD?

19. In the number 45,823, is the value in the thousands place 10 times the value in the hundreds place? Explain.

20. Write the greatest number possible using each number card once. Then write the least six-digit number possible.

7	2	4	6	5	8

Greatest: _____   Least: _____

21. In the number 32,376, is the value in the ten thousands place 10 times the value in the hundreds place? Explain.

22. Write the greatest number possible using each number card once. Then write the least four-digit number possible.

8	1	3	9

Greatest: _____   Least: _____

Use the table.

23. The land area of which state has a 2 in the thousands place?

_____

24. What is the value of the digit 9 in the land area of Georgia? in the land area of Hawaii? How do these values relate to each other?

U.S. State	Land Area (square miles)
Georgia	59,425
Hawaii	10,931
Kentucky	40,410
Ohio	44,825
South Carolina	32,030
West Virginia	24,230

25. Compare the value of the 3s in the land area of South Carolina.

Name _____

> A **place value chart** shows the value of each digit in a number. The value of each place is 10 times the value of the place to the right.
>
> The place value chart shows how the place values are grouped. Each group is called a period. In a number, periods are separated by commas.

> The 5 in this number is in the ten thousands place. It has a value of 5 ten thousands, or 50,000.

Thousands Period			Ones Period		
Hundreds	**Tens**	**Ones**	**Hundreds**	**Tens**	**Ones**
2	5	4,	9	3	6
2 hundred thousands	5 ten thousands	4 thousands	9 hundreds	3 tens	6 ones
200,000	50,000	4,000	900	30	6

Example

Thousands Period			Ones Period		
Hundreds	**Tens**	**Ones**	**Hundreds**	**Tens**	**Ones**
3	6	2,	2	4	7

- The number in standard form is 362,247.
- The value of the digit 3 is 3 hundred thousands, or 300,000.
- The value of the digit 2 in the thousands place is 2,000.
- The value of the digit 2 in the hundreds place is 200.
- The value of the digit 2 in the thousands place is 10 times the value of the digit 2 in the hundreds place.

Write the value of the underlined digit.

1. 46,931

2. 256,780

3. 581,429

4. 726,439

Compare the values of the underlined digits.

5. 30 and 300

6. 8,000 and 800

Name _____

Write a number to answer each riddle.

1. I have 5 digits.
   One digit has a value of 3,000.
   One digit has a value of 70,000.
   One digit has a value of 400 and is 10 times the value of another digit.
   What is the greatest number I can be?

_____

2. I have 5 digits.
   One digit has a value of 50.
   One digit has a value of 80,000.
   The thousands digit is 100 times the value of the tens digit.
   What is the least number I can be?

_____

3. I have 6 digits.
   One digit has a value of 9.
   One digit has a value of 300.
   The digit with the greatest place value is 7.
   The thousands digit is 10 times the value of the hundreds digit.
   What is the least number I can be?

_____

4. I have 5 digits.
   One digit has a value of 5,000.
   The digit with the greatest place value is 6.
   The digit with the least place value is 4.
   The hundreds digit is 100 times the value of another digit.
   What is the greatest number I can be?

1. Find the product.

   0 × 5 = _____

1. Write what you know about this word. Give an example.

   period

Write the value of the underlined digit.

1. 41,<u>3</u>07

2. 5<u>6</u>4,901

Name _____

Write the number in two other forms.

1. Standard form:

Word form:

Expanded form: 200,000 + 50,000 + 4,000 + 300 + 90 + 7

_____

2. Standard form:

Word form: thirty-five thousand, forty-seven

Expanded form:

_____

3. Standard form: 923,706

Word form:

Expanded form:

_____

4. Standard form:

Word form: sixty-one thousand, three hundred fifteen

Expanded form:

_____

5. Complete the table.

Standard Form	Word Form	Expanded Form
5,426		
		70,000 + 2,000 + 10 + 3
407,023		
	eight hundred three thousand, twelve	

Big Ideas Math: Modeling Real Life Grade 4   13
Resources by Chapter

6. Your teacher asks the class to write twenty thousand, four hundred seventy-five in standard form. Which student wrote the correct number? What mistake did the other student make?

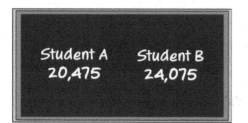

Student A   Student B
20,475   24,075

7. What is the number? The number has two periods. The thousands period is written as five hundred ten thousand in word form. The ones period is written as 90 + 8 in expanded form.

8. Use the table to write the number in standard form, word form, and expanded form.

| Braille Numbers |
1	2	3	4	5	6	7	8	9	0

9. Use the table above to write the number in standard form, word form, and expanded form.

10. Use the number 7,000 + 200 + 3 to complete the check.

PAY TO THE ORDER OF *Save the Whales* $ [ ] ← standard form

word form →

DOLLARS

MEMO *Donation*

AUTHORIZED SIGNATURE

123456789 09 02   12346694566 0003

0000
DATE

Name _____

Use place value to write numbers in expanded form.

Example Write the number in standard form, word form, and expanded form.

Thousands Period			Ones Period		
Hundreds	Tens	Ones	Hundreds	Tens	Ones
		4,	7	2	5

Standard form: 4,725

Word form: four thousand, seven hundred twenty-five

Expanded form: 4,000 + 700 + 20 + 5

Use a comma between periods in standard form and word form. Use a hyphen between two-word numbers from 21 to 99 when writing in word form.

Example Write the number in standard form, word form, and expanded form.

Thousands Period			Ones Period		
Hundreds	Tens	Ones	Hundreds	Tens	Ones
7	0	2,	0	5	1

Standard form: 702,051

Word form: seven hundred two thousand, fifty-one

Expanded form: 700,000 + 2,000 + 50 + 1

Write the number in two other forms.

1. Standard form: 24,520

Word form:

Expanded form:

_____

2. Standard form:

Word form: three hundred two thousand, four hundred

Expanded form:

Name _____

Enrichment and Extension

Use the code below to represent a number. Write the number in standard form, word form, and expanded form. Use each digit only once in each number.

1	2	3	4	5	6	7	8	9	0
★	▲	♥	☾	♦	●	■	❯	↑	✚

1. Create a 4-digit number using the code.

   Code:

   Standard form:

   Word form:

   Expanded form:

_____

2. Create a 5-digit number using the code.

   Code:

   Standard form:

   Word form:

   Expanded form:

_____

3. Create a 6-digit number using the code.

   Code:

   Standard form:

   Word form:

   Expanded form:

1. Use the number line to solve.

   For an activity, 15 students are divided into 3 groups. How many students are in each group?

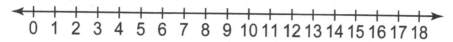

   15 ÷ 3 = _____

1. Write what you know about this word. Give an example.

   equivalent

Compare.

1. 475 $\bigcirc$ 481

2. 305 $\bigcirc$ 35

Name _____

Write which place to use when comparing the numbers.

1. 31,492 31,681	**2.** 725,124 732,063	**3.** 194,025 192,376
4. 20,954 20,937	**5.** 528,620 379,201	**6.** 954,677 955,892
7. 471,204 463,017	**8.** 14,381 12,515	**9.** 267,462 267,530

Compare.

10. 4,521 ◯ 4,530	**11.** 48,250 ◯ 49,123	**12.** 613,426 ◯ 612,578
13. 300,000 ◯ 30,000	**14.** 2,237 ◯ 3,136	**15.** 73,841 ◯ 80,950
16. 917,333 ◯ 917,421	**17.** 940,713 ◯ 876,924	**18.** 55,328 ◯ 55,327
19. 6,358 ◯ 6,361	**20.** 92,605 ◯ 92,506	**21.** 7,000 ◯ 600,000
22. 36,431 ◯ 36,413	**23.** 8,830 ◯ 8,645	**24.** 521,984 ◯ 507,699

Compare.

25. 24,650 ◯ 20,000 + 4,000 + 600 + 5 | **26.** thirty-five thousand ◯ 350,000

27. seven hundred thousand, twenty-six ◯ 726,000

28. four hundred ten thousand, sixty-five ◯ 410,605

29. 675,419 ◯ 600,000 + 70,000 + 5,000 + 400 + 10 + 9

30. 307,982 ◯ 300,000 + 70,000 + 900 + 80 + 2

31. Two different canoes cost $2,275 and $2,075. Which is the lesser price?

32. If the leftmost digits of two multi-digit numbers are both 7, can you explain which number is greater? Explain.

33. Which digits do you compare first when comparing multi-digit numbers? Explain.

34. Use the table to answer the questions.

Name two cities that have a greater population than Seattle. Name two cities that have a population that is less than Boston.

City Population	
Boston, MA	673,184
Baltimore, MD	614,664
Charlotte, NC	842,051
Detroit, MI	672,795
Fort Worth, TX	854,113
Seattle, WA	704,352

Name _____

Example Compare 7,245 and 7,218.

Start at the left. Compare the digits in each place value until the digits are different.

Thousands Period			Ones Period		
Hundreds	**Tens**	**Ones**	**Hundreds**	**Tens**	**Ones**
		7,	2	4	5
		7,	2	1	8

Step 1: Compare the thousands.
7 thousands = 7 thousands

Step 2: Compare the hundreds.
2 hundreds = 2 hundreds

Step 3: Compare the tens.
4 tens > 1 ten

The tens digits are different, so you don't have to compare the ones digits.

So, 7,245 > 7,218.

Write which place value to use when comparing the numbers.

1. 3,524
   3,810

2. 8,315
   7,920

3. 25,781
   25,726

Compare.

4. 6,348 6,572

5. 8,270 8,291

6. 57,011 ◯ 56,123

Name _____

1. Use the digits below to make two numbers that are compared by looking at the thousands digits. Use the numbers to complete the comparisons.

6 7 1 4 3 8 7 4 2 6

___ ___ , ___ ___ ___ > ___ ___ , ___ ___ ___

2. Use the digits below to make two numbers that are compared by looking at the hundreds digits. Use the numbers to complete the comparisons.

2 7 5 4 9 1 3 4 3 8 3 5

___ ___ ___ , ___ ___ ___ < ___ ___ ___ , ___ ___ ___

3. Use the digits below to make two numbers that are compared by looking at the ten thousands digits. Use the numbers to complete the comparisons.

8 2 3 2 3 6 5 8 9 6 9 5

___ ___ ___ , ___ ___ ___ > ___ ___ ___ , ___ ___ ___

1. Round to the nearest ten to estimate the difference.

$$
\begin{array}{r}
502 \\
-127 \\
\hline
\end{array}
$$

Lesson 1.4 **Vocabulary Practice**
For use before Lesson 1.4

1. Write what you know about this phrase. Give an example.

place value

Big Ideas Math: Modeling Real Life Grade 4   **23**
Resources by Chapter

Round the number to the nearest ten.

1. 347

_____

Round the number to the nearest hundred.

2. 648

Name _____

Round the number to the place of the underlined digit.

1. 7,9<u>3</u>2	**2.** 4,<u>1</u>76	**3.** <u>9</u>,531	**4.** 3<u>1</u>,427
5. <u>6</u>7,025	**6.** 13,<u>6</u>20	**7.** 73,8<u>5</u>4	**8.** 1<u>0</u>7,231
9. 4<u>9</u>5,148	**10.** 524,3<u>2</u>7	**11.** 925,<u>7</u>38	**12.** <u>3</u>61,950

Round the number to the nearest thousand.

13. 2,395	**14.** 54,614
15. 47,208	**16.** 8,542

Round the number to the nearest ten thousand.

17. 206,324	**18.** 784,675
19. 873,615	**20.** 125,399

Round the number to the nearest hundred thousand.

21. 471,302

22. 82,427

23. 147,319

24. 728,916

25. Round ★ to the nearest thousand and to the nearest ten thousand.

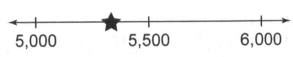

5,000   5,500   6,000

Nearest thousand: _____

Nearest ten thousand: _____

26. Which numbers round to 500,000 when rounded to the nearest hundred thousand?

| 526,725 | 583,000 | 548,900 |
| 453,215 | 445,999 | 54,285 |

27. When discussing the price of a video game, should you round to the nearest ten or the nearest hundred? Explain.

28. Newton says 29,675 rounds to 20,000 when rounded to the nearest thousand. Is he correct? Explain.

29. A car sales person sells several cars. The price of each car, rounded to the nearest thousand, is $24,000. Which could be the prices of the cars he sells?

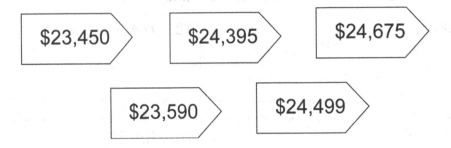

$23,450 $24,395 $24,675

$23,590 $24,499

Name _____

You can use a number line or place value to round a number. Find the multiple of 10, 100, 1,000, and so on, that is closest to the number.

Example Use a number line to round 6,820 to the nearest thousand.

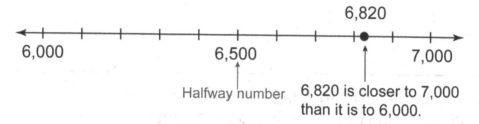

6,820 is closer to 7,000 than it is to 6,000.

So, 6,820 rounded to the nearest thousand is 7,000.

- -

Example Use place value to round 425,350 to the nearest ten thousand.

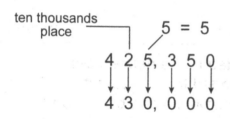

Look at the digit to the right of the rounding digit. If it is 5 or greater, the rounding digit increases by 1.

The digit to the right of the ten thousands place is 5. The ten thousands digit increases by 1.

So, 425,350 rounded to the nearest ten thousand is 430,000.

Round the number to the place of the underlined digit.

1. 3,725	**2.** 54,103	**3.** 39,650	**4.** 273,475

5. Round 671,340 to the nearest hundred thousand.	**6.** Round 8,215 to the nearest thousand.

Name _____

Enrichment and Extension

1. A number rounds to 6,500 when rounded to the nearest hundred. It rounds to 6,000 when rounded to the nearest thousand. What is one number that it could be? Round the number to the nearest ten.

_____

2. A number rounds to 45,000 when rounded to the nearest thousand. It rounds to 50,000 when rounded to the nearest ten thousand. What is one number that it could be? Round the number to the nearest hundred and the nearest ten.

_____

3. A number rounds to 750,000 when rounded to the nearest ten thousand. It rounds to 700,000 when rounded to the nearest hundred thousand. What is the greatest number it can be? Round the number to the nearest thousand, the nearest hundred, and the nearest ten.

_____

4. A number rounds to 350,000 when rounded to the nearest ten thousand. It rounds to 400,000 when rounded to the nearest hundred thousand. What is the least number it can be? Round the number to the nearest thousand, the nearest hundred, and the nearest ten.

Name _____

Chapter Self-Assessment

Use the scale below to rate your understanding of the learning target and the success criteria.

1	**2**	**3**	**4**
I do not understand.	I can do it with help.	I can do it on my own.	I can teach someone else.

	Rating
1.1 Understand Place Value	
Learning Target: Identify the values of digits in multi-digit numbers.	1 2 3 4
I can identify the first six place value names.	1 2 3 4
I can identify the value of each digit in a number.	1 2 3 4
I can compare the values of two of the same digits in a number.	1 2 3 4
1.2 Read and Write Multi-Digit Numbers	
Learning Target: Read and write multi-digit numbers in different forms.	1 2 3 4
I can write a number in standard form.	1 2 3 4
I can read and write a number in word form.	1 2 3 4
I can write a number in expanded form.	1 2 3 4
1.3 Compare Multi-Digit Numbers	
Learning Target: Use place value to compare two multi-digit numbers.	1 2 3 4
I can explain how to compare two numbers with the same number of digits.	1 2 3 4
I can use the symbols <, >, and = to compare two numbers.	1 2 3 4
1.4 Round Multi-Digit Numbers	
Learning Target: Use place value to round multi-digit numbers.	1 2 3 4
I can explain which digit I use to round and why.	1 2 3 4
I can round a multi-digit number to any place.	1 2 3 4

Chapter 2

Name _____

Dear Family,

In this chapter, your student is learning various strategies for adding and subtracting numbers with up to six digits. The lessons address estimating sums and differences, using estimates to check whether an answer is reasonable, choosing a strategy to add or subtract, and using addition to check subtraction. The vocabulary word associated with this chapter is *estimate*.

You and your student can practice addition and subtraction and review geography at the same time! Have your student think of places you have visited, cities where friends and family live, or landmarks he or she finds interesting. Then, use the Internet to learn about these places while practicing math.

- Have your student find the distance between your home and a chosen location. Then, have your student add to find how many miles it would be to travel from home to that location and back. Ask, "Did you have to regroup any place values? Which ones? Why did you need to regroup?" Extend this by including another location and finding the total distance. Say, "Suppose we travel to Chicago, then to Atlanta, then come home. How could you find how many miles we travel in all?"

- Have your student find the distances to two different locations. Have him or her estimate the difference in the distances, then subtract and see if the answer is reasonable. For example, "Aunt Gwen lives 540 miles away. Grandma lives 172 miles away. How can you estimate how much farther Aunt Gwen lives?" After subtracting, have your student explain why the answer is reasonable, then use addition to check the subtraction.

- Have your student read about interesting landmarks, then think of and solve addition and subtraction word problems related to the information. For example, "Mount Fuji is 12,388 feet tall. Mount Everest is 29,029 feet tall. How much taller is Mount Everest?" or "How many feet would you climb if you climbed both mountains?" Ask your student to explain how to use compensation and counting on to subtract, or partial sums and compensation to add.

By the end of this chapter, your student should feel confident with the learning targets and success criteria on the next page. Encourage your student to look for opportunities to add and subtract multi-digit numbers throughout the day.

Have a great time practicing math and geography!

Add and Subtract Multi-Digit Numbers

Lesson	Learning Target	Success Criteria
2.1 Estimate Sums and Differences	Use rounding to estimate sums and differences.	• I can use rounding to estimate a sum. • I can use rounding to estimate a difference. • I can explain what happens when I round to different place values.
2.2 Add Multi-Digit Numbers	Add multi-digit numbers and check whether the sum is reasonable.	• I can use place value to line up the numbers in an addition problem. • I can add multi-digit numbers, regrouping when needed. • I can estimate a sum to check whether my answer is reasonable.
2.3 Subtract Multi-Digit Numbers	Subtract multi-digit numbers and check my answer.	• I can use place value to line up the numbers in a subtraction problem. • I can subtract multi-digit numbers, regrouping when needed. • I can estimate a difference or use addition to check my answer.
2.4 Use Strategies to Add and Subtract	Use strategies to add and subtract multi-digit numbers.	• I can use strategies to add multi-digit numbers. • I can use strategies to subtract multi-digit numbers.
2.5 Problem Solving: Addition and Subtraction	Use the problem-solving plan to solve two-step addition and subtraction word problems.	• I can understand a problem. • I can make a plan to solve a problem using letters to represent the unknown numbers. • I can solve a problem and check whether my answer is reasonable.

Nombre _____

Querida familia:

En este capítulo, su estudiante está aprendiendo varias estrategias para sumar y restar números de hasta seis dígitos. Las lecciones se centran en estimaciones de sumas y diferencias, usar estimaciones para verificar si una respuesta es razonable, escoger una estrategia para sumar o restar y usar la suma para verificar una resta. Las palabras de vocabulario asociadas con este capítulo es *estimar*.

¡Usted y su estudiante pueden practicar sumar y restar, y revisar geografía al mismo tiempo! Haga que su estudiante piense en los lugares que ha visitado, ciudades donde viven amigos y familiares o puntos de referencia que encuentre interesantes. Luego, use internet para aprender acerca de estos lugares mientras practica matemática.

- Haga que su estudiante encuentre la distancia entre su casa y un lugar seleccionado. Luego, haga que su estudiante sume para determinar cuántas millas se viajarían desde casa hasta ese lugar y después de regreso. Pregunte, "¿Tuviste que reagrupar alguna posición de valor? ¿Cuáles? ¿Por qué necesitaste reagrupar?". Extienda esto incluyendo otros lugares y hallando la distancia total. Diga, "Supongamos que viajamos a Chicago, luego a Atlanta y después regresamos a casa ¿Cómo podrías determinar cuántas millas en total viajamos?".

- Haga que su estudiante encuentre las distancias entre dos lugares diferentes. Haga que estime la diferencia en las distancias, luego reste y verifique si su respuesta es razonable. Por ejemplo, "Tía Gwen vive a 540 millas de distancia. Abuela vive a 172 millas de distancia. ¿Cómo podrías estimar cuánto más lejos vive la tía Gwen?". Después de restar, haga que su estudiante explique por qué su respuesta es razonable, luego use la suma para verificar la resta.

- Haga que su estudiante lea acerca de puntos de referencia interesantes, luego piense y resuelva sumando y restando enunciados de problemas con la información. Por ejemplo, "Monte Fuji tiene 12,388 pies de altura. Monte Everest tiene 29,029 pies de altura ¿Cuánto más alto es el Monte Everest?" o "¿Cuántos pies escalarías si subieras hasta el tope ambas montañas?". Haga que su estudiante explique cómo usar compensación y llevar para restar, o sumas parciales y compensación para sumar.

Al final de este capítulo, su estudiante debe sentirse seguro sobre los objetivos de aprendizaje y criterios de éxito que se indican en la siguiente página. Anime a su estudiante a que esté pendiente durante el día de situaciones para sumar y restar números de varios dígitos.

¡Disfruten practicando juntos matemáticas y geografía!

Suma y resta de números de varios dígitos
(continuación)

Lección	Objetivo de aprendizaje	Criterios de éxito
2.1 Estimar sumas y diferencias	Usar redondeo para estimar sumas y diferencias.	• Sé usar redondeo para estimar una suma. • Sé usar redondeo para estimar una diferencia. • Sé explicar que sucede cuando redondeo a posiciones de valor diferentes.
2.2 Sumar números de varios dígitos	Sumar números de varios dígitos y verificar si el resultado es razonable.	• Sé usar el valor de la posición para alinear números es un problema de adición. • Sé sumar números de varios dígitos, reagruparlos cuando sea necesario. • Sé estimar una suma verificando si mi respuesta es razonable.
2.3 Restar números de varios dígitos	Restar números de varios dígitos y verificar el resultado.	• Sé usar el valor de la posición para alinear números es un problema de substracción. • Sé restar números de varios dígitos, reagruparlos cuando sea necesario. • Sé estimar una diferencia verificando si mi respuesta es razonable.
2.4 Usar estrategias para sumar y restar	Usar estrategias para sumar y restar números de varios dígitos.	• Sé usar estrategias para sumar números de varios dígitos. • Sé usar estrategias para restar números de varios dígitos.
2.5 Resolver problemas: Sumando y restando	Resolver enunciados de problemas usando el plan de sumando y restando a dos pasos.	• Sé entender un problema. • Sé hacer un plan para resolver un problema usando letras para representar los números desconocidos. • Sé resolver un problema y verificar si mi respuesta es razonable.

1. You buy a net and 3 jars. You spend $28. The net costs $10.
   Each jar costs the same amount. How much is each jar?

   Each jar costs $_____.

1. Write what you know about this phrase. Give an example.

   hundreds place

Prerequisite Skills Practice
For use before Lesson 2.1

Round the number to the place of the underlined digit.

1. <u>4</u>,395

---

2. 6<u>1</u>7,450

Name_____

Estimate the sum or difference.

1.   9,143 ⟶ [ ]
    + 5,437 ⟶ + [ ]
    _____
              [ ]

2.   17,328 ⟶ [ ]
    + 25,689 ⟶ + [ ]
    _____
                [ ]

3.   8,076 ⟶ [ ]
    − 2,715 ⟶ − [ ]
    _____
              [ ]

4.   72,345 ⟶ [ ]
    − 34,703 ⟶ − [ ]
    _____
                [ ]

5.   93,721
    − 65,283
    _____

6.   48,078
    + 86,715
    _____

7.   36,751
    − 14,329
    _____

8.   59,372
    + 42,363
    _____

9.   725,740
    − 236,419
    _____

10.   460,553
     + 108,332
     _____

11.   916,463
     − 368,275
     _____

12.   583,620
     + 254,681
     _____

13.   643,227
     − 158,341
     _____

Estimate the sum or difference.

14. 418,734 − 293,415 = _____

15. 531,862 + 54,163 = _____

16. 382,061 + 421,625 = _____

17. 627,183 − 33,426 = _____

18. Newton estimates a difference by rounding each number to the nearest hundred thousand. His estimate is 300,000. Which problems could he have estimated?

782,315 − 52,498	437,964 − 85,376
822,763 − 362,180	476,208 − 183,115

19. When might you estimate the sum of 715,385 and 298,721 to the nearest thousand? to the nearest hundred thousand?

20. During an election, 41,736 people voted for the one of the candidates and 57,412 people voted for the other candidate. About how many people voted in the election?

21. You read 12,356 pages in a year. Your friend reads 3,682 fewer pages than you. About how many pages does your friend read?

22. There are 28,135 fiction books checked out of the library. There are 17,892 non-fiction books checked out. About how many books are checked out of the library in all?

23. You earn 6,285 points at the arcade. Your friend earns 8,791 points. About how many points do you and your friend earn altogether?

Name_____

An **estimate** is a number that is close to an exact number. You can use rounding to estimate when you add and subtract.

Look at the hundreds digit to round to the nearest thousand.

Look at the tens digit to round to the nearest hundred.

Example Estimate: 7,325 + 5,864.

One Way: Round each addend to the nearest hundred. Then add.

7,325 →	7,300
+ 5,864 → +	5,900
	13,200

So, 7,325 + 5,864 is about 13,200.

Another Way: Round each addend to the nearest thousand. Then add.

7,325 →	7,000
+ 5,864 → +	6,000
	13,000

So, 7,325 + 5,864 is about 13,000.

Example Estimate: 432,530 − 21,305.

One Way: Round each number to the nearest thousand. Then subtract.

432,530 →	433,000
− 21,305 → −	21,000
	412,000

So, 432,530 − 21,305 is about 412,000.

Another Way: Round each number to nearest ten thousand. Then subtract.

432,530 →	430,000
− 21,305 → −	20,000
	410,000

So, 432,530 − 21,305 is about 410,000.

Estimate the sum or difference.

1.
52,695 →	
+ 37,215 → +	

2.
6,328 →	
− 3,871 → −	

Name _____

Enrichment and Extension

1. Which does *not* show 8,736 rounded to a nearest place value?

   9,000   8,700   8,800

---

2. Which do *not* show 62,395 rounded to a nearest place value?

   62,000   63,000   62,400   63,400   100,000

---

3. Which do *not* show 46,271 rounded to a nearest place value?

   47,000   46,200   100,000   46,000   46,300   47,300

---

4. Which do *not* show 235,418 rounded to a nearest place value?

   300,000   240,000   200,000   236,000   235,400

---

5. Which do *not* show 457,283 rounded to a nearest place value?

   460,000   458,000   500,000   457,300   400,000   450,000

Daily Skills Practice
For use before Lesson 2.2

1. Find the equivalent fraction.

$$\frac{2}{3} = \frac{\square}{6}$$

Lesson 2.2 **Vocabulary Practice**
For use before Lesson 2.2

1. Write what you know about this word. Give an example.

addend

Estimate the sum or difference.

1.
```
    4 2 3,7 1 9
  + 3 8 1,0 9 6
  _____
```

2.
```
    7 4 6,8 5 2
  - 2 7 3,9 1 5
  _____
```

Name_____

Find the sum. Check whether your answer is reasonable.

1. Estimate: _____

$$\begin{array}{r} 7,436 \\ +\ 5,815 \\ \hline \end{array}$$

2. Estimate: _____

$$\begin{array}{r} 9,238 \\ +\ 6,572 \\ \hline \end{array}$$

3. Estimate: _____

$$\begin{array}{r} 62,482 \\ +\ \ \ 2,941 \\ \hline \end{array}$$

4. Estimate: _____

$$\begin{array}{r} 24,175 \\ +\ \ \ 4,537 \\ \hline \end{array}$$

5. Estimate: _____

$$\begin{array}{r} 53,810 \\ +\ 38,726 \\ \hline \end{array}$$

6. Estimate: _____

$$\begin{array}{r} 43,804 \\ +\ 76,318 \\ \hline \end{array}$$

7. Estimate: _____

$$\begin{array}{r} 85,436 \\ +\ 92,775 \\ \hline \end{array}$$

8. Estimate: _____

$$\begin{array}{r} 625,319 \\ +\ \ \ 73,742 \\ \hline \end{array}$$

9. Estimate: _____

$$\begin{array}{r} 817,856 \\ +\ \ \ 45,390 \\ \hline \end{array}$$

10. Estimate: _____

$$\begin{array}{r} 228,363 \\ +\ 704,683 \\ \hline \end{array}$$

11. Estimate: _____

$$\begin{array}{r} 385,712 \\ +\ 532,184 \\ \hline \end{array}$$

12. Estimate: _____

$$\begin{array}{r} 447,650 \\ +\ 176,351 \\ \hline \end{array}$$

Find the sum. Check whether your answer is reasonable.

13. Estimate: _____

921,934 + 3,581 = _____

14. Estimate: _____

764,325 + 68,903 = _____

15. Estimate: _____

138,463 + 29,648 = _____

16. Estimate: _____

658,103 + 215,899 = _____

17. Find and explain the error. What is the correct sum?

```
   3 4 6,7 1 2
+     2 4,3 3 4
_____
   3 7 0,0 4 6
```

18. Write a word problem that can be solved by finding the sum of 34,781 and 48,227.

19. A school wants to collect 3,500 pounds of items to recycle. They collect 1,928 pounds of plastic and 1,579 pounds of glass. Did the school collect enough items to meet its goal?

20. The high score on Video Game A is 42,872 points less than the high score on Video Game B. What is the high score on Video Game B?

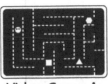

Video Game A: 364,739 points

Video Game B: ?

Name_____

Lesson 2.2 **Reteach**

When you add:

- Estimate the sum.
- Line up the addends by place value.
- Regroup when the sum of a place value is 10 or more.

Example Add: 209,580 + 75,040.

Estimate: 210,000 + 75,000 = 285,000

```
        1
   2 0 9, 5 8 0    Add the ones first then the tens.
 +   7 5, 0 4 0    Regroup 12 tens as 1 hundred
 ─────────────     and 2 tens.
            2 0
```

Start with the ones. Line up the addends by place value.

```
     1   1
   2 0 9, 5 8 0    Add the hundreds then the thousands.
 +   7 5, 0 4 0    Regroup 14 thousands as 1 ten
 ─────────────     thousand and 4 thousands.
        4, 6 2 0
```

```
     1   1
   2 0 9, 5 8 0    Add the ten thousands then
 +   7 5, 0 4 0    hundred thousands.
 ─────────────
   2 8 4, 6 2 0
```

The sum is 284,620. This is close to the estimate of 285,000, so the answer is reasonable.

Find the sum. Check whether your answer is reasonable.

1. Estimate: _____

```
   1 5, 3 7 5
 + 8 2, 6 3 4
 ───────────
```

2. Estimate: _____

```
   4 6 3, 8 2 5
 +     9, 0 8 3
 ─────────────
```

Name _____

Newton completed the problems below. Is his work correct? If not, explain.

1. Estimate: 400,000

$$\begin{array}{r} \overset{1}{}\overset{1}{} \\ 3\,6\,4,3\,2\,5 \\ +\ 2\,7,1\,8\,6 \\ \hline 6\,3\,6,1\,8\,5 \end{array}$$

2. Estimate: 390,000

$$\begin{array}{r} \overset{1}{}\overset{1}{} \\ 1\,4\,5,7\,9\,2 \\ +\ 2\,3\,9,6\,0\,4 \\ \hline 3\,8\,5,3\,9\,6 \end{array}$$

3. Estimate: 920,000

$$\begin{array}{r} \overset{1}{}\overset{1}{}\overset{1}{} \\ 8\,7\,6,9\,1\,2 \\ +\ \ \ 4\,3,1\,7\,5 \\ \hline 9\,2\,0,0\,8\,7 \end{array}$$

4. Estimate: 760,000

$$\begin{array}{r} \overset{1}{} \\ 5\,2\,8,1\,9\,3 \\ +\ 2\,3\,4,1\,5\,3 \\ \hline 7\,6\,2,2\,4\,6 \end{array}$$

Daily Skills Practice
For use before Lesson 2.3

1. What is the total mass shown?

The total mass is _____ grams.

Vocabulary Practice
For use before Lesson 2.3

1. Write what you know about this word. Give an example.

difference

Big Ideas Math: Modeling Real Life Grade 4   **49**
Resources by Chapter

Prerequisite Skills Practice

Find the sum. Check whether your answer is reasonable.

1. Estimate:

542,935 + 7,419 = _____

2. Estimate:

315,208 + 34,628 = _____

Name_____

Find the difference. Then check your answer.

1.   7,235
    − 2,940
    _____

2.   5,612
    − 3,621
    _____

3.   82,705
    −   6,432
    _____

4.   45,143
    −   4,089
    _____

5.   70,381
    − 14,203
    _____

6.   92,175
    − 35,698
    _____

7.   38,206
    − 24,715
    _____

8.   67,112
    − 39,018
    _____

9.   725,300
    −   52,225
    _____

10.   146,375
    −   72,193
    _____

11.   536,041
    − 172,131
    _____

12.   974,215
    − 882,042
    _____

13.   215,871
    − 203,184
    _____

14.   495,307
    − 186,573
    _____

15.   600,395
    − 227,608
    _____

Find the difference. Then check your answer.

16. 875,419 − 9,325 = _____

17. 603,200 − 8,535 = _____

18. 328,416 − 31,605 = _____

19. 455,866 − 48,783 = _____

20. Write and solve a subtraction word problem using the numbers 27,305 and 9,413.

Use the time line to answer the questions.

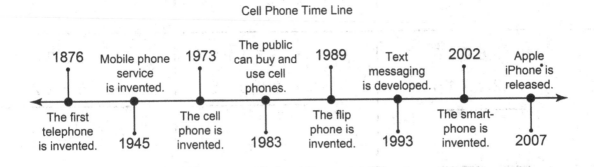

Cell Phone Time Line

21. How many years after mobile phone service was invented was text messaging developed?

22. How many years passed from the invention of the first telephone to the year the public could buy and use cell phones?

Name_____

Lesson 2.3 Reteach

When you subtract:

- Line up the numbers by place value.
- Subtract the ones, then move to the next place value.
- Regroup if necessary.
- Add to check your answer.

Example Subtract: 74,875 − 6,129.

$$\begin{array}{r} {}^{6\ 15} \\ 7\,4,\,8\,\cancel{7}\,\cancel{5} \\ -\quad 6,\,1\,2\,9 \\ \hline 4\ 6 \end{array}$$

Start with the ones. Regroup 7 tens and 5 ones as 6 tens and 15 ones.

Subtract the ones, then the tens.

$$\begin{array}{r} {}^{6\ 14}\quad {}^{6\ 15} \\ \cancel{7}\,\cancel{4},\,8\,\cancel{7}\,\cancel{5} \\ -\quad 6,\,1\,2\,9 \\ \hline 7\ 4\ 6 \end{array}$$

Subtract the hundreds.

Regroup 7 ten thousands and 4 thousands as 6 ten thousands and 14 thousands.

$$\begin{array}{r} {}^{6\ 14}\quad {}^{6\ 15} \\ \cancel{7}\,\cancel{4},\,8\,\cancel{7}\,\cancel{5} \\ -\quad 6,\,1\,2\,9 \\ \hline 6\,8,\,7\,4\,6 \end{array}$$

Subtract the thousands, then the ten thousands.

The difference is 68,746.

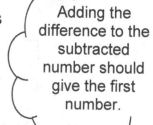

Adding the difference to the subtracted number should give the first number.

Add to check your answer.

$$\begin{array}{r} {}^{1}\qquad {}^{1} \\ 6\,8,\,7\,4\,6 \\ +\quad 6,\,1\,2\,9 \\ \hline 7\,4,\,8\,7\,5 \end{array}$$

Find the difference. Then check your answer.

1.
$$\begin{array}{r} 8,3\,2\,5 \\ -6,2\,4\,0 \\ \hline \end{array}$$

2.
$$\begin{array}{r} 4\,5,9\,7\,2 \\ -1\,8,2\,0\,3 \\ \hline \end{array}$$

Name _____

Use each set of numbers to create two subtraction problems. Add
to check your work.

1.

10,100	15,375	20,480

8,500	11,980	5,275

```
    ┌──────────┐          ┌──────────┐
    │          │          │          │
    └──────────┘          └──────────┘
    ┌──────────┐          ┌──────────┐
  - │          │        - │          │
    └──────────┘          └──────────┘
    ──────────            ──────────
    ┌──────────┐          ┌──────────┐
    │          │          │          │
    └──────────┘          └──────────┘
```

2.

37,415	25,750	18,115

19,500	19,300	45,250

```
    ┌──────────┐          ┌──────────┐
    │          │          │          │
    └──────────┘          └──────────┘
    ┌──────────┐          ┌──────────┐
  - │          │        - │          │
    └──────────┘          └──────────┘
    ──────────            ──────────
    ┌──────────┐          ┌──────────┐
    │          │          │          │
    └──────────┘          └──────────┘
```

3.

316,475	304,945	48,750

350,795	45,850	365,225

```
    ┌──────────┐          ┌──────────┐
    │          │          │          │
    └──────────┘          └──────────┘
    ┌──────────┐          ┌──────────┐
  - │          │        - │          │
    └──────────┘          └──────────┘
    ──────────            ──────────
    ┌──────────┐          ┌──────────┐
    │          │          │          │
    └──────────┘          └──────────┘
```

Daily Skills Practice
For use before Lesson 2.4

1. Find the product.

   $2 \times 6 =$ _____

Vocabulary Practice
For use before Lesson 2.4

1. Write what you know about this word. Give an example.

   sum

Prerequisite Skills Practice
For use before Lesson 2.4

Find the difference. Then check your answer.

1.
$$\begin{array}{r} 8,325 \\ -\ 2,746 \\ \hline \end{array}$$

2.
$$\begin{array}{r} 54,10 \\ -\ 7,34 \\ \hline \end{array}$$

Name_____

Lesson 2.4 Extra Practice

Find the sum or difference. Then check your answer.

1.
```
   8,4 1 9
 + 3,7 2 5
 _____
```

2.
```
   9,5 4 3
 - 6,2 1 3
 _____
```

3.
```
   6,7 8 2
 + 7,0 0 9
 _____
```

4.
```
   7,5 8 2
 - 1,4 8 3
 _____
```

5.
```
  1 6,3 1 5
 +   8,5 2 7
 _____
```

6.
```
   6,3 0 0
 - 4,2 7 5
 _____
```

7.
```
  1 9,3 4 5
 -   3,7 2 1
 _____
```

8.
```
  2 4 5,8 6 0
 +   3 6,1 7 3
 _____
```

9.
```
  4 2 8,3 3 0
 +   5 4,2 8 1
 _____
```

10. 634,726 − 45,218 = _____

11. 827,306 + 62,813 = _____

12. 325,090 + 127,305 = _____

13. 731,062 − 534,713 = _____

14. 902,470 − 410,625 = _____

15. 186,304 + 326,278 = _____

16. Your friend uses partial sums to add. Is your friend correct? Explain.

$$
\begin{array}{rcrcrcrcrcr}
35,204 & = & 30,000 & + & 5,000 & & & + & 20 & + & 4 \\
+\ 14,365 & = & 10,000 & + & 4,000 & + & 300 & + & 60 & + & 5 \\
\hline
& & 40,000 & + & 9,000 & + & 300 & + & 80 & + & 9 \\
\end{array}
$$

$= 49,389$

17. Your friend uses compensation to add. Is your friend correct? Explain.

$$
\begin{array}{ccccc}
73,236 - 36 & & 73,200 & & 88,650 \\
+\ 15,450 & \longrightarrow & +\ 15,450 & \longrightarrow & +\quad\ \ 36 \\
\cline{3-3}\cline{5-5}
& & 88,650 & & 88,686 \\
\end{array}
$$

18. Which strategy would you use to subtract 7,075 from 63,109? Explain.

19. There are about 700,000 students in a city. About 89,300 of the students are in the fourth grade. How many of the students are *not* in the fourth grade?

20. Students turn in a total of $43,975 from selling candles for a fundraiser. They turn in $9,250 on Monday. Then they turn in $7,175 each day on Tuesday and Wednesday. The rest of the money is turned in on Thursday. How much money is turned in on Thursday?

Name_____

You can choose a strategy to use to add or subtract.

Example Add: 4,015 + 1,230.

One Way: Use partial sums to add.

Use the expanded form of each addend.

$$4,015 = 4,000 \qquad + 10 + 5$$
$$+ \ 1,230 = 1,000 + 200 + 30 +$$
$$\overline{5,000 + 200 + 40 + 5 = 5,245}$$

Example Subtract: 15,000 − 4,975.

One Way: Count on to subtract.

- Start at the number being taken away.
- Count on to the first number.
- Add the amount of each jump.

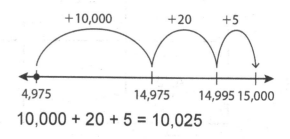

$$10,000 + 20 + 5 = 10,025$$

Another Way: Use compensation.

$$\begin{array}{r} 4,015 - 15 \\ + 1,230 \end{array} \longrightarrow \begin{array}{r} 4,000 \\ + 1,230 \\ \hline 5,230 \end{array}$$

Add or subtract to make a number that is easy to use.

You added 15 less than 4,015. Now add 15 to the answer.

$$\begin{array}{r} 5,230 \\ + \quad 15 \\ \hline 5,245 \end{array}$$

So, 4,015 + 1,230 = 5,245.

Another Way: Use compensation.

$$\begin{array}{r} 15,000 \\ - \ 4,975 + 25 \end{array} \longrightarrow \begin{array}{r} 15,000 \\ - \ 5,000 \\ \hline 10,000 \end{array}$$

You subtracted 25 more than 4,975. Now add 25 to the answer.

$$\begin{array}{r} 10,000 \\ + \quad 25 \\ \hline 10,025 \end{array}$$

So, 15,000 − 4,975 = 10,025.

Find the sum or difference. Then check your answer.

1. $\begin{array}{r} 8,300 \\ + 7,435 \end{array}$

2. $\begin{array}{r} 6,510 \\ - 4,105 \end{array}$

Name _____

Enrichment and Extension

1. Fill in the missing numbers. The sum of each row and each column should match the number beside the arrow.

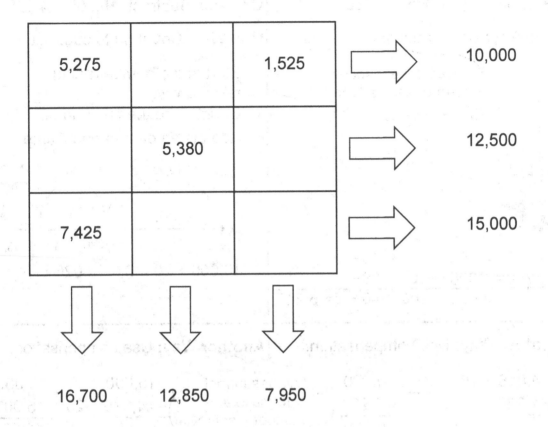

2. Explain how you found the missing numbers.

_____

_____

3. Choose one of the sums for the rows. Write three different addends that have that sum.

_____

Lesson 2.5 Daily Skills Practice
For use before Lesson 2.5

1. Compare.

7,786  7,807

Lesson 2.5 Vocabulary Practice
For use before Lesson 2.5

1. Write what you know about this word. Give an example.

compensation

Find the sum or difference. Then check your answer.

1.
$$\begin{array}{r} 7,425 \\ +\ 6,810 \\ \hline \end{array}$$

2.
$$\begin{array}{r} 34,609 \\ -\ \ 8,243 \\ \hline \end{array}$$

Name_____

Understand the problem. Then make a plan. How will you solve? Explain.

1. A music sales company receives a shipment of 200,000 CDs. At the end of the first day of a sale, 135,697 of the CDs are left. The company sells 47,319 more CDs. How many CDs were sold during the sale?

2. An elephant eats about 2,400 pounds of food each week. A large dog eats about 182 pounds of food each year. How much more food does an elephant eat in 1 week than a dog eats in 2 years?

3. A theme park sold 52,000 tickets one day. The park sold 7,531 tickets before it opened in the morning. By noon, 34,493 more tickets were sold. How many more tickets did the theme park sell for the day?

4. A water park uses 18,000 gallons of water per day. A golf course uses 854 gallons of water per day. A car wash uses 3,360 gallons of water per day. How many more gallons of water does the water park use each day than the golf course and car wash combined?

5. A farmer has 1,217 pounds of vegetables. After selling some vegetables to a restaurant, he has 843 pounds left. Then he sells 326 pounds of vegetables at the farmers' market. How many pounds of vegetables does he sell in all?

6. There are 1,468 students at Lakeside School. There are 376 more students at Oak Hill School. How many students are there in all in both schools?

7. A national park has 215,378 fewer visitors in July than in May and June combined. The park has 323,419 visitors in May and 438,756 visitors in June. How many visitors does the national park have in July?

8. Write and solve a two-step word problem that can be solved using both addition and subtraction.

9. George Washington lived from 1732 to 1799. Abraham Lincoln lived from 1809 to 1865. How many years longer did Washington live than Lincoln?

10. Your class sells 60 adult tickets and 80 children's tickets for the school play. Adult tickets cost $7 each and children's tickets cost $5 each. Your class wants to sell a total of $1,200 worth of tickets. How many more dollars worth of tickets does your class need to sell?

11. Your family travels 1,549 miles from Dallas, Texas, to Boston, Massachusetts. Then, your family travels another 1,257 miles from Boston to Miami, Florida. Your uncle travels 8,581 miles from Dallas to Sydney, Australia, for business. Then, your uncle travels another 7,332 miles from Sydney to Anchorage, Alaska. How many more miles does your uncle travel than your family?

12. After your trip, your family travels 1,119 miles from Miami back to Dallas. Your uncle travels 3,043 miles from Anchorage back to Dallas. How many miles have your family and your uncle traveled in all?

Name _____

Lesson 2.5 Reteach

Example There are 3,500 adults and 2,150 children at the zoo. 750 people leave. How many people are still at the zoo?

Understand the Problem

Think: What do I know?
- There are 3,500 adults.
- There are 2,150 children.
- 750 people leave.

Think: What do I need to find?
- How many people are left.

Make a Plan

Think: What will I do to find the answer?
- Step 1: Add to find the total number of people.
- Step 2: Subtract to find how many are left.

Solve

Step 1:

3,500 adults	2,150 children

k = total number of people

$$
\begin{array}{r}
3,500 \\
+\,2,150 \\
\hline
5,650
\end{array}
$$

k is the unknown sum.
$3,500 + 2,150 = k$
$5,650 = k$

Step 2:

n	750

$5,650$ = total number of people

$$
\begin{array}{r}
5,650 \\
-\,\ \ \ 750 \\
\hline
4,900
\end{array}
$$

n is the unknown difference.
$5,650 - 750 = n$
$4,900 = n$

So, there are 4,900 people still at the zoo.

1. 350 more people come to the zoo, but 730 more people leave. How many people are at the zoo now? How will you solve? Explain.

Name _____

1. The county fair was from Thursday through Sunday. On Thursday, 13,256 people went to the fair. On Friday, 4,718 more people went than on Thursday. Twice as many people went on Saturday as on Thursday. A total of 75,000 people went to the fair in all. How many people went on Sunday?

2. Descartes surveyed people about their favorite color. 1,275 people chose blue and 3,834 people chose green. 986 fewer people chose yellow than green. 2,315 more people chose red than blue. What color did the most people choose? How many people did Descartes survey in all?

3. What are two different ways to solve the problem below? Explain both plans and find the answer.

   Newton's class collects 12,725 items to recycle. They collect 3,481 aluminum cans and 2,591 more glass bottles than cans. The rest of the items they collect are plastic. How many plastic items does the class collect?

   One Way:

   Another Way:

Name _____

Chapter 2 | Chapter Self-Assessment

Use the scale below to rate your understanding of the learning target and the success criteria.

1	2	3	4
I do not understand.	I can do it with help.	I can do it on my own.	I can teach someone else.

	Rating
2.1 Estimate Sums and Differences	
Learning Target: Use rounding to estimate sums and differences.	1 2 3 4
I can use rounding to estimate a sum.	1 2 3 4
I can use rounding to estimate a difference.	1 2 3 4
I can explain what happens when I round to different place values.	1 2 3 4
2.2 Add Multi-Digit Numbers	
Learning Target: Add multi-digit numbers and check whether the sum is reasonable.	1 2 3 4
I can use place value to line up the numbers in an addition problem.	1 2 3 4
I can add multi-digit numbers, regrouping when needed.	1 2 3 4
I can estimate a sum to check whether my answer is reasonable.	1 2 3 4
2.3 Subtract Multi-Digit Numbers	
Learning Target: Subtract multi-digit numbers and check my answer.	1 2 3 4
I can use place value to line up the numbers in a subtraction problem.	1 2 3 4
I can subtract multi-digit numbers, regrouping when needed.	1 2 3 4
I can estimate a difference or use addition to check my answer.	1 2 3 4

Name _____

	Rating
2.4 Use Strategies to Add and Subtract	
Learning Target: Use strategies to add and subtract multi-digit numbers.	1 2 3 4
I can use strategies to add multi-digit numbers.	1 2 3 4
I can use strategies to subtract multi-digit numbers.	1 2 3 4
2.5 Problem Solving: Addition and Subtraction	
Learning Target: Use the problem-solving plan to solve two-step addition and subtraction word problems.	1 2 3 4
I can understand a problem.	1 2 3 4
I can make a plan to solve a problem using letters to represent the unknown numbers.	1 2 3 4
I can solve a problem and check whether my answer is reasonable.	1 2 3 4

Chapter 3

Name_____

Dear Family,

In this chapter, your student is learning how to multiply one-digit numbers by tens, hundreds, and thousands. The lessons address how to estimate products by rounding, and to multiply using properties, expanded form, and partial products. The vocabulary words associated with this chapter are: Distributive Property and partial products.

Your student can practice multiplying by one-digit numbers while looking at prices at home or at the store!

- While shopping, look at whole-number price tags. For items that are less than $10, ask your student to name a two-digit number, then find the total cost of that many of the item. For example, if a jar of peanut butter costs $4, ask, "How could you find the total cost of 23 jars of peanut butter? What would the total cost be?" Encourage your student to explain more than one strategy for finding the answer. Have your student draw an area model and explain how it can be used to multiply.

- At home, look through advertisements for items that have a three-digit price. Have your student point out the digits in each place value. Then, have him or her use partial products to find the total cost of several of the items. Remember to select a single-digit number of items. For example, your student might select a $425 TV. Guide your student to find the total cost of 3 TVs. Ask, "What is the product of 3 and 4 hundreds? What is the product of 3 and 2 tens? What is the product of 3 and 5 ones?" Then, have your student add the partial products. Continue by asking, "Can you find an item that costs about 3 times as much as your item? Is there an item that costs about 8 times as much?"

- Ask your student to name an item that might have a four-digit price. Look up the cost of the item online. Roll a number cube and have your student estimate the total cost of that many of the item. Then, have your student choose a strategy to multiply. Have your student compare the total cost with the estimate and explain whether the answer is reasonable. Encourage your student to think of word problems involving multiplication that you can solve together.

By the end of this chapter, your student should feel confident with the learning targets and success criteria on the next page. Encourage your student to think of other contexts in which he or she can multiply by one-digit numbers, such as finding the number of minutes in the hours of school each day, and then the minutes each week.

Have a great time practicing multiplication!

Lesson	Learning Target	Success Criteria
3.1 Understand Multiplicative Comparisons	Use multiplication to compare two numbers.	• I can write addition or multiplication equations given a comparison sentence. • I can write a comparison sentence given an addition or a multiplication sentence. • I can solve comparison word problems involving multiplication.
3.2 Multiply Tens, Hundreds, and Thousands	Use place value to multiply by tens, hundreds, or thousands.	• I can find the product of a one-digit number and a multiple of ten, one hundred, or one thousand. • I can describe a pattern when multiplying by tens, hundreds, or thousands.
3.3 Estimate Products by Rounding	Use rounding to estimate products.	• I can use rounding to estimate a product. • I can find two estimates that a product is between. • I can tell whether a product is reasonable.
3.4 Use the Distributive Property to Multiply	Use the Distributive Property to Multiply.	• I can draw an area model to multiply. • I can use known facts to find a product. • I can explain how to use the Distributive Property.
3.5 Use Expanded Form to Multiply	Use expanded form and the Distributive Property to multiply.	• I can use an area model to multiply. • I can use expanded form and the Distributive Property to find a product.
3.6 Use Partial Products to Multiply	Use place value and partial products to multiply.	• I can use place value to tell the value of each digit in a number. • I can write the partial products for a multiplication problem. • I can add the partial products to find a product.
3.7 Multiply Two-Digit Numbers by One-Digit Numbers	Multiply two-digit numbers by one-digit numbers.	• I can multiply to find the partial products. • I can show 10 ones regrouped as 1 ten. • I can find the product.
3.8 Multiply Three- and Four-Digit Numbers by One-Digit Numbers	Multiply multi-digit numbers by one-digit numbers.	• I can multiply to find the partial products. • I can show how to regroup more than 10 tens. • I can find the product.
3.9 Use Properties to Multiply	Use properties to multiply.	• I can use the Commutative Property of Multiplication to multiply. • I can use the Associative Property of Multiplication to multiply. • I can use the Distributive Property to multiply.
3.10 Problem Solving: Multiplication	Solve multi-step word problems involving multiplication.	• I can understand a problem. • I can make a plan to solve using letters to represent the unknown numbers. • I can solve a problem using an equation.

Capítulo 3 · Multiplicar por un dígito

Querida familia:

En este capítulo, el alumno aprende a multiplicar números de un dígito por decenas, centenas y unidades de mil. La lección aborda la manera de estimar productos por redondeo y multiplicar usando propiedades, en forma desarrollada y como productos parciales. El vocabulario asociado con este capítulo es: propiedad distributiva y productos parciales.

¡El estudiante puede practicar multiplicar por números de un dígito mientras mira los precios en casa o en el supermercado!

- Al hacer las compras, mire etiquetas de precios que tengan números enteros. Con los artículos que valen menos de $10, pídale al estudiante que mencione un número de dos dígitos y, después, que halle el costo total de esa cantidad de artículos. Por ejemplo, un frasco de manteca de maní cuesta $4; pregúntele: "¿Cómo hallas el costo total de 23 frascos? ¿Cuál sería el costo total?". Anímelo a que explique más de una estrategia para hallar la respuesta. Pídale que prepare un modelo y que explique cómo usarlo para multiplicar.

- En casa busque anuncios de artículos que tengan un precio de tres dígitos. Pídale al estudiante que señale los dígitos de cada valor posicional. Después pídale que use los productos parciales para hallar el costo total de varios artículos. Recuerde elegir una cantidad de artículos de un solo dígito. Por ejemplo, si el estudiante elige un televisor de $425, guíelo para hallar el costo total de tres televisores. Pregúntele: "¿Cuál es el producto de 3 y 4 centenas? ¿Cuál es el producto de 3 y 2 decenas? ¿Cuál es el producto de 3 y 5 unidades?". Después pídale que sume los productos parciales. Siga preguntando: "¿Puedes hallar un artículo que cueste 3 veces lo que cuesta tu artículo? ¿Hay algún artículo que cueste 8 veces eso?".

- Pídale al estudiante que mencione un artículo con un precio de cuatro dígitos. Verifiquee en línea el precio. Lance un dado y pídale que estime el costo total de esa cantidad de artículos. Después pídale que elija una estrategia para multiplicar, que compare el costo total con el estimado y que explique si la respuesta es razonable. Anímelo a que piense enunciados de problemas con multiplicación y resuélvanlos juntos.

Hacia el final de este capítulo, el estudiante debe sentirse confiado con el objetivo de aprendizaje y el criterio de evaluación de la próxima página. Anímelo a pensar en otros contextos en los que pueda multiplicar por números de un dígito, como averiguar cuántos minutos tienen las horas que pasan por día en la escuela y, después, los minutos de cada semana.

¡Disfruten con la práctica de la multiplicación!

Multiplicar por un dígito (continuación)

Lección	Objetivo de aprendizaje	Criterios de éxito
3.1 Comprender la comparación multiplicativa	Usar la multiplicación para comparar dos números.	• Sé escribir ecuaciones de suma o multiplicación dado un enunciado comparativo. • Sé escribir un enunciado comparativo dado un enunciado de suma o multiplicación. • Sé resolver problemas comparativos de multiplicación.
3.2 Multiplicar decenas, centenas y unidades de mil	Usar valor preposicional para multiplicar por decenas, centenas o unidades de mil.	• Sé hallar el producto de un número de un dígito y un múltiplo de diez, cien o mil. • Sé describir un modelo para multiplicar por decenas, centenas o unidades de mil.
3.3 Estimar productos por redondeo	Estimar productos por redondeo.	• Sé usar el redondeo para estimar un producto. • Sé hallar dos estimaciones entre las que está el producto. • Sé decir si un producto es razonable.
3.4 Usar la propiedad distributiva para multiplicar	Usar la propiedad distributiva para multiplicar.	• Sé preparar un modelo para multiplicar. • Sé usar factores conocidos para hallar un producto. • Sé explicar el uso de la propiedad distributiva.
3.5 Usar la forma desarrollada para multiplicar	Usar la forma desarrollada y la propiedad distributiva para multiplicar.	• Sé usar un modelo para multiplicar. • Sé usar la forma desarrollada y la propiedad distributiva para hallar un producto.
3.6 Usar productos parciales para multiplicar	Usar el valor posicional y los productos parciales para multiplicar.	• Sé usar valor posicional para indicar el valor de cada dígito de un número. • Sé escribir los productos parciales de un problema de multiplicación. • Sé sumar los productos parciales para hallar un producto.
3.7 Multiplicar números de dos dígitos por un dígito	Multiplicar números de dos dígitos por números de un dígito.	• Sé multiplicar para hallar productos parciales. • Sé mostras 10 unidades reagrupadas en 1 decena. • Sé hallar el producto.
3.8 Multiplicar números de tres y cuatro dígitos por un dígito	Multiplicar números de varios dígitos por números de un dígito.	• Sé multiplicar para hallar productos parciales. • Sé mostrar cómo reagrupar más de 10 decenas. • Sé hallar el producto.
3.9 Usar propiedades para multiplicar	Usar propiedades para multiplicar.	• Sé usar la propiedad conmutativa de la multiplicación para multiplicar. • Sé usar la propiedad asociativa de la multiplicación para multiplicar. • Sé usar la propiedad distributiva de la multiplicación para multiplicar.
3.10 Resolución de problemas: Multiplicación	Resolver problemas de varios pasos con la multiplicación.	• Sé comprender un problema. • Sé hacer un plan de resolución con letras que representen los números desconocidos. • Sé resolver un problema con una ecuación.

1. Compare the values of the underlined digits.

   7,000 and 700

   The value of the 7 in 7,000 is _____ times the value of the 7 in 700.

1. Write what you know about this word. Give an example.

   estimate

Prerequisite Skills Practice

For use before Lesson 3.1

1. Write two equations that show the Commutative Property of Multiplication.

____ × ____ = ____ × ____ | ____ × ____ = ____ × ____

Name _____

 Extra Practice

Write two comparison sentences for the equation.

1. $35 = 5 \times 7$	**2.** $16 = 2 \times 8$
3. $72 = 8 \times 9$	**4.** $54 = 9 \times 6$
5. $28 = 7 \times 4$	**6.** $45 = 5 \times 9$

Write an equation for the comparison sentence.

7. 24 is 6 times as many as 4.	**8.** 14 is 5 more than 9.
9. 9 is 3 times as many as 3.	**10.** 21 is 7 times as many as 3.
11. 13 is 6 more than 7.	**12.** 40 is 8 times as many as 5.

13. Hillside School has 275 more students than Lakeview School. Lakeview School has 300 students. How many students attend Hillside school?

14. A car can hold 3 students for a field trip. A bus can hold 8 times as many students as the car. How many students can the bus hold?

15. Descartes says the equation 560 = 70 × 8 means 560 is 70 times as many as 8. Newton says 560 is 8 times as many as 70. Explain how you know both are correct.

16. Compare the giraffe's height to the tiger's height using multiplication and addition.

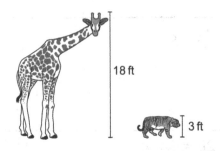

18 ft

3 ft

17. Write a comparison statement for a sum of 36.

18. There are 20 students in the library. There are 4 times as many girls as boys. How many boys are there?

19. Newton plays sports for 2 times as long as Descartes each week. Descartes plays sports for 6 hours each week. How many hours does Newton play sports each week?

20. You have 7 times as many nickels as pennies. You have 16 nickels and pennies altogether. How much money do you have in all?

21. Write a comparison statement for a sum of 24.

22. You read for 4 times as long as you watch TV each week. You watch TV for 5 hours each week. How many hours do you read each week?

Name _____

You can use multiplication to compare two numbers.

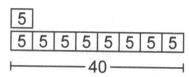

You can multiply in any order. 5 × 8 is the same as 8 × 5.

Example Write two comparison sentences for 40 = 5 × 8.

8
8	8	8	8	8
├————— 40 —————┤

The model shows that 5 groups of 8 is 40. 40 is 5 times as many as 8.

5
5	5	5	5	5	5	5	5
├————— 40 —————┤

The model shows that 8 groups of 5 is 40. 40 is 8 times as many as 5.

- -

You can use addition or multiplication to compare two numbers.

Example Write an equation for each comparison sentence.

More than tells you to add. Times as many tells you to multiply.

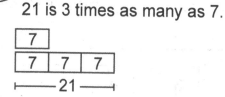

21 is 14 more than 7.

21
7	14

Use addition to find *how many more* or *how many fewer*.

21 = 7 + 14

21 is 3 times as many as 7.

7
7	7	7
├——— 21 ———┤

Use multiplication to find *how many times* as much.

21 = 3 × 7

Write two comparison sentences for the equation.

1. 56 = 7 × 8

2. 36 = 4 × 9

Draw a model for the comparison sentence. Then write an equation.

3. 16 is 4 more than 12.

4. 30 is 5 times as many as 6.

Name _____

Use the numbers to complete each comparison.

1.

| 6 | 18 | 24 | 24 |

_____ is _____ more than 6.

_____ is 4 times as many as _____.

2.

| 5 | 7 | 15 | 20 | 35 |

_____ is _____ more than _____.

35 is _____ times as many as _____.

3.

| 3 | 4 | 5 | 11 | 15 | 15 |

_____ is _____ more than _____.

_____ is _____ times as many as _____.

4.

| 2 | 4 | 6 | 8 | 12 | 12 |

_____ is _____ more than _____.

_____ is _____ times as many as _____.

---

1. Find the sum.

```
     63,468
+    47,930
_____
```

1. Write what you know about this phrase. Give an example.

place value

Prerequisite Skills Practice
For use before Lesson 3.2

Write two comparison sentences for the equation.

1. $20 = 4 \times 5$

2. $12 = 2 \times 6$

Name _____

Lesson 3.2 Extra Practice

Find each product.

1. $4 \times 7 =$ _____

   $4 \times 70 =$ _____

   $4 \times 700 =$ _____

   $4 \times 7,000 =$ _____

2. $6 \times 2 =$ _____

   $6 \times 20 =$ _____

   $6 \times 200 =$ _____

   $6 \times 2,000 =$ _____

3. $9 \times 3 =$ _____

   $9 \times 30 =$ _____

   $9 \times 300 =$ _____

   $9 \times 3,000 =$ _____

4. $5 \times 8 =$ _____

   $5 \times 80 =$ _____

   $5 \times 800 =$ _____

   $5 \times 8,000 =$ _____

Find the product.

5. $3 \times 40 =$ _____	6. $9,000 \times 2 =$ _____	7. $7 \times 500 =$ _____
8. $8,000 \times 1 =$ _____	9. $8 \times 300 =$ _____	10. $2 \times 30 =$ _____
11. $5 \times 400 =$ _____	12. $60 \times 8 =$ _____	13. $3 \times 7,000 =$ _____

Find the missing factor.

14. _____ $\times 600 = 4,200$	15. $2 \times$ _____ $= 8,000$	16. _____ $\times 400 = 400$
17. $4 \times$ _____ $= 3,200$	18. _____ $\times 1,000 = 3,000$	19. $6 \times$ _____ $= 2,400$

Compare.

20. $4 \times 20 \bigcirc 800$	**21.** $9 \times 500 \bigcirc 4{,}500$	**22.** $5{,}000 \times 3 \bigcirc 1{,}500$
23. $8 \times 900 \bigcirc 7{,}200$	**24.** $6 \times 70 \bigcirc 450$	**25.** $3 \times 8{,}000 \bigcirc 8{,}300$

26. Describe and complete the pattern.

$1 \times 5 = \underline{\hspace{2cm}}$

$2 \times 50 = \underline{\hspace{2cm}}$

$3 \times 500 = \underline{\hspace{2cm}}$

$\underline{\hspace{1.5cm}} \times \underline{\hspace{1.5cm}} = \underline{\hspace{1.5cm}}$

$\underline{\hspace{1.5cm}} \times \underline{\hspace{1.5cm}} = \underline{\hspace{1.5cm}}$

$\underline{\hspace{1.5cm}} \times \underline{\hspace{1.5cm}} = \underline{\hspace{1.5cm}}$

27. Without calculating, tell whether the product of 6 and 700 or the product of 6 and 7,000 is greater. Explain how you know.

28. How does 2×9 help you find $2{,}000 \times 9$? Explain.

29. Write a multiplication equation with a product of 360.

30. A second grade student reads about 600 minutes each month. A fourth grade student reads about 900 minutes each month. How many total minutes would 5 second grade students and 9 fourth grade students read in one month?

31. A pet store sells 7 bags of dog food that each weigh 40 pounds. They also sell 6 bags of cat food that each weigh 30 pounds. They sell one bag of hamster food that weighs 15 pounds. How many pounds of pet food are sold in all?

Name _____

You can use place value to multiply by tens, hundreds, or thousands.

Example Find each product.

Think: What multiplication fact can I use to find the product?

$4 \times 600 = 4 \times 6$ hundreds

= 24 hundreds

= 2,400

So, $4 \times 600 = 2,400$.

$5 \times 3,000 = 5 \times 3$ thousands.

= 15 thousands

= 15,000

So, $5 \times 3,000 = 15,000$.

Example Find each product.

$7 \times 9 = 63$ Multiplication fact

$7 \times 90 = 630$ Find 7×9; write 1 zero to show tens.

$7 \times 900 = 6,300$ Find 7×9; write 2 zeros to show hundreds.

$7 \times 9,000 = 63,000$ Find 7×9; write 3 zeros to show thousands.

Notice the Pattern: Write the multiplication fact. Then write the same number of zeros that are in the second factor.

Find each product.

1. $2 \times 8 = $ _____

    $2 \times 80 = $ _____

    $2 \times 800 = $ _____

    $2 \times 8,000 = $ _____

2. $6 \times 5 = $ _____

    $6 \times 50 = $ _____

    $6 \times 500 = $ _____

    $6 \times 5,000 = $ _____

Name _____

Fill in the missing numbers to complete each pattern.

1. $2 \times$ _____ $= 14$

   $2 \times 70 =$ _____

   _____ $\times 700 = 1{,}400$

   $2 \times 7{,}000 =$ _____

   $2 \times 70{,}000 =$ _____

   $2 \times$ _____ $= 1{,}400{,}000$

2. $9 \times 4 =$ _____

   $9 \times$ _____ $= 360$

   _____ $\times$ _____ $= 3{,}600$

   _____ $\times 4{,}000 =$ _____

   $9 \times$ _____ $= 360{,}000$

   $9 \times$ _____ $=$ _____

3. $8 \times$ _____ $=$ _____

   _____ $\times 30 = 240$

   $8 \times$ _____ $=$ _____

   _____ $\times 3{,}000 =$ _____

   _____ $\times 30{,}000 =$ _____

   $8 \times$ _____ $=$ _____

4. _____ $\times$ _____ $= 45$

   $9 \times$ _____ $=$ _____

   _____ $\times 500 =$ _____

   _____ $\times$ _____ $=$ _____

   _____ $\times 50{,}000 =$ _____

   _____ $\times$ _____ $=$ _____

5. Complete the pattern two different ways.

   _____ $\times$ _____ $= 18$ _____ $\times$ _____ $= 18$

   _____ $\times$ _____ $= 180$ _____ $\times$ _____ $= 180$

   _____ $\times$ _____ $= 1{,}800$ _____ $\times$ _____ $= 1{,}800$

   _____ $\times$ _____ $= 18{,}000$ _____ $\times$ _____ $= 18{,}000$

Lesson 3.3 Daily Skills Practice
For use before Lesson 3.3

1. Find the difference.

$$\begin{array}{r} 5{,}179 \\ -2{,}931 \\ \hline \end{array}$$

Lesson 3.3 Vocabulary Practice
For use before Lesson 3.3

1. Write what you know about this word. Give an example.

round

Lesson 3.3

Prerequisite Skills Practice

For use before Lesson 3.3

Find the product.

1. $4 \times 500 =$ _____

2. $7,000 \times 8 =$ _____

Name _____

Estimate the product.

1. 5 × 37	**2.** 66 × 8	**3.** 9 × 438
4. 3 × 572	**5.** 2,341 × 7	**6.** 8,562 × 6
7. 690 × 4	**8.** 2 × 1,832	**9.** 6 × 85

Find two estimates that the product is between.

10. 4 × 55	**11.** 68 × 9	**12.** 7 × 362
13. 2 × 574	**14.** 425 × 6	**15.** 837 × 8
16. 3 × 819	**17.** 5 × 6,247	**18.** 9 × 3,350

19. A school orders 63 cases of workbooks with 8 books in each case. To determine whether there are enough books for each of 500 students, can you use an estimate or is an exact answer required? Explain.

20. A student finds the product. Is his answer reasonable? Estimate to check.

$$4 \times 5{,}823 \stackrel{?}{=} 23{,}292$$

21. A company pays $3,245 per month rent for office space. You estimate that the company will pay $18,000 in 6 months. Is the amount of rent paid in 6 months greater than or less than your estimate? Explain.

22. Your teacher asks you to estimate by rounding to check your work when multiplying. Explain how this can be helpful.

Use the graph to answer the questions.

23. Which tree has an average height that is about 2 times as tall as an oak?

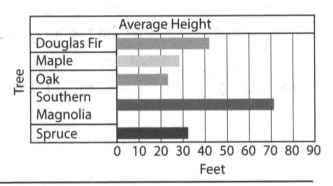

24. About how tall is a tree that is 4 times the height of a spruce tree? Find two estimates that the answer is between.

25. A redwood tree can grow to about 5 times as tall as a southern magnolia. About how tall can a redwood tree grow?

 Big Ideas Math: Modeling Real Life Grade 4
Resources by Chapter

Name _____

Lesson 3.3 Reteach

You can estimate a product by rounding one of the factors.

Example Estimate 5 × 387.

Round 387 to the nearest hundred.
Then multiply.

hundreds place ──────┐   8 > 5

3 8 7
↓ ↓ ↓
4 0 0

When you estimate, choose a number that is close to the exact number.

5 × 400 = 2,000

So, 5 × 387 is about 2,000.

- -

You can check whether a product is reasonable by finding two estimates that a product is between.

Example Find two estimates that the product of 6 × 47 is between.

Think: 47 is between 40 and 50, so 6 × 47 is between 6 × 40 and 6 × 50.

6 × 40 = 240   6 × 50 = 300

So, the product of 6 × 47 is between 240 and 300.

Estimate the product.

1. 2 × 88

2. 7 × 642

3. 8 × 3,625

Find two estimates that the product is between.

4. 3 × 65

5. 9 × 527

6. 4 × 7,381

Name _____

Enrichment and Extension

The table shows the prices of items at a sporting goods store.

Sporting Goods	
Item	**Price**
Bicycle	$319
Bike Helmet	$37
Basketball Hoop	$165
Canoe	$1,585
Golf Club Set	$925
Skateboard	$48

1. A store clerk sold 5 of the same item. The total cost was between $200 and $250. What items did the clerk sell?

2. The store sold 4 of the same item. The total cost was greater than $3,600 but less than $4,000. What item was sold?

3. A customer bought 4 bicycles and 4 bike helmets. Describe two ways to estimate the total cost. Then use both ways to estimate the total cost. Which way seems easier? Which way gives a closer estimate?

Daily Skills Practice
For use before Lesson 3.4

1. Round the number to the place of the underlined digit.

   9<u>5</u>,042

Vocabulary Practice
For use before Lesson 3.4

1. Write what you know about this phrase. Give an example.

   thousands period

Prerequisite Skills Practice
For use before Lesson 3.4

Estimate the product.

1. 6×37

2. $5,821 \times 9$

Name _____

Draw an area model. Then find the product.

1. $4 \times 15 =$ _____

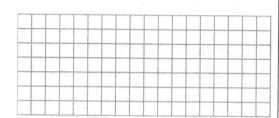

2. $6 \times 17 =$ _____

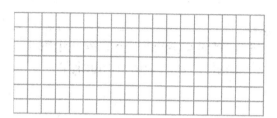

3. $5 \times 12 =$ _____

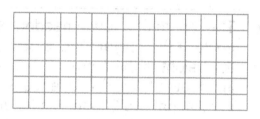

4. $3 \times 14 =$ _____

5. $7 \times 25 =$ _____

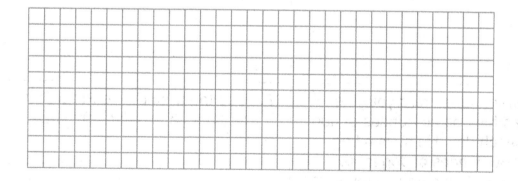

6. $3 \times 32 =$ _____

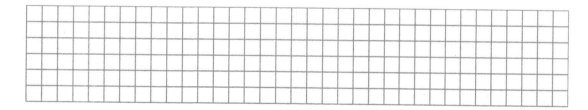

Find the product.

7. $8 \times 47 =$ _____	8. $65 \times 2 =$ _____	9. $83 \times 9 =$ _____
10. $53 \times 4 =$ _____	11. $5 \times 74 =$ _____	12. $6 \times 39 =$ _____

13. How does using the Distributive Property help you multiply?

14. Use the Distributive Property to find 8×29 two different ways.

15. To find 7×24, would you rather break apart the factor 24 as $20 + 4$ or as $12 + 12$? Explain.

16. The length of a fence needed to enclose the playground is 38 times the height of the fence. The fence is 5 feet in height. The fence is sold in rolls that are 200 feet in length. Is one roll of fence long enough to enclose the playground? Explain.

17. The veterinarian tells your friend to feed his dog 36 ounces of dog food each day. He buys a bag with 160 ounces of dog food. Does your friend have enough to feed his dog for 4 days? Explain.

18. Use the Distributive Property to find 3×25 two different ways.

Name _____

Lesson 3.4 **Reteach**

To multiply a two-digit number, you can break apart the number. Then use the Distributive Property.

5 × 14 = 5 × (10 + 4)

5 × (10 + 4) = (5 × 10) + (5 × 4)   **Distributive Property**

= 50 + 20

= 70

Break 14 apart into 10 + 4.

Example Use an area model to find 7 × 16.

Model the expression. Break apart 16 as 10 + 6.

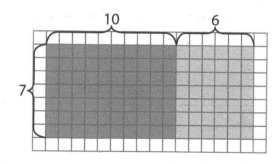

7 × 16 = 7 × (10 + 6)   Rewrite 16 as 10 + 6.

= (7 × 10) + (7 × 6)   Distributive Property: Multiply 7 by 10 and by 6.

= 70 + 42   7 × 10 = 70 and 7 × 6 = 42.

= 112   Add.

Draw an area model. Then find the product.

1. 4 × 13 = _____

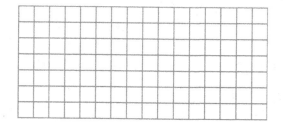

2. 6 × 17 = _____

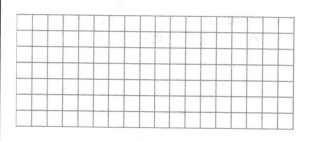

Name _____

Use the Distributive Property to find 5 × 25 in three different ways.
Draw an area model to represent each.

1. 5 × 25 = 5 × (10 + _____)

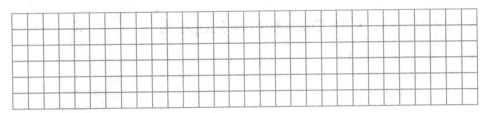

2. 5 × 25 = 5 × (_____ + _____)

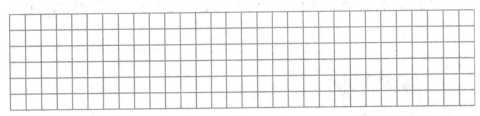

3. 5 × 25 = 5 × (_____ − _____)

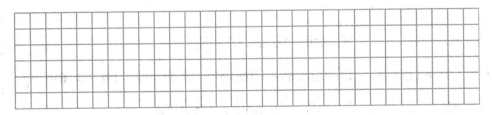

4. How are the models in questions 1–3 alike? How are they
different?

5. Could you use the Distributive Property by breaking apart 5
rather than 25? Explain.

1. A warehouse has 4,462 packages. It receives 2,579 packages. Then it ships 884 packages. How many packages does it have now?

   The warehouse has _____ packages now.

1. Write what you know about this phrase. Give an example.

Distributive Property

Prerequisite Skills Practice

For use before Lesson 3.5

Find the product.

1. $5 \times 38 =$ _____

2. $62 \times 8 =$ _____

Name _____

Find the product.

1. $8 \times 406 = $ _____

400	6
8	8 ×	8 ×

2. $901 \times 3 = $ _____

900	1
3	3 ×	3 ×

3. $4 \times 2{,}308 = $ _____

2,000	300	8
4	4 ×	4 ×	4 ×

4. $3{,}075 \times 6 = $ _____

3,000	70	5
6	6 ×	6 ×	6 ×

5. $56 \times 7 = (50 + 6) \times 7$

$= ($ ____ $\times 7) + ($ ____ $\times 7)$

$= $ ____ $+$ ____

$= $ ____

6. $2 \times 594 = 2 \times ($ ___ $+$ ___ $+$ ___ $)$

$= (2 \times$ ___ $) + (2 \times$ ___ $) + (2 \times$ ___ $)$

$= $ ___ $+$ ___ $+$ ___

$= $ ____

7. $9 \times 623 = $ _____

8. $7{,}481 \times 5 = $ _____

9. A florist puts 6 tulips in each of 237 vases for a banquet. How many tulips are there in all?

10. A commercial airliner can fly 550 miles per hour. How many miles can it fly in 3 hours?

11. Rewrite the expression as a product of two factors.

$(4,000 \times 7) + (600 \times 7) + (2 \times 7)$

12. Explain how you can find $9 \times 6,075$ using expanded form.

13. A farmer plants 45 rows of beans. He plants 4 times as many rows of tomatoes as beans. How many more rows of tomatoes than beans does he plant?

14. A baker uses 5 eggs in each batch of muffins he bakes. He plans to bake 22 batches of muffins. He buys 6 cartons of eggs. There are 18 eggs in each carton. Will 6 cartons of eggs be enough to bake the muffins?

15. Rewrite the expression as a product of two factors.

$(500 \times 8) + (20 \times 8) + (6 \times 8)$

16. An art teacher orders 72 markers. She orders 3 times as many colored pencils. How many more colored pencils than markers does she order?

Name _____

Use expanded form to separate the number.

You can use the Distributive Property to multiply.

Example Find 5 × 63.

Think 63 = 60 + 3

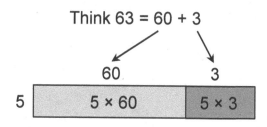

| 5 | 5 × 60 | 5 × 3 |

5 × 63 = 5 × (60 + 3)   Write 63 in expanded form.

= (5 × 60) + (5 × 3)   Distributive Property

= 300 + 15   5 × 60 = 300 and 5 × 3 = 15.

= 315   So, 5 × 63 = 315.

Example Find 3 × 7,408. Think: 7,408 = 7,000 + 400 + 8.

| 3 | 3 × 7,000 | 3 × 400 | 3 × 8 |

3 × 7,408 = 3 × (7,000 + 400 + 8)   Write 7,408 in expanded form.

= (3 × 7,000) + (3 × 400) + (3 × 8)   Distributive Property

= 21,000 + 1,200 + 24

= 22,224   So, 3 × 7,408 = 22,224.

Find the product.

1. 7 × 204 = 7 × (_____ + _____)

= (7 × _____) + (7 × _____)

= _____ + _____

= _____

2. 8 × 374

Name _____

Determine whether each model is correct. If not, explain the error and find the correct product.

1. 4 × 523 = 283

	50	20	3
4	4 × 50	4 × 20	4 × 3

2. 8 × 236 = 4,048

	200	300	6
8	8 × 200	8 × 300	8 × 6

3. 5 × 6,432 = 32,160

	6,000	400	30	2
5	5 × 6,000	5 × 400	5 × 30	5 × 2

4. 7 × 3,605 = 25,585

	3,000	600	50	5
7	7 × 3,000	7 × 600	7 × 50	7 × 5

1. Write the number in two other forms.

    Word form: fifty-six thousand, three hundred five

    Standard form:

    Expanded form:

1. Write what you know about this word. Give an example.

    factors

Prerequisite Skills Practice

For use before Lesson 3.6

Find the product.

1. $3 \times 154 =$ _____

2. $5,273 \times 7 =$ _____

Name _____

Find the product.

1. $\begin{array}{r} 43 \\ \times\ \ 6 \\ \hline \end{array}$	**2.** $\begin{array}{r} 75 \\ \times\ \ 9 \\ \hline \end{array}$	**3.** $\begin{array}{r} 358 \\ \times\ \ 4 \\ \hline \end{array}$
4. $\begin{array}{r} 726 \\ \times\ \ 8 \\ \hline \end{array}$	**5.** $\begin{array}{r} 6,289 \\ \times\ \ 5 \\ \hline \end{array}$	**6.** $\begin{array}{r} 8,903 \\ \times\ \ 7 \\ \hline \end{array}$
7. $\begin{array}{r} 247 \\ \times\ \ 3 \\ \hline \end{array}$	**8.** $\begin{array}{r} 96 \\ \times\ \ 2 \\ \hline \end{array}$	**9.** $\begin{array}{r} 7,582 \\ \times\ \ 4 \\ \hline \end{array}$

Find the product.

10. $\begin{array}{r} 856 \\ \times \quad 6 \\ \hline \end{array}$	**11.** $\begin{array}{r} 491 \\ \times \quad 9 \\ \hline \end{array}$	**12.** $\begin{array}{r} 3{,}217 \\ \times \quad 8 \\ \hline \end{array}$
13. $\begin{array}{r} 5{,}485 \\ \times \quad 3 \\ \hline \end{array}$	**14.** $\begin{array}{r} 9{,}437 \\ \times \quad 2 \\ \hline \end{array}$	**15.** $\begin{array}{r} 2{,}098 \\ \times \quad 5 \\ \hline \end{array}$

16. Which four numbers are the partial products that you add to find the product of 4,935 and 7?

28,000   6,300   630

280   210   35

17. The sum of a three-digit number and a one-digit number is 642. The product of the numbers is 5,072. What are the numbers?

18. The length of the Amazon River is 295 miles less than 2 times the length of the Mississippi River. The length of the Mississippi River is 2,320 miles. What is the length of the Amazon River?

19. A pilot flies 416 miles from Tampa to Atlanta 5 times in one week. She flies 721 miles from Atlanta to Dallas 8 times. What is the total number of miles she flies?

Flight	Distance
Tampa to Atlanta	416 miles
Atlanta to Dallas	721 miles

Name _____

You can use *partial products* to multiply. **Partial products** are found by breaking apart a factor into ones, tens, hundreds, and so on, and multiplying each of these by the other factor.

Add the partial products to find the product in the problem.

Example Use an area model and partial products to find 6 × 235.

Think: 235 = 200 + 30 + 5.

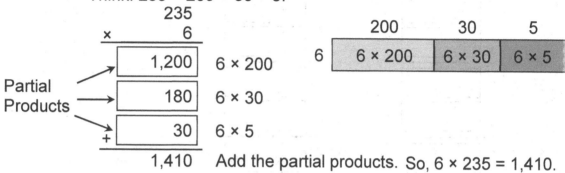

```
        235
    ×     6
     ┌─────────┐
     │  1,200  │  6 × 200
     ├─────────┤
     │    180  │  6 × 30
     ├─────────┤
   + │     30  │  6 × 5
     └─────────┘
        1,410    Add the partial products.  So, 6 × 235 = 1,410.
```

200	30	5
6 × 200	6 × 30	6 × 5

6

Example Use place value and partial products to find 5,237 × 4.

```
      5,237
   ×      4
    ┌──────────┐
    │  20,000  │  4 × 5 thousands = 20 thousands
    ├──────────┤
    │     800  │  4 × 2 hundreds = 8 hundreds
    ├──────────┤
    │     120  │  4 × 3 tens = 12 tens
    ├──────────┤
  + │      28  │  4 × 7 ones = 28 ones
    └──────────┘
      20,948    Add the partial products.    So, 5,237 × 4 = 20,948.
```

Find the product.

1.
```
        58
   ×     3
   ┌────────┐
   │        │
   ├────────┤
 + │        │
   └────────┘
```

2.
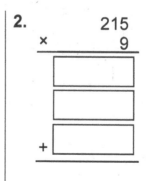
```
       215
   ×     9
   ┌────────┐
   │        │
   ├────────┤
   │        │
   ├────────┤
 + │        │
   └────────┘
```

3.
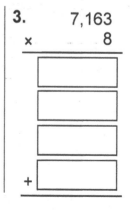
```
      7,163
   ×      8
   ┌────────┐
   │        │
   ├────────┤
   │        │
   ├────────┤
   │        │
   ├────────┤
 + │        │
   └────────┘
```

Name _____

  Enrichment and Extension

Use the numbers to complete the equations using partial products.

1.   3   8   400   120   16

        15   52   45   135   416

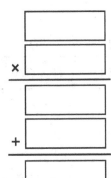

2.   1,400   1,981   5   21   45   2,000

        50   560   283   7   419   2,095

Daily Skills Practice
For use before Lesson 3.7

1. Compare.

266,042 ( ) 299,042

Vocabulary Practice
For use before Lesson 3.7

1. Write what you know about this phrase. Give an example.

partial products

Prerequisite Skills Practice
For use before Lesson 3.7

Find the product.

1.
$$\begin{array}{r} 92 \\ \times \quad 7 \\ \hline \end{array}$$

$$\begin{array}{r} \boxed{} \\ + \boxed{} \\ \hline \end{array}$$

2.
$$\begin{array}{r} 326 \\ \times \quad 5 \\ \hline \end{array}$$

$$\begin{array}{r} \boxed{} \\ \boxed{} \\ + \boxed{} \\ \hline \end{array}$$

Name _____

1. Use the model to find the product.

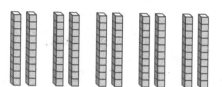

$5 \times 23 =$ _____

2. Use the model to find the product.

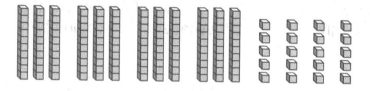

$4 \times 35 =$ _____

Find the product. Check whether your answer is reasonable.

3. Estimate: __70__

$$\begin{array}{r} \square \\ 1\,4 \\ \times \quad 7 \\ \hline \end{array}$$

4. Estimate: _____

$$\begin{array}{r} \square \\ 4\,8 \\ \times \quad 9 \\ \hline \end{array}$$

5. Estimate: _____

$$\begin{array}{r} \square \\ 7\,2 \\ \times \quad 6 \\ \hline \end{array}$$

6. Estimate: _____

$$\begin{array}{r} \square \\ 8\,6 \\ \times \quad 3 \\ \hline \end{array}$$

7. Estimate: _____

$$\begin{array}{r} \square \\ 6\,7 \\ \times \quad 2 \\ \hline \end{array}$$

8. Estimate: _____

$$\begin{array}{r} \square \\ 5\,9 \\ \times \quad 8 \\ \hline \end{array}$$

Find the product. Check whether your estimate is reasonable.

9. Estimate: _____ $45 \times 3 =$ _____	10. Estimate: _____ $8 \times 27 =$ _____	11. Estimate: _____ $19 \times 4 =$ _____
12. Estimate: _____ $7 \times 53 =$ _____	13. Estimate: _____ $85 \times 2 =$ _____	14. Estimate: _____ $8 \times 32 =$ _____

15. There are 3 checkerboards. Each board has 24 checkers. How many checkers are there in all?

16. The sum of two numbers is 26. The product of the two numbers is 88. What are the two numbers?

17. There are 14 teams playing in a volleyball tournament. There are 6 students on each team. How many students are playing volleyball?

18. The difference between two numbers is 9. The product of the two numbers is 36. What are the two numbers?

19. Your friend multiplies 92 by 5 and says that the product is 4,500. Is your friend's answer reasonable? Explain.

20. How much less is 8×23 than 9×23? Explain how you know without multiplying.

21. A teacher travels 3 miles to school each day. The principal travels 13 times as far as the teacher. The coach travels 35 miles. Who travels the farthest?

22. The distance from Washington D.C. to Alexandria, Virginia, is 8 miles. The distance from Washington D.C. to New York City is about 29 times as far. How many miles is it from Washington D.C. to New York City?

Name _____

Reteach

You can regroup 10 or more ones as tens when you multiply.

Example Find 3 × 46.

Estimate: 3 × 50 = 150

Step 1: Multiply the ones. Regroup.

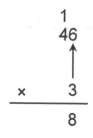

- 3 × 6 ones = 18 ones
- Think: How do I regroup 18 ones when I add?
- Regroup 18 ones as 1 ten and 8 ones.

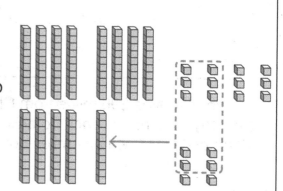

Step 2: Multiply the tens. Add any regrouped tens.

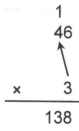

- 3 × 4 tens = 12 tens
- 12 tens + 1 regrouped ten = 13 tens
- 13 tens is 1 hundred and 3 tens

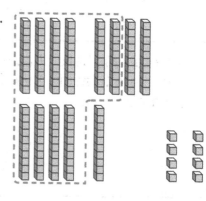

So, 3 × 46 = 138.

Check: Because 138 is close to the estimate, 150, the answer is reasonable.

1. Find 5 × 23. Check whether your answer is reasonable.

Estimate: _____

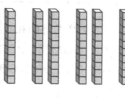

Name _____

1. A farmer picks 48 baskets of apples each day for 7 days. There
    are 9 apples in each basket. How many apples does the farmer
    pick?

2. A woman drives 296 miles from Chicago to St. Louis every
    Monday. She drives back from St. Louis to Chicago every
    Wednesday. How many miles does she drive in 4 weeks?

3. A store sells balls of yarn that each have 125 yards of yarn.
    There are 3 feet in 1 yard. How many feet of yarn are in 9 balls
    of yarn?

4. There are 245 bracelets for sale at a craft show. Each bracelet
    has 6 red beads, along with 4 times as many blue beads as red
    beads. How many beads are there in all?

5. There are 178 apple juice boxes for a school picnic. There are
    also 5 times as many grape juice boxes. Each juice box holds
    8 ounces of juice. How many ounces of juice are there in all?

Lesson 3.8 Daily Skills Practice
For use before Lesson 3.8

1. Find the difference.

$$
\begin{array}{r}
50,756 \\
-28,519 \\
\hline
\end{array}
$$

Lesson 3.8 Vocabulary Practice
For use before Lesson 3.8

1. Write what you know about this word. Give an example.

product

Prerequisite Skills Practice

For use before Lesson 3.8

Find the product. Check whether your answer is reasonable.

1. Estimate: _____

   $58 \times 3 =$ _____

2. Estimate: _____

   $6 \times 74 =$ _____

Name _____

Extra Practice

Find the product. Check whether your answer is reasonable.

1. Estimate: _____

$$\begin{array}{r} 295 \\ \times \quad 6 \\ \hline \end{array}$$

2. Estimate: _____

$$\begin{array}{r} 953 \\ \times \quad 4 \\ \hline \end{array}$$

3. Estimate: _____

$$\begin{array}{r} 578 \\ \times \quad 2 \\ \hline \end{array}$$

4. Estimate: _____

$$\begin{array}{r} 4{,}276 \\ \times \quad 9 \\ \hline \end{array}$$

5. Estimate: _____

$$\begin{array}{r} 2{,}485 \\ \times \quad 3 \\ \hline \end{array}$$

6. Estimate: _____

$$\begin{array}{r} 7{,}049 \\ \times \quad 8 \\ \hline \end{array}$$

7. Estimate: _____

$$\begin{array}{r} 317 \\ \times \quad 5 \\ \hline \end{array}$$

8. Estimate: _____

$$\begin{array}{r} 9{,}264 \\ \times \quad 7 \\ \hline \end{array}$$

9. Estimate: _____

$$\begin{array}{r} 4{,}791 \\ \times \quad 2 \\ \hline \end{array}$$

10. Estimate: _____

$$\begin{array}{r} 1{,}532 \\ \times \quad 6 \\ \hline \end{array}$$

11. Estimate: _____

$$\begin{array}{r} 913 \\ \times \quad 8 \\ \hline \end{array}$$

12. Estimate: _____

$$\begin{array}{r} 237 \\ \times \quad 7 \\ \hline \end{array}$$

13. Estimate: _____

$$\begin{array}{r} 6{,}403 \\ \times \quad 3 \\ \hline \end{array}$$

14. Estimate: _____

$$\begin{array}{r} 147 \\ \times \quad 9 \\ \hline \end{array}$$

15. Estimate: _____

$$\begin{array}{r} 2{,}790 \\ \times \quad 4 \\ \hline \end{array}$$

Find the product. Check whether your answer is reasonable.

16. Estimate: _____ $427 \times 6 =$ _____	**17.** Estimate: _____ $5 \times 6,215 =$ _____	**18.** Estimate: _____ $439 \times 2 =$ _____
19. Estimate: _____ $1,442 \times 3 =$ _____	**20.** Estimate: _____ $2,760 \times 7 =$ _____	**21.** Estimate: _____ $4 \times 168 =$ _____

Compare.

22. $5 \times 2,185$ $\bigcirc$ $3 \times 5,216$

23. $7 \times 3,228$ $\bigcirc$ $6 \times 4,137$

24. There are 4 performances of a play. The theater sells 2,145 tickets for each performance. How many tickets are sold in all?

25. What number is 725 less than the product of 6,128 and 9?

26. Descartes says that the product of a four-digit number and a one-digit number is always a four-digit number. Is Descartes correct? Explain.

27. The numbers of stairs Newton and Descartes climbed in a day are shown. You climbed 3 times as many stairs as Descartes. Who climbed the most stairs?

Newton: 964 stairs

Descartes: 317 stairs

Name _____

You can regroup any place value when you multiply.

Example Find 3 × 847.

Step 1: Multiply the ones. Regroup.

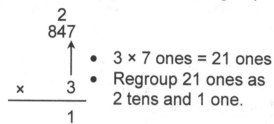

- 3 × 7 ones = 21 ones
- Regroup 21 ones as 2 tens and 1 one.

> Estimate 3 × 800 = 2,400 to check whether the answer is reasonable.

Step 2: Multiply the tens. Add any regrouped tens.

- 3 × 4 tens = 12 tens
- 12 tens + 2 tens = 14 tens; Regroup 14 tens as 1 hundred and 4 tens.

Step 3: Multiply the hundreds. Add any regrouped hundreds.

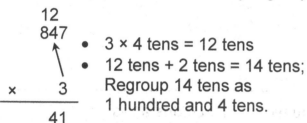

- 3 × 8 hundreds = 24 hundreds
- 24 hundreds + 1 hundred = 25 hundreds, or 2 thousands 5 hundreds.

So, 3 × 847 = 2,541.

Example Find 6 × 2,048. Estimate: 6 × 2,000 = 12,000.

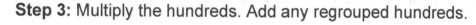

```
  24
2,048
×    6
───────
12,288
```

- Multiply the ones, tens, hundreds, and thousands by 6. Regroup as necessary.
- Check: Because 12,288 is close to the estimate, 12,000, the answer is reasonable.

Find the product. Check whether your answer is reasonable.

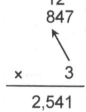

1. Estimate: _____

```
  415
×   8
```

2. Estimate: _____

```
  276
×   5
```

3. Estimate: _____

```
3,693
×    4
```

Name _____

Enrichment and Extension

1. Newton multiplies 537 and 3. He says he will regroup only the ones. Is he correct? Explain.

_____

2. Descartes multiplies 4,105 and 2. He says he will not regroup any place value because all of the digits are small. Is he correct? Explain.

_____

3. Write and solve a multiplication equation that includes a 3-digit number and does not involve any regrouping.

_____

4. Write and solve a multiplication equation that includes a 4-digit number and involves regrouping ones and tens.

_____

5. Write and solve a multiplication equation that includes a 4-digit number that involves regrouping 1 ten and 3 hundreds.

Lesson 3.9 Daily Skills Practice
For use before Lesson 3.9

1. Round the number to the place of the underlined digit.

7̲,865

Lesson 3.9 Vocabulary Practice
For use before Lesson 3.9

1. Write what you know about this word. Give an example.

equation

Prerequisite Skills Practice
For use before Lesson 3.9

Find the product. Check whether your answer is reasonable.

1. Estimate: _____

   $715 \times 8 =$ _____

2. Estimate: _____

   $4 \times 3,276 =$ _____

Name_____

Extra Practice

Use properties to find the product. Explain your reasoning.

1. 7 × 295	**2.** 43 × 6	**3.** 4 × 630
4. 8 × 76	**5.** 6 × 450	**6.** 9 × 507
7. 4 × 3 × 25	**8.** 899 × 2	**9.** 6 × 392
10. 8 × 503	**11.** 50 × 9 × 2	**12.** 5 × 197
13. 7 × 604	**14.** 15 × 6 × 2	**15.** 3 × 2,995
16. 2 × 83 × 5	**17.** 6,005 × 9	**18.** 4 × 396

19. Is Newton correct? Explain.

$$403 \times 6 = (400 + 3) \times 6$$
$$= (400 \times 6) + (3 \times 6)$$
$$= 2,400 + 18$$
$$= 2,418$$

20. Complete the square so that the product of each row and column is 1,800.

		3
300		2
2		

21. The height of the tip of the Empire State Building is 234 feet taller than 4 times the height of the Statue of Liberty. How tall is the Empire State Building?

305 ft

22. Descartes's favorite football player can throw the ball 30 feet more than 3 times the distance Descartes can throw. How far can the football player throw the ball?

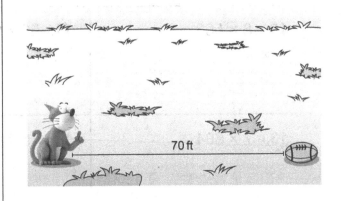

70 ft

23. The record speed for a human marathon runner is about 13 miles per hour. A cheetah makes a short run that is 9 miles an hour faster than 4 times the marathon runner's speed. How fast does the cheetah run?

24. Newton collects 197 cans to recycle. Descartes collects 15 less than 3 times as many as Newton. How many cans does Descartes collect?

Name _____

You can use properties to multiply.

Example Find 5 × 180.

5 × 180 = 5 × (2 × 90)	Think: How can I break apart the factors to make a simpler problem? 180 = 2 × 90
= (5 × 2) × 90	Associative Property of Multiplication: You can multiply any two factors first.
= 10 × 90	
= 900	So, 5 × 180 = 900.

Example Find 6 × 397.

6 × 397 = 6 × (400 − 3)	Think: 397 = 400 − 3
= (6 × 400) − (6 × 3)	Distributive Property
= 2,400 − 18	
= 2,382	So, 6 × 397 = 2,382.

Example Find 4 × 6 × 25.

4 × 6 × 25 = 6 × 4 × 25	Commutative Property of Multiplication: Reorder factors to multiply more easily.
= 6 × 100	4 × 25 = 100
= 600	So, 4 × 6 × 25 = 600.

Use properties to find the product. Explain your reasoning.

1. 6 × 250

2. 8 × 296

3. 25 × 3 × 4

Name _____

Enrichment and Extension

Write and solve a word problem to match each product.

1. 8 × 450

_____

2. 9 × 692

_____

3. 2 × 84 × 50

_____

4. 16 × 25

1. Find the sum.

```
    68,013
 +  64,691
 _____
```

1. Write what you know about this word. Give an example.

multiplication

Prerequisite Skills Practice
For use before Lesson 3.10

Write an equation for the comparison sentence.

1. 36 is 4 times as many as 9.

2. 56 is 7 times as many as 8.

Name _____

Understand the problem. Then make a plan. How will you solve? Explain.

1. A carnival sells 1,235 tickets for the Ferris wheel on Thursday. They sell 362 less than 4 times as many tickets on Friday. You want to find the number of tickets sold on Friday.

2. You read your library book for 45 minutes each day. You read books on your e-reader for a total of 185 minutes each week. You want to find how many minutes you read in all each week.

3. A movie theater sells 317 adult tickets for $9 each. It sells 548 children's tickets for $6 each. You want to find the total cost of the tickets.

4. A photo album has 56 pages. Each page holds 8 photos. You put some photos in the album and have room for 135 more photos. You want to find how many photos are in the album.

5. A baker makes 275 wheat rolls. He fills 9 boxes with 24 rolls in each box. You want to find how many rolls are not in boxes.

6. Your friend makes 65 vanilla scented candles and 82 pine scented candles for a craft sale. She charges $8 for each. At the end of the sale, she has 39 candles left. You want to find how much money she made.

7. You buy 5 sets of sports cards. There are 42 cards in each set. You give some away and have 187 left. How many cards did you give away?

8. Your teacher buys 6 packs of drinking straws for the school picnic. There are 75 straws in each pack. She needs 460 straws. Are there enough? Explain.

9. There are 5 small paintbrushes and 2 large paintbrushes in a set. The art teacher orders 36 sets. How many paintbrushes does he order in all?

10. Newton practices playing the piano 5 days this week. He practices 45 minutes each day. He needs to practice for a total of at least 220 minutes. Has Newton practiced the piano enough this week? Explain.

11. Write and solve a two-step word problem that can be solved using multiplication and addition.

12. The students collected $2,437 in donations for a new school playground. Each of the 5 fourth grade classes collected $178. Each of the 6 third grade classes collected $154. The rest of the donation money was collected by the fifth grade students. How much money did the fifth grade students collect?

13. A man drives 24 miles each week for work. His wife drives 43 miles each week for work. How many miles do they drive in 4 weeks?

14. A scout troop with 7 members earns $1,245 to spend on a camping trip for 4 nights. They buy $112 of camping gear for each person and $43 of food for each person. How much money does the scout troop have left?

Name _____

Use these steps to solve a word problem:

1. Understand the problem. → Think about what you know and what you need to find.

2. Make a plan. → Think about which operations you need to use. Which operation should you use first? next?

3. Solve. → Follow the steps in your plan.

Example A school principal buys 8 packages of glitter pens and spends $72. Each package has 24 pens. She gives 97 pens to the students. How many glitter pens are left?

1. Understand the problem.

What you know:	What you need to find:
• The principal buys 8 packages. • The total cost is $72. • Each package has 24 pens. • She gives out 97 pens.	• How many pens are left?

2. Make a plan.
- First, multiply 8 by 24 to find the total number of glitter pens.
- Then subtract 97 pens from the total to find how many are left.
- The cost is not needed to solve the problem.

3. Solve.

Step 1: Find the total number of glitter pens.

24	24	24	24	24	24	24	24

├──────────── k ────────────┤

k is the unknown product.

$8 \times 24 = k$
$8 \times 24 = 192$
$k = 192$

Step 2: Use k to find how many pens are left.

97	n

├──── $k = 192$ ────┤

n is the unknown difference.

$192 - 97 = n$
$192 - 97 = 95$
$n = 95$

There are 95 pens left.

1. Find how many pens are left if the principal gives out 111 glitter pens.

Lesson 3.10 **Enrichment and Extension**

1. There are 5 classes of third grade students with 26 students in each class. There are 7 classes of fourth grade students with 28 students in each class. There are 8 classes of fifth grade students with 31 students in each class. How many fourth and fifth grade students are there in all?

2. On Saturday 245 adults and 179 children visited the museum. On Sunday 376 adults and 228 children visited the museum. Each person paid $6 for a museum ticket. What is the total cost of the tickets for both days?

3. On the days that he jogs, Descartes jogs 3 miles. He jogged 340 days last year. Newton jogs 4 miles each day. He jogged for 365 days last year. How many more miles did Newton jog than Descartes?

4. You play soccer 6 days each week for 25 minutes per day. You play basketball 5 days each week for 15 minutes per day. Your friend plays soccer 4 days each week for 35 minutes per day. How many total minutes do you and your friend play soccer in 8 weeks?

5. 7 buses bring students to Lakeside School. Each bus travels 62 miles per day, 5 days per week. How many total miles do the 7 buses travel in 4 weeks?

Name_____

Chapter Self-Assessment

Use the scale below to rate your understanding of the learning target and the success criteria.

1	2	3	4
I do not understand.	I can do it with help.	I can do it on my own.	I can teach someone else.

	Rating
3.1 Understand Multiplicative Comparisons	
Learning Target: Use multiplication to compare two numbers.	1 2 3 4
I can write addition or multiplication equations given a comparison sentence.	1 2 3 4
I can write a comparison sentence given an addition or a multiplication equation.	1 2 3 4
I can solve comparison word problems involving multiplication.	1 2 3 4
3.2 Multiply Tens, Hundreds, and Thousands	
Learning Target: Use place value to multiply by tens, hundreds, or thousands.	1 2 3 4
I can find the product of a one-digit number and a multiple of ten, one hundred, or one thousand.	1 2 3 4
I can describe a pattern when multiplying by tens, hundreds, or thousands.	1 2 3 4
3.3 Estimate Products by Rounding	
Learning Target: Use rounding to estimate products.	1 2 3 4
I can use rounding to estimate a product.	1 2 3 4
I can find two estimates that a product is between.	1 2 3 4
I can tell whether a product is reasonable.	1 2 3 4
3.4 Use the Distributive Property to Multiply	
Learning Target: Use the Distributive Property to multiply.	1 2 3 4
I can draw an area model to multiply.	1 2 3 4
I can use known facts to find a product.	1 2 3 4
I can explain how to use the Distributive Property.	1 2 3 4

Name _____

	Rating

3.5 Use Expanded Form to Multiply

Learning Target: Use expanded form and the Distributive Property to multiply.	1	2	3	4
I can use an area model to multiply.	1	2	3	4
I can use expanded form and the Distributive Property to find a product.	1	2	3	4

3.6 Use Partial Products to Multiply

Learning Target: Use place value and partial products to multiply.	1	2	3	4
I can use place value to tell the value of each digit in a number.	1	2	3	4
I can write the partial products for a multiplication problem.	1	2	3	4
I can add the partial products to find a product.	1	2	3	4

3.7 Multiply Two-Digit Numbers by One-Digit Numbers

Learning Target: Multiply two-digit numbers by one-digit numbers.	1	2	3	4
I can multiply to find the partial products.	1	2	3	4
I can show 10 ones regrouped as 1 ten.	1	2	3	4
I can find the product.	1	2	3	4

3.8 Multiply Three- and Four-Digit Numbers by One-Digit Numbers

Learning Target: Multiply multi-digit numbers by one-digit numbers.	1	2	3	4
I can multiply to find the partial products.	1	2	3	4
I can show how to regroup more than 10 tens.	1	2	3	4
I can find the product.	1	2	3	4

3.9 Use Properties to Multiply

Learning Target: Use properties to multiply.	1	2	3	4
I can use the Commutative Property of Multiplication to multiply.	1	2	3	4
I can use the Associative Property of Multiplication to multiply.	1	2	3	4
I can use the Distributive Property to multiply.	1	2	3	4

3.10 Problem Solving: Multiplication

Learning Target: Solve multi-step word problems involving multiplication.	1	2	3	4
I can understand a problem.	1	2	3	4
I can make a plan to solve using letters to represent the unknown numbers.	1	2	3	4
I can solve a problem using an equation.	1	2	3	4

Chapter 4

Name_____

Dear Family,

In this chapter, your student is learning to multiply two-digit numbers. Your student will learn multiplication strategies for estimating, using area models, using the Distributive Property, and using partial products. The vocabulary phrase for this chapter is compatible numbers. Compatible numbers are numbers that are easy to multiply and are close to the actual numbers being multiplied.

You can practice multiplication at a warehouse club store where people buy large quantities of items. For example, 1 large box contains 10 smaller boxes, and each smaller box contains 8 packages of fruit snacks. Here are some questions to ask your student.

- What expression would you use to find the total number of fruit snacks in 1 large box? In 5 large boxes?

- What are some additional examples of items that are packaged and sold this way?

Another way to help your student practice multiplication is to go online and find the ticket prices for a nearby attraction, such as a movie theater, museum, or theme park. The tickets should have at least two different prices—for example, adults and children. Then use the information to complete the following exercises.

- Create a group of at least 10 individuals attending the event.

- Write an expression to find the cost of tickets for the group. Find the cost.

- Suppose the price for one type of ticket goes up. Explain how your expression should change and how the total cost changes.

By the end of this chapter, your student should feel confident with the learning targets and success criteria on the next page. Encourage your student to think of other reasons to multiply numbers, such as finding the number of seats in an auditorium.

Have a great time practicing multiplication!

Lesson	Learning Target	Success Criteria
4.1 Multiply by Tens	Use place value and properties to multiply by multiples of ten.	• I can use place value to multiply by multiples of ten. • I can use the Associative Property to multiply by multiples of ten. • I can describe a pattern with zeros when multiplying by multiples of ten.
4.2 Estimate Products	Use rounding and compatible numbers to estimate products.	• I can use rounding to estimate a product. • I can use compatible numbers to estimate a product. • I can explain different ways to estimate a product.
4.3 Use Area Models to Multiply Two-Digit Numbers	Use area models and partial products to multiply.	• I can use an area model to break apart the factors of a product. • I can relate an area model to partial products. • I can add partial products to find a product.
4.4 Use the Distributive Property to Multiply Two-Digit Numbers	Use area models and the Distributive Property to multiply.	• I can use an area model and partial products to multiply. • I can use an area model and the Distributive Property to multiply.
4.5 Use Partial Products to Multiply Two-Digit Numbers	Use place value and partial products to multiply.	• I can use place value to tell the value of each digit in a number. • I can write the partial products for a multiplication problem. • I can add the partial products to find a product.
4.6 Multiply Two-Digit Numbers	Multiply two-digit numbers.	• I can multiply to find the partial products. • I can show how to regroup ones, tens, and hundreds. • I can add the partial products to find the product.
4.7 Practice Multiplication Strategies	Use strategies to multiply two-digit numbers.	• I can choose a strategy to multiply. • I can multiply two-digit numbers. • I can explain the strategy I used to multiply.
4.8 Problem Solving: Multiplication with Two-Digit Numbers	Solve multi-step word problems involving two-digit multiplication.	• I can understand a problem. • I can make a plan to solve using letters to represent the unknown numbers. • I can solve a problem using an equation.

Nombre _____

Multiplicar números de dos dígitos

En este capítulo su estudiante está aprendiendo a multiplicar números de dos dígitos. Su estudiante aprenderá estrategias de multiplicación por estimación, usando modelos de área, la Propiedad Distributiva y usando productos parciales. El vocabulario de frase para este capítulo es: números compatibles. Números compatibles son números que son fáciles para multiplicar y están cerca de los números que están siendo multiplicados.

Usted puede practicar multiplicación al ir a una tienda o al consultar sitios en línea donde se compran entradas para eventos.

En las tiendas al por mayor, las personas compran grandes cantidades de artículos. Por ejemplo, 1 caja grande contiene 10 cajas más pequeñas y cada caja más pequeña contiene 8 paquetes de gomitas de frutas. Aquí están algunas sugerencias de preguntas para su estudiante.

- ¿Qué expresión usaría para hallar el número total de paquetes de gomitas de frutas en 1 caja grande? ¿En 5 cajas grandes?

- ¿Cuáles otros ejemplos adicionales de artículos son empacados y vendidos de esta manera?

Ayude a su estudiante a hallar precios de entradas para un espectáculo cercano, como un cine, museo o parque de atracciones. Las entradas deberían tener al menos dos precios diferentes—por ejemplo, adultos y niños. Luego use la información para completar los siguientes ejercicios.

- Organice un grupo de al menos 10 personas que irán al evento.

- Escriba una expresión para hallar el costo de las entradas para el grupo. Determine el costo.

- Suponga que el precio para un tipo de entrada aumenta su valor. Explique cómo su expresión cambiaría y cómo se modifica el costo total.

Al final de este capítulo, su estudiante debe sentirse seguro sobre los objetivos de aprendizaje y criterios de éxito que se indican en la siguiente página. Anime a su estudiante a pensar en otros casos para multiplicar números, como hallar el número de sillas en una sala de conferencias.

¡Disfruten juntos practicando multiplicación!

Lección	Objetivo de aprendizaje	Criterios de éxito
4.1 Multiplicar por decenas	Usar el valor de lugar y propiedades para multiplicar por múltiplos de diez.	• Sé usar el valor de lugar para multiplicar por múltiplos de diez. • Sé usar la Propiedad Asociativa para multiplicar por múltiplos de diez. • Sé describir un patrón con ceros cuando multiplico por múltiplos de diez.
4.2 Estimación de productos	Usar redondeo y números compatibles para estimación de productos.	• Sé usar redondeo para estimación de productos. • Sé usar números compatibles para estimación de productos. • Sé explicar diferentes maneras para estimación de productos.
4.3 Usar modelos de área para multiplicar números de dos dígitos	Usar modelos área y productos parciales para multiplicar.	• Sé usar modelos de área para separar los factores de un producto. • Sé relacionar un modelo de área a productos parciales. • Sé sumar productos parciales para hallar un producto.
4.4 Usar la propiedad distributiva para multiplicar números de dos dígitos	Usar modelos de área y la Propiedad Distributiva para multiplicar.	• Sé usar un modelo área y productos parciales para multiplicar. • Sé usar un modelo de área y la Propiedad Distributiva para multiplicar.
4.5 Usar productos parciales para multiplicar números de dos dígitos	Usar el valor de lugar y productos parciales para multiplicar.	• Sé usar el valor de lugar para decir el valor de cada dígito en un número. • Sé escribir los productos parciales para un problema de multiplicación. • Sé sumar los productos parciales para hallar un producto.
4.6 Multiplicar números de dos dígitos	Multiplicar números de dos dígitos.	• Sé multiplicar para hallar los productos parciales. • Sé mostrar cómo reagrupar unidades, decenas y centenas. • Sé sumar los productos parciales para hallar un producto.
4.7 Practicar estrategias de multiplicación	Usar estrategias para multiplicar números de dos dígitos.	• Sé escoger una estrategia para multiplicar. • Sé multiplicar números de dos dígitos. • Sé explicar la estrategia que usé para multiplicar.
4.8 Resolver problemas: Multiplicación con números de dos dígitos	Resolver enunciados de problemas de múltiples pasos incluyendo multiplicación de números de dos dígitos.	• Sé entender un problema. • Sé hacer un plan para resolver usando letras para representar números desconocidos. • Sé resolver un problema usando una ecuación.

Lesson 4.1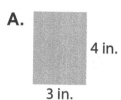

Daily Skills Practice

For use before Lesson 4.1

1. Which two rectangles have the same area?

   A.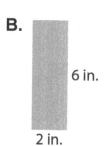

   4 in.

   3 in.

   B.

   6 in.

   2 in.

   C.

   2 in.

   10 in.

Lesson 4.1

Vocabulary Practice

For use before Lesson 4.1

1. Write what you know about this phrase. Give an example.

   ones period

Find the product.

1. $3 \times (6 \times 5) =$

2. $(8 \times 5) \times 5 =$

Name_____

Lesson 4.1 Extra Practice

Find the product.

1. $10 \times 70 =$ _____	**2.** $30 \times 80 =$ _____	**3.** $40 \times 60 =$ _____
4. $50 \times 22 =$ _____	**5.** $38 \times 20 =$ _____	**6.** $70 \times 62 =$ _____
7. $45 \times 30 =$ _____	**8.** $38 \times 40 =$ _____	**9.** $25 \times 90 =$ _____
10. $60 \times 81 =$ _____	**11.** $10 \times 37 =$ _____	**12.** $17 \times 90 =$ _____

Find the missing factor.

13. $40 \times$ _____ $= 1,600$	**14.** _____ $\times 50 = 1,000$	**15.** _____ $\times 30 = 1,800$
16. $90 \times$ _____ $= 7,200$	**17.** $20 \times$ _____ $= 600$	**18.** _____ $\times 10 = 800$

Compare.

19. 50×43 ◯ $2,000$	**20.** 62×40 ◯ $2,500$	**21.** 45×60 ◯ $2,700$
22. 40×24 ◯ $1,000$	**23.** 54×50 ◯ $2,700$	**24.** 36×40 ◯ $1,500$

25. A driver makes a daily work commute of 44 total miles. He worked 20 days during the month. How many total miles did he drive for his work commute for the month?

_____

26. A school has 35 classrooms with 30 seats in each classroom. How many students can fit in the school?

_____

Write the multiplication equation represented by the number line.

27.

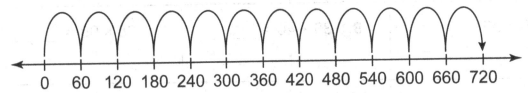

0   60   120   180   240   300   360   420   480   540   600   660   720

_____ × _____ =

28.

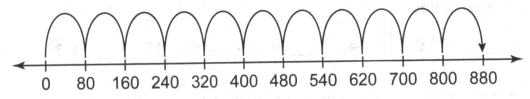

0   80   160   240   320   400   480   540   620   700   800   880

_____ × _____ =

29. Explain how you can use $30 \times 20 = 600$ to find 30×22.	**30.** The product of a number and three times that number is 2,700. What are the numbers?
31. In a hotel, there are 17 floors and 60 rooms on each floor. There are 1,108 guests registered for a conference at the hotel. How many guests will not have a room?	**32.** There are 50 more wrestlers at the county wrestling meet than at the city wrestling meet. The city meet has 30 teams, each with 14 wrestlers. How many wrestlers are at the county meet?

Name_____

You can use place value and properties to multiply two-digit numbers by multiples of ten.

Example Find 20 × 18.

One Way: Use place value.

20 × 18 = 2 tens × 18

= 36 tens

= 360

So, 20 × 18 = 360.

Another Way: Use the Associative Property of Multiplication.

20 × 18 = (10 × 2) × 18   Rewrite 20 as 10 × 2.

= 10 × (2 × 18)   Associative Property of Multiplication

= 10 × 36

= 360

So, 20 × 18 = 360.

Rewrite the product so that one of the factors is 10.

Find the product.

1. 30 × 90 =

2. 50 × 70 =

3. 60 × 23 =

4. 78 × 30 =

Name _____

Enrichment and Extension

A baker uses different sized boxes to sell healthy baked goods.

- A muffin box holds 30 muffins.

- A scone box holds 24 scones.

- A bagel box holds 12 bagels.

The following table shows the number of boxes sold of each item.

	Muffin Boxes	Scone Boxes	Bagel Boxes
Friday	12	20	30
Saturday	18	40	20
Sunday	11	10	10

Write an expression to find the number of items sold each day.
Then find the number.

	Muffins	Scones	Bagels
Friday	1.	2.	3.
Saturday	4.	5.	6.
Sunday	7.	8.	9.

Find the quotient.

1. 54 ÷ 9 = _____

2. 21 ÷ 7 = _____

Lesson 4.2 Vocabulary Practice
For use before Lesson 4.2

1. Write what you know about this word. Give an example.

round

Find the product.

1. $30 \times 80 =$ _____

2. $60 \times 37 =$ _____

Name_____

Use rounding to estimate the product.

1. 52×14

2. 38×62

3. 47×39

4. 61×78

5. 36×38

6. 25×72

Use compatible numbers to estimate the product.

7. 24×69

8. 47×81

9. 30×92

10. 74×26

11. 21×94

12. 57×42

Estimate the product.

13. 81×74 | **14.** 68×91 | **15.** 76×71

Write two possible factors that could be estimated as shown.

16. 4,800

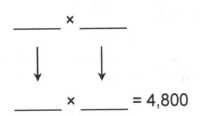

_____ × _____ = 4,800

17. 1,400

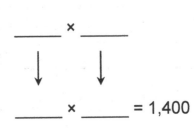

_____ × _____ = 1,400

18. 2,000

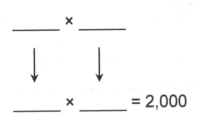

_____ × _____ = 2,000

19. 4,500

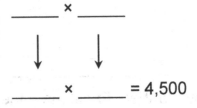

_____ × _____ = 4,500

---

20. You use 70×80 to estimate 67×79. Will your estimate be greater than or less than the actual product? Explain.

---

21. You use 80×90 to estimate 78×88. Will your estimate be greater than or less than the actual product? Explain.

---

22. About how many candles come in 22 medium boxes of candles?

Number of Candles in a Box	
Box Size	**Number**
Small	16
Medium	25
Large	36

Name_____

You can estimate products by using rounding or compatible numbers. **Compatible numbers** are numbers that are easy to multiply and are close to the actual numbers.

Example Use rounding to estimate 22×38.

Step 1: Round each factor to the nearest ten.

$$22 \times 38$$
$$\downarrow \quad \downarrow$$
$$20 \times 40$$

Step 2: Multiply the rounded factors.

$$20 \times 40 = 20 \times 4 \text{ tens}$$
$$= 80 \text{ tens}$$
$$= 800$$

So, 22×38 is about 800.

Example Use compatible numbers to estimate 23×42.

Step 1: Choose compatible numbers.

$$23 \times 42$$
$$\downarrow \quad \downarrow$$
$$25 \times 40$$

Step 2: Multiply the compatible numbers.

$$25 \times 40 = 25 \times 4 \text{ tens}$$
$$= 100 \text{ tens}$$
$$= 1,000$$

So, 23×42 is about 1,000.

Use rounding to estimate the product.

1. 19×31

2. 27×42

3. 68×75

Use compatible numbers to estimate the product.

4. 28×57

5. 91×28

6. 94×21

Name _____

Enrichment and Extension

The list below shows the daily average number of volunteers in a community.

- January: Daily average of 23 volunteers

- February: Daily average of 18 volunteers

- March: Daily average of 27 volunteers

- April: Daily average of 43 volunteers

Write an expression to estimate the number of volunteers for the month by the given method. Then find the estimate.

	Rounding	Compatible Numbers
January	1.	2.
February	3.	4.
March	5.	6.
April	7.	8.

9. Which method of estimating do you prefer? Explain.

1. What is the total mass shown?

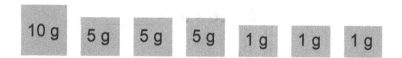

The total mass is _____ grams.

1. Write what you know about this word. Give an example.

area

Estimate the product.

1. $49 \times 72 = \underline{\hspace{1cm}}$

2. $56 \times 91 = \underline{\hspace{1cm}}$

Name_____

Use the area model to find the product.

1. 35 × 22 = _____

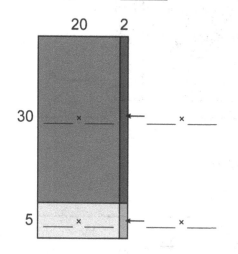

☐ + ☐ + ☐ + ☐

2. 16 × 18 = _____

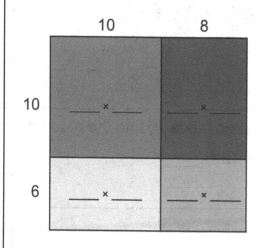

☐ + ☐ + ☐ + ☐

3. 19 × 33 = _____

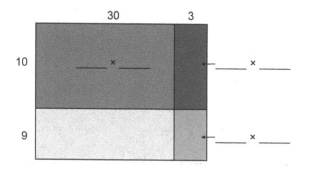

☐ + ☐ + ☐ + ☐

4. 41 × 24 = _____

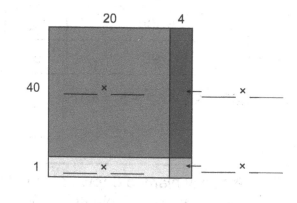

☐ + ☐ + ☐ + ☐

Use the area model to find the product.

5. 27 × 17 = _____

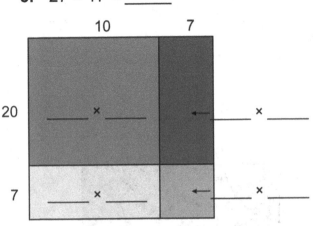

6. 34 × 32 = _____

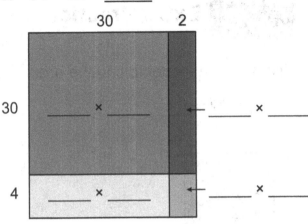

Draw an area model to find the product.

7. 11 × 18 = _____

8. 16 × 20 = _____

9. 13 × 25 = _____

10. 32 × 41 = _____

11. Your friend finds 13 times 32. Is your friend correct?

	30	2
10	300	12
3	90	5

300 + 90 + 12 + 5 = 407

12. Explain how to use an area model to find the partial products when you multiply 14 × 23.

13. A family planted 6 rows of tomato plants in April and 7 more rows in May. Each row has 12 plants. How many tomato plants are there in all?

14. A company buys 21 boxes of bagged snacks. There are 18 bagged snacks in each box. Draw an area model to find the total number of bagged snacks.

Name_____

Example Use an area model and partial products to find 19 × 11.

Model the expression. Break apart 19 as 10 + 9 and 11 as 10 + 1.

Add the area of each rectangle
to find the product for the whole model.

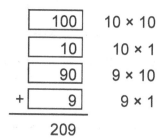

100	10 × 10
10	10 × 1
90	9 × 10
+ 9	9 × 1
209	

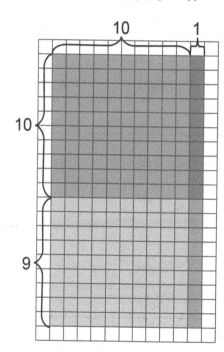

Add the partial products.

So, 19 × 11 = 209.

Use the area model to find the product.

1. 31 × 25 = _____

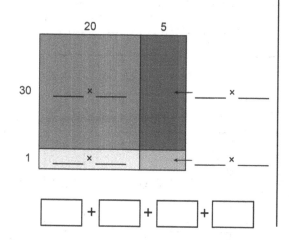

☐ + ☐ + ☐ + ☐

2. 53 × 42 = _____

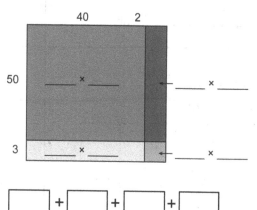

☐ + ☐ + ☐ + ☐

Name _____

Lesson 4.3   **Enrichment and Extension**

Write the multiplication equation represented by the area model.

1. _____ × _____ = _____

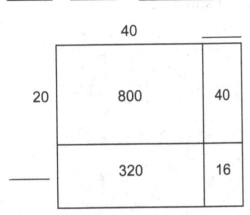

	40	_____
20	800	40
_____	320	16

2. _____ × _____ = _____

	30	_____
20	600	60
	270	27

3. _____ × _____ = _____

	60	_____
_____	3,000	100
6	360	12

4. _____ × _____ = _____

	40	4
_____	1,600	160
_____	160	16

5. _____ × _____ = _____

	50	_____
_____	1,500	30
_____	30	1

6. _____ × _____ = _____

	60	_____
_____	4,200	350
	60	5

Lesson 4.4 **Daily Skills Practice**
For use before Lesson 4.4

1. Find the equivalent fraction.

$$\frac{8}{8} = \frac{\square}{6}$$

Lesson 4.4 **Vocabulary Practice**
For use before Lesson 4.4

1. Write what you know about this phrase. Give an example.

Distributive Property

Draw an area model to find the product.

1. $38 \times 34 =$ _____

2. $61 \times 52 =$ _____

Name_____

1. Use the area model and the
   Distributive Property to find 32×47.

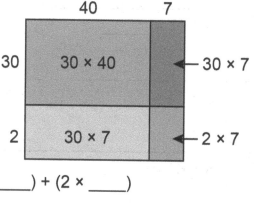

$32 \times 47 = 32 \times (40 + 7)$

$\qquad = (32 \times 40) + (32 \times 7)$

$\qquad = (30 + 2) \times \underline{\quad} + (30 + 2) \times \underline{\quad}$

$\qquad = (30 \times \underline{\quad}) + (2 \times \underline{\quad}) + (30 \times \underline{\quad}) + (2 \times \underline{\quad})$

$\qquad = \underline{\quad} + \underline{\quad} + \underline{\quad} + \underline{\quad}$

$\qquad = \underline{\quad}$

Use the Distributive Property to find the product.

2. $53 \times 38 = $

$53 \times 38 = 53 \times (30 + 8)$

$\qquad = (53 \times 30) + (53 \times 8)$

$\qquad = (50 + 3) \times \underline{\quad} + (50 + 3) \times \underline{\quad}$

$\qquad = (50 \times \underline{\quad}) + (3 \times \underline{\quad}) + (50 \times \underline{\quad}) + (3 \times \underline{\quad})$

$\qquad = \underline{\quad} + \underline{\quad} + \underline{\quad} + \underline{\quad}$

$\qquad = \underline{\quad}$

---

3. $64 \times 55 = $

$64 \times 55 = 64 \times (50 + 5)$

$\qquad = (64 \times 50) + (64 \times 5)$

$\qquad = (60 + 4) \times \underline{\quad} + (60 + 4) \times \underline{\quad}$

$\qquad = (60 \times \underline{\quad}) + (4 \times \underline{\quad}) + (60 \times \underline{\quad}) + (4 \times \underline{\quad})$

$\qquad = \underline{\quad} + \underline{\quad} + \underline{\quad} + \underline{\quad}$

$\qquad = \underline{\quad}$

Use the Distributive Property to find the product.

4. $43 \times 53 =$ _____

5. $21 \times 67 =$ _____

6. $59 \times 17 =$ _____

7. $38 \times 49 =$ _____

8. $66 \times 71 =$ _____

9. $23 \times 95 =$ _____

10. $58 \times 62 =$ _____

11. $64 \times 88 =$ _____

12. $75 \times 83 =$ _____

13. $92 \times 74 =$ _____

14. $91 \times 84 =$ _____

15. $70 \times 95 =$ _____

16. Find 67×34 by breaking apart 34 first.

17. A lot has dimensions of 75 feet by 86 feet. There must be 2,200 square feet for each dog to play in the lot. Is the lot large enough for 3 dogs to play? Explain.

18. At a basketball game there are 85 boxes of towels to give to fans. There are 68 towels in each box. If there are 5,678 fans attending the game, will each fan get a towel? Explain.

19. There were 92 buyers of $23 tickets for a show in the first hour. The show wanted to sell $2,000 worth of tickets in the first hour. Did the show meet its goal? Explain.

Name_____

Use an area model and the Distributive Property to find 28 × 19.

One Way: Use an area model and partial products.

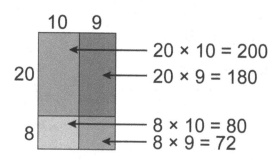

20 × 10 = 200
20 × 9 = 180
8 × 10 = 80
8 × 9 = 72

Add the partial products:

200 + 180 + 80 + 72 = 532

So, 28 × 19 = 532.

Another Way: Use an area model and the Distributive Property.

28 × 19 = (20 + 8) × 19	Break apart 28.
= (20 × 19) + (8 × 19)	Distributive Property
= 20 × (10 + 9) + 8 × (10 + 9)	Break apart 19.
= (20 × 10) + (20 × 9) + (8 × 10) + (8 × 9)	Distributive Property
= 200 + 180 + 80 + 72	Multiply.
= 532	Add.

So, 28 × 19 = 532.

1. Use the area model and the Distributive Property to find 34 × 46.

$$34 × 46 = 34 × (40 + 6)$$

40	30
30 × 40	30 × 6
4 × 40	4 × 6

30
4

= (34 × 40) + (34 × 6)

= (30 + 4) × ___ + (30 + 4) × ___

= (30 × ___) + (4 × ___) + (30 × ___) + (4 × ___)

= ___ + ___ + ___ + ___

= ___

Name _____

Lesson 4.4 Enrichment and Extension

Complete the missing steps.

1.   _____ × 36 = _____ × (30 + 6)

                = (_____ × 30) + (_____ × 6)

                = (20 + _____) × 30 + (20 + _____) × 6

                = (20 × 30) + (6 × 30) + (20 × 6) + (6 × 6)

                = 600 + 180 + 120 + 36

                = 936

2. 81 × _____ = _____ × (_____ + 1)

                = (81 × _____) + (81 × _____)

                = (_____ + 1) × 70 + (_____ + 1) × 1

                = (_____ × 70) + (1 × 70) + (_____ × 1) + (1 × 1)

                = _____ + 70 + 80 + 1

                = 5,751

3.   _____ × _____ = _____ × (90 + _____)

                = (_____ × 90) + (_____ × 2)

                = (70 + _____) × 90 + (70 + _____) × 2

                = (70 × _____) + (5 × _____) + (70 × _____) + (5 × _____)

                = _____ + _____ + _____ + _____

                = _____

1.   What is the total liquid volume shown?

A.   1 liter 700 milliliters

B.   1 liter 900 milliliters

C.   2 liters

D.   1 liter 300 milliliters

Lesson 4.5 **Vocabulary Practice** For use before Lesson 4.5

1.   Write what you know about this phrase. Give an example.

place value

Prerequisite Skills Practice

For use before Activity 4.5

Use the Distributive Property to find the product.

1. $24 \times 37 =$ _____

2. $59 \times 38 =$ _____

Name_____

Find the product. Check whether your answer is reasonable.

1. Estimate: _____

$$\begin{array}{r} 23 \\ \times\ 18 \\ \hline \end{array}$$

☐
☐
☐
+ ☐
_____

2. Estimate: _____

$$\begin{array}{r} 32 \\ \times\ 27 \\ \hline \end{array}$$

☐
☐
☐
+ ☐
_____

3. Estimate: _____

$$\begin{array}{r} 43 \\ \times\ 47 \\ \hline \end{array}$$

☐
☐
☐
+ ☐
_____

4. Estimate: _____

$$\begin{array}{r} 29 \\ \times\ 62 \\ \hline \end{array}$$

☐
☐
☐
+ ☐
_____

5. Estimate: _____

$$\begin{array}{r} 53 \\ \times\ 71 \\ \hline \end{array}$$

☐
☐
☐
+ ☐
_____

6. Estimate: _____

$$\begin{array}{r} 38 \\ \times\ 93 \\ \hline \end{array}$$

☐
☐
☐
+ ☐
_____

Find the product. Check whether your answer is reasonable.

7. Estimate: _____	8. Estimate: _____	9. Estimate: _____
33 × 41	28 × 44	52 × 58

10. Estimate:	11. Estimate:	12. Estimate:
92 × 23 = _____	64 × 32 = _____	58 × 45 = _____

13. Estimate:	14. Estimate:	15. Estimate:
49 × 73 = _____	38 × 91 = _____	53 × 52 = _____

16. Find the missing digits.
Then find the product.

```
      □8
×    1□
    100
     80
     40
     32
    [    ]
```

17. If you reach your goal each week, how many miles will you run in 12 weeks?

Weekly Running Goal	
You	★★★★
Newton	★
Descartes	★★↗

Each ★ = 4 miles

18. Use the table in Exercise 17. If you and Descartes meet your goal each week, how many more miles will you run in 4 weeks than Descartes?

Name_____

Example Use place value and partial products to find 22×36.

Estimate: $20 \times 40 = 800$

Step 1: Multiply the tens by the tens: $20 \times 30 = 600$

Step 2: Multiply the ones by the tens: $2 \times 30 = 60$

Step 3: Multiply the tens by the ones: $20 \times 6 = 120$

Step 4: Multiply the ones by the ones: $2 \times 6 = 12$

Step 5: Add the partial products: $600 + 60 + 120 + 12 = 792$

NOTE: You can do these steps in any order.

Check: Because 792 is close to the estimate of 800, the answer is reasonable.

```
    22
  × 36
   600
    60
   120
  +  12
   792
```

Find the product. Check whether your answer is reasonable.

1. Estimate:

_____

```
    42
  × 18
```
☐
☐
☐
+ ☐

2. Estimate:

_____

```
    33
  × 52
```
☐
☐
☐
+ ☐

3. Estimate:

_____

```
    76
  × 49
```
☐
☐
☐
+ ☐

Name _____

Use place value and partial products to find the total number of
seats in the rows described for a stadium.

1. The first 32 rows have 94 seats in each row.

_____

2. The next 27 rows have 86 seats in each row.

_____

3. The next 24 rows have 82 seats in each row.

_____

4. The next 19 rows have 75 seats in each row.

_____

5. The next 17 rows have 68 seats in each row.

_____

6. The last 12 rows have 54 seats in each row.

_____

7. Find the total number of seats in the stadium.

_____

Write the multiplication equation shown by the partial products.

8. $3,200 + 120 + 560 + 21$

_____

9. $3,000 + 540 + 50 + 9$

_____

10. $5,600 + 160 + 490 + 14$

_____

11. $4,500 + 720 + 200 + 32$

_____

12. $5,400 + 420 + 270 + 21$

_____

13. $5,600 + 560 + 560 + 56$

1. Round to the nearest hundred to estimate the difference.

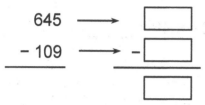

$$
\begin{array}{r}
645 \longrightarrow \boxed{} \\
-\ 109 \longrightarrow -\boxed{} \\
\hline
\boxed{}
\end{array}
$$

1. Write what you know about this word. Give an example.

perimeter

Prerequisite Skills Practice

For use before Lesson 4.6

Find the product using partial products.

1. 35 × 56 = _____

2. 91 × 48 = _____

Name_____

Find the product. Check whether your answer is reasonable.

1. Estimate: _____

    42
    × 31
    _____

2. Estimate: _____

    71
    × 81
    _____

3. Estimate: _____

    ☐
    5 3
    × 3 7
    _____

4. Estimate: _____

    ☐
    8 4
    × 2 8
    _____

5. Estimate: _____

    ☐
    ☐
    4 7
    × 5 4
    _____

6. Estimate: _____

    ☐
    ☐
    8 6
    × 3 9
    _____

7. Estimate: _____

    72
    × 38
    _____

8. Estimate: _____

    35
    × 64
    _____

9. Estimate: _____

    57
    × 61
    _____

10. Estimate: _____

    19
    × 82
    _____

11. Estimate: _____

    33
    × 72
    _____

12. Estimate: _____

    78
    × 52
    _____

Find the product. Check whether your answer is reasonable.

13. Estimate: _____

    21 × 19 = _____

14. Estimate: _____

    34 × 42 = _____

15. Estimate: _____

    45 × 28 = _____

16. Estimate: _____

    51 × 27 = _____

17. Estimate: _____

    62 × 37 = _____

18. Estimate: _____

    39 × 32 = _____

19. A class of 16 students takes a field trip to an aquarium. The price for tickets is $21. What is the total cost of admission for the students?

20. When you multiply two-digit numbers, is regrouping needed when the ones digits are 3 or less? Why?

21. Find the missing digits.

```
      4 ☐
  ×   5 4
  ─────────
    1 7 ☐
  2 1 ☐
  ─────────
  2 3 ☐ 2
```

22. A tree is 18 feet tall. An office building is 13 times taller than the tree. A cell phone tower is 228 feet tall. Is the office building or the cell phone tower taller?

Name_____

Example Find 79 × 56.

Estimate: 80 × 60 = 4,800

Step 1: Multiply 79 by 6 ones, or 6.

```
      5
     79
  ×  56
     474
```
6 × 79 ⟶ 474

- 6 × 9 ones = 54 ones
  Regroup as 5 tens and 4 ones.
- 6 × 7 tens = 42 tens
  Add the regrouped tens:
  42 + 5 = 47.

Step 2: Multiply 79 by 5 tens, or 50.

```
     4
     5̸
     79
  ×  56
     474
```
50 × 79 ⟶ 3,950

- 5 tens × 9 = 45 tens
  Regroup as
  4 hundreds and
  5 tens or 50.
- 5 tens × 70 = 350 tens, or 35 hundreds
  Add the regrouped hundreds:
  35 + 4 = 39.

So, 79 × 56 = 4,424.

Step 3: Add the partial products.

```
     4
     5̸
     79
  ×  56
     474
  + 3,950
    4,424
```

Make sure the partial products are aligned in the correct place values.

Check: Because 4,424 is close to the estimate of 4,800, the answer is reasonable.

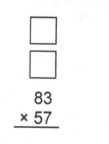

Find the product. Check whether your answer is reasonable.

1. Estimate: _____

```
     22
  × 43
```

2. Estimate: _____

```
  ☐
     46
  × 13
```

3. Estimate: _____

```
  ☐
  ☐
     83
  × 57
```

Name _____

Enrichment and Extension

Use four of the numbers 4, 5, 6, 7, 8, and 9 to make two
two-digit numbers that have a product as close as possible
to the number given, but not greater than the number.
Write the multiplication equation.

1. 5,000

_____

2. 6,000

_____

3. 7,000

_____

4. 8,000

_____

5. 9,000

1. Identify the property.

   17 + 22 = 22 + 17

   A. Commutative Property of Addition

   B. Associative Property of Addition

   C. Addition Property of Zero

1. Write what you know about this word. Give an example.

   rhombus

Find the product. Check if your answer is reasonable.

1. Estimate: _____

   $82 \times 73 =$

2. Estimate: _____

   $64 \times 71 =$

Name_____

Lesson 4.7 **Extra Practice**

Find the product.

1. $28 \times 41 =$ _____

2. $54 \times 31 =$ _____

3. $64 \times 82 =$ _____

4. $65 \times 52 =$ _____

5. $13 \times 88 =$ _____

6. $24 \times 27 =$ _____

7. $32 \times 14 =$ _____

8. $41 \times 19 =$ _____

9. $72 \times 76 =$ _____

10. $64 \times 48 =$ _____

11. $61 \times 35 =$ _____

12. $46 \times 75 =$ _____

Find the product.

13. $42 \times 73 =$ _____

14. $58 \times 84 =$ _____

_____

15. $84 \times 84 =$ _____

16. $95 \times 95 =$ _____

---

17. What number can you multiply the number of bowling balls by to find the total weight? Use this pattern to complete the table.

Number of Bowling Balls	6	12	18	24	30
Total Weight (in Pounds)	60	120	180		

---

18. A box of golf balls contains 3 balls. The boxes come in a case, with 16 boxes per case. The cases are shipped in a crate, with 12 cases per crate. How many golf balls are there in a crate?

Name_____

Example Find 57 × 60.

One Way: Use an area model and partial products.

	60
50	50 × 60
7	7 × 60

Add the partial products:

3,000 + 420 = 3,420

So, 57 × 60 = 3,420.

Another Way: Use place value.

57 × 60 = 57 × 6 tens

= 342 tens

= 3,420

So, 57 × 60 = 3,420.

Example Find 62 × 29.

One Way: Use place value and partial products.

```
      62
    × 29
   1,200   20 × 60
      40   20 × 2
     540   9 × 60
      18   9 × 2
   1,798
```

So, 62 × 29 = 1,798.

Another Way: Use regrouping.

Multiply 62 by 9 ones. Then multiply 62 by 2 tens. Regroup if necessary.

```
    1
      62
    × 29
     558
   1,240
   1,798
```

So, 62 × 29 = 1,798.

Find the product using any method.

1. 12 × 22 = _____

2. 58 × 40 = _____

3. 66 × 13 = _____

4. 83 × 15 = _____

5. 41 × 64 = _____

6. 63 × 33 = _____

Name _____

Enrichment and Extension

Find the missing factor.

1.
```
   42
×  [    ]
  252
+1,260
 1,512
```

2.
```
   57
×  [    ]
  228
+2,850
 3,078
```

3.
```
   38
×  [    ]
   38
+2,280
 2,318
```

4.
```
   72
×  [    ]
  216
+5,760
 5,976
```

5.
```
   64
×  [    ]
  128
+3,200
 3,328
```

6.
```
   85
×  [    ]
  340
+3,400
 3,740
```

Find the missing digit so both products are the same.

7.
```
   42        5 0
×  25      × 2 [ ]
```

8.
```
   42        7 5
×  25      × 1 [ ]
```

9.
```
   42        7 0
×  25      × 1 [ ]
```

10.
```
   58        6 8
×  34      × 2 [ ]
```

11.
```
   44        8 8
×  68      × 3 [ ]
```

12.
```
   72        6 4
×  56      × 6 [ ]
```

1. You buy a bookmark and 3 books. You spend $29.
   The bookmark costs $2. Each book costs the same amount.
   How much is each book?

   Each book costs $_____.

Lesson 4.8 **Vocabulary Practice**
For use before Lesson 4.8

1. Write what you know about this word. Give an example.

   kilogram

Prerequisite Skills Practice

For use before Lesson 4.8

Find the product. Check if your answer is reasonable.

1. $38 \times 83 =$ _____

2. $97 \times 29 =$ _____

Name_____

Lesson 4.8 **Extra Practice**

Understand the problem. Then make a plan. How will you solve? Explain.

1. There are 36 drivers in an automobile race. Each driver will use 12 tires. How many more tires are used than the number of drivers in the race?

_____

2. A box of fig bars contains 16 two-packs. A concession stand orders 15 boxes. How many fig bars are there in all?

_____

3. A teacher has 24 students take a 27-question test. The teacher has graded the answers for 3 tests. How many more answers does the teacher need to grade?

_____

4. A warehouse club sells water in packages of 32 sixteen-fluid-ounce bottles. You buy 3 packages. How many fluid ounces of water did you buy in all?

_____

5. A school has 48 buses. Each bus has 23 rows of 2 seats. How many passengers can travel by bus?

_____

6. A parking lot has 28 rows that can hold 44 cars and 32 rows that can hold 27 cars. How many cars can be parked in the lot?

7. An airline has 52 small planes. Each plane has 18 rows with 3 seats in each row. How many passengers can the planes carry in all?

8. An employee lives 37 miles from work. The employee works 18 days each month. How many miles does the employee drive to and from work each month?

9. A child ticket to a play is $13, which is $18 less than an adult ticket. There are 54 child tickets and 45 adult tickets sold. What is the total cost of the tickets?

10. A child has a wall of building blocks. There are 28 blocks in each row and the wall is 34 blocks high. The child has knocked down 655 blocks. How many blocks are standing?

11. An auditorium has 72 rows of 54 seats on the ground level. There are 44 rows of 44 seats in the balcony. How many more seats are there on the floor of the auditorium?

12. The edge of a stained glass window is a pattern made of alternating shorter and longer rectangular tiles. The pattern has 11 shorter tiles and 10 longer tiles. How long is the edge of the stained glass window?

Name_____

Reteach

Example A store receives a shipment of 4 boxes of snacks. Each box is 2 feet long and contains 24 bags. Each bag has 21 ounces of snacks. How many total ounces of snacks are in the shipment?

Understand the Problem

What do you know?	What do you need to find?
• The store receives 4 boxes. • Each box contains 24 bags. • Each bag has 21 ounces of snacks.	• You need to find how many ounces of snacks are in the shipment.

Make a Plan

How will you solve?

- Multiply 24 by 4 to find the total number of bags.
- Then multiply the product by 21 to find the total number of ounces.

Solve

Step 1: How many bags are in the shipment?

$$\begin{array}{r} 1 \\ 24 \\ \times\ \ 4 \\ \hline 96 \end{array}$$

There are 96 bags in the shipment.

Step 2: How many ounces are in the shipment?

$$\begin{array}{r} 1 \\ 96 \\ \times\ \ 21 \\ \hline 96 \\ 192 \\ \hline 2{,}016 \end{array}$$

There are 2,016 ounces in the shipment.

1. Find how many ounces of snacks there are in a shipment of 3 boxes of snacks.

Name _____

Lesson 4.8   **Enrichment and Extension**

Write two expressions that can be used to solve the problem.

1. There are 10 players in a game. They each receive 15 cards from a deck of 275 cards. How many cards are left in the deck?

_____

2. An athlete in training runs 12 miles per day and bikes 33 miles per day. The athlete trains for 3 full weeks. How many miles does the athlete travel in all by running and biking?

_____

3. A T-shirt company prints 22 white shirts and 34 blue shirts. Each shirt has 12 characters. What is the total number of characters on all the shirts?

_____

4. A store sells 56 pairs of jeans for $25 each and 84 shirts for $18 each. How much money does the store receive in all for the items?

_____

5. You have 50 pictures that measure 8 inches by 11 inches. You are placing string around the outside edge of each picture. How much string do you need in all?

_____

6. A bookstore receives a shipment of 8 boxes with 8 books inside each box. Each book weighs 14 ounces. What is the total weight?

_____

7. A family uses 1,423 kilowatt-hours of electricity in a month. They receive a credit of 46 kilowatt-hours from each of the 22 solar panels they have. How many kilowatt-hours does the family have to pay for?

_____

8. There are 18 classes in a school that are testing. Each class has 24 students who each have 3 pencils. How many pencils are being used in all?

Name _____

Chapter 4 Chapter Self-Assessment

Use the scale below to rate your understanding of the learning target and the success criteria.

1	**2**	**3**	**4**
I do not understand.	I can do it with help.	I can do it on my own.	I can teach someone else.

	Rating
4.1 Multiply by Tens	
Learning Target: Use place value and properties to multiply by multiples of ten.	1 2 3 4
I can use place value to multiply by multiples of ten.	1 2 3 4
I can use the Associative Property to multiply by multiples of ten.	1 2 3 4
I can describe a pattern with zeros when multiplying by multiples of ten.	1 2 3 4
4.2 Estimate Products	
Learning Target: Use rounding and compatible numbers to estimate products.	1 2 3 4
I can use rounding to estimate a product.	1 2 3 4
I can use compatible numbers to estimate a product.	1 2 3 4
I can explain different ways to estimate a product.	1 2 3 4
4.3 Use Area Models to Multiply Two-Digit Numbers	
Learning Target: Use area models and partial products to multiply.	1 2 3 4
I can use an area model to break apart the factors of a product.	1 2 3 4
I can relate an area model to partial products.	1 2 3 4
I can add partial products to find a product.	1 2 3 4

Name _____

	Rating
4.4 Use the Distributive Property to Multiply Two-Digit Numbers	
Learning Target: Use area models and the Distributive Property to multiply.	1 2 3 4
I can use an area model and partial products to multiply.	1 2 3 4
I can use an area model and the Distributive Property to multiply.	1 2 3 4
4.5 Use Partial Products to Multiply Two-Digit Numbers	
Learning Target: Use place value and partial products to multiply.	1 2 3 4
I can use place value to tell the value of each digit in a number.	1 2 3 4
I can write the partial products for a multiplication problem.	1 2 3 4
I can add the partial products to find a product.	1 2 3 4
4.6 Multiply Two-Digit Numbers	
Learning Target: Multiply two-digit numbers.	1 2 3 4
I can multiply to find partial products.	1 2 3 4
I can show how to regroup ones, tens, and hundreds.	1 2 3 4
I can add partial products to find a product.	1 2 3 4
4.7 Practice Multiplication Strategies	
Learning Target: Use strategies to multiply two-digit numbers.	1 2 3 4
I can choose a strategy to multiply.	1 2 3 4
I can multiply two-digit numbers.	1 2 3 4
I can explain the strategy I used to multiply.	1 2 3 4
4.8 Problem Solving: Multiplication with Two-Digit Numbers	
Learning Target: Solve multi-step word problems involving two-digit multiplication.	1 2 3 4
I can understand a problem.	1 2 3 4
I can make a plan to solve using letters to represent the unknown numbers.	1 2 3 4
I can solve a problem using an equation.	1 2 3 4

Chapter 5

Chapter 5 Divide Multi-Digit Numbers by One-Digit Numbers

Dear Family,

In this chapter, your student is learning about dividing multi-digit numbers by one-digit numbers. Students will use tape diagrams, counters, and area diagrams when dividing. Students will explore division problems with and without a remainder. Students will use a division strategy involving partial quotients, where quotients are found in parts until the remainder is less than the divisor. You can help your student learn about dividing multi-digit numbers by one-digit numbers by practicing in real-life settings. Vocabulary terms associated with this chapter include *remainder* and *partial quotients*.

At the grocery store, you can find items to help model division. For example, there may be a cereal box containing 80 ounces. The box of cereal may have a serving size of 3 ounces. Here are some questions to ask your student at the store.

- What expression can you use to find the total number of servings?

- What other items are packaged and sold this way?

Help your student find items that can be shared with many people. There should be at least 3 items available. Then ask your student to complete the following.

- Determine the number of people sharing the items.

- Find the number of items that each person would receive.

- Suppose there is one less person to share the items with. Explain how you would change your expression to model the new situation. Explain the meaning of the remainder (if any).

By the end of this chapter, your student should feel confident with the learning targets and success criteria on the next page. Encourage your student to think of other contexts in which to use division.

Have fun exploring division!

Lesson	Learning Target	Success Criteria
5.1 Divide Tens, Hundreds, and Thousands	Use place value to divide tens, hundreds, or thousands.	• I can divide a multiple of ten, one hundred, or one thousand by a one-digit number. • I can explain how to use place value and division facts to divide tens, hundreds, or thousands.
5.2 Estimate Quotients	Use division facts and compatible numbers to estimate quotients.	• I can use division facts and compatible numbers to estimate a quotient. • I can find two estimates that a quotient is between.
5.3 Understand Division and Remainders	Use models to find quotients and remainders.	• I can use models to divide numbers that do not divide evenly. • I can find a quotient and a remainder. • I can interpret the quotient and the remainder in a division problem.
5.4 Use Partial Quotients	Use partial quotients to divide.	• I can explain how to use an area model to divide. • I can write partial quotients for a division problem. • I can add the partial quotients to find a quotient.
5.5 Use Partial Quotients with a Remainder	Use partial quotients to divide and find remainders.	• I can use partial quotients to divide. • I can find a remainder.
5.6 Divide Two-Digit Numbers by One-Digit Numbers	Divide two-digit numbers by one-digit numbers.	• I can divide to find the partial quotients. • I can show how to regroup 1 or more tens. • I can use place value to record the partial quotients.
5.7 Divide Multi-Digit Numbers by One-Digit Numbers	Divide multi-digit numbers by one-digit numbers.	• I can use place value to divide. • I can show how to regroup thousands, hundreds, or tens. • I can find a quotient and a remainder.
5.8 Divide by One-Digit Numbers	Divide by one-digit numbers.	• I can use place value to divide. • I can explain why there might be a 0 in the quotient. • I can find a quotient and a remainder.
5.9 Problem Solving: Division	Solve multi-step word problems involving division.	• I can understand a problem. • I can make a plan to solve using letters to represent the unknown numbers. • I can solve a problem using an equation.

Nombre _____

Capítulo 5 — Dividir números de varios dígitos entre números de un dígito

Querida familia:

En este capítulo, su estudiante está aprendiendo sobre división de números de varios dígitos entre números de un dígito. Estudiantes usarán diagramas de cinta, contadores y diagramas de área cuando dividan. Estudiantes explorarán problemas de división con y sin resto. Estudiantes usarán una estrategia para dividir incluyendo cocientes parciales, donde los cocientes son hallados por partes hasta que el resto es menor que el divisor. Puede ayudar a su estudiante a aprender a dividir números de varios dígitos entre números de un dígito practicando con situaciones de la vida real. Palabras de vocabulario asociadas con este capítulo incluyen *resto* y *cocientes parciales*.

En la tienda, usted puede hallar artículos para ayudar a modelar la operación de división. Por ejemplo, podría haber una caja de cereal que contenga 80 onzas y con un tamaño de porción de 3 onzas. Aquí algunas preguntas para hacer a su estudiante en la tienda. (Puede escoger cualquier producto, pero que pueda redondear su precio al valor de dólar más cercano.)

- ¿Qué expresión puedes usar para hallar el número total de porciones?

- ¿Cuáles otros artículos están empacados y se venden de esta misma manera?

Ayude a su estudiante a encontrar artículos que puedan ser compartidos con muchas personas. Debería haber al menos 3 artículos disponibles. Luego pregunte a su estudiante que complete lo siguiente.

- Determina el número de personas para compartir los artículos.

- Halla el número de artículos que cada persona recibirá.

- Vamos a suponer que hay una persona menos con quien compartir los artículos. Explica cómo cambiarías tu expresión para representar la nueva situación. Explica el significado del resto (si lo hay).

Al final de este capítulo, su estudiante debe sentirse seguro sobre los objetivos de aprendizaje y criterios de éxito que se indican en la siguiente página. Anime a su estudiante a pensar en otros contextos para usar división.

¡Diviértanse explorando a través de la operación de división!

Lección	Objetivo de aprendizaje	Criterios de éxito
5.1 Dividir decenas, centenas y miles	Usar el valor de la posición para dividir decenas, centenas o miles.	• Sé dividir un múltiplo de diez, cien o mil entre un número de un dígito. • Sé explicar cómo usar el valor de la posición y datos de la división para dividir decenas, centenas o miles.
5.2 Estimar cocientes	Usar datos de la división y números compatibles para estimar cocientes.	• Sé usar datos de la división y números compatibles para estimar un cociente. • Sé hallar dos estimados entre los que esté un cociente.
5.3 Entender división y resto	Usar modelos para hallar cocientes y restos.	• Sé usar modelos para dividir números cuya división no es exacta. • Sé hallar un cociente y un resto. • Sé interpretar el cociente y el resto en un problema de división.
5.4 Usar cocientes parciales	Usar cocientes parciales para dividir.	• Sé explicar cómo usar un modelo de área para dividir. • Sé escribir cocientes parciales para un problema de división. • Sé sumar cocientes parciales para hallar un cociente.
5.5 Usar cocientes parciales con un resto	Usar cocientes parciales para dividir y hallar restos.	• Sé usar cocientes parciales para dividir. • Sé hallar un resto.
5.6 Dividir números de dos dígitos entre números de un dígito	Dividir números de dos dígitos entre números de un dígito.	• Sé dividir para hallar los cocientes parciales. • Sé mostrar cómo agrupar una o más decenas. • Sé usar el valor de la posición para registrar cocientes parciales.
5.7 Dividir números de varios dígitos entre números de un dígito	Dividir números de varios dígitos entre números de un dígito.	• Sé usar el valor de la posición para dividir. • Sé mostrar como agrupar miles, centenas o decenas. • Sé encontrar un cociente y un resto.
5.8 Dividir entre números de un dígito	Dividir entre números de un dígito.	• Sé usar el valor de la posición para dividir. • Sé explicar por qué debe haber un 0 en el cociente. • Sé encontrar un cociente y un resto.
5.9 Resolver problemas: División	Resolver enunciados de problemas de múltiples pasos que incluyan la división.	• Sé entender un problema. • Sé hacer un plan para resolver problemas usando letras para representar los números desconocidos. • Sé resolver un problema usando una ecuación.

Daily Skills Practice

For use before Lesson 5.1

Find the product.

1. 8,686
    ×   8
    _____

2. 7,899
    ×   8
    _____

Lesson 5.1

Vocabulary Practice

For use before Lesson 5.1

1. Write what you know about this word. Give an example.

numerator

Big Ideas Math: Modeling Real Life Grade 4   **199**
Resources by Chapter

Prerequisite Skills Practice

For use before Lesson 5.1

Find the product.

1. 70 × 20 = _____

2. 40 × 15 = _____

Name_____

1. Find 600 ÷ 4.

   Think: _____ ÷ _____ = _____

   600 ÷ 4 = _____ tens ÷ 4

   = _____ tens

   = _____

   So, 600 ÷ 4 = _____.

2. Find 7,200 ÷ 9.

   Think: _____ ÷ _____ = _____

   7,200 ÷ 9 = _____ hundreds ÷ 9

   = _____ hundreds

   = _____

   So, 7,200 ÷ 9 = _____.

Find each quotient.

3. 20 ÷ 5 = _____

   200 ÷ 5 = _____

   2,000 ÷ 5 = _____

4. 18 ÷ 6 = _____

   180 ÷ 6 = _____

   1,800 ÷ 6 = _____

5. 32 ÷ 4 = _____

   320 ÷ 4 = _____

   3,200 ÷ 4 = _____

6. 21 ÷ 3 = _____

   210 ÷ 3 = _____

   2,100 ÷ 3 = _____

Find the quotient.

7. 320 ÷ 8 = _____	8. 80 ÷ 4 = _____	9. 4,000 ÷ 4 = _____
10. 450 ÷ 5 = _____	11. 1,000 ÷ 5 = _____	12. 900 ÷ 3 = _____
13. 1,600 ÷ 8 = _____	14. 1,400 ÷ 7 = _____	15. 900 ÷ 9 = _____
16. 4,000 ÷ 5 = _____	17. 700 ÷ 7 = _____	18. 180 ÷ 2 = _____

Find the missing number.

19. $100 \div \underline{\hspace{1cm}} = 10$	**20.** $\underline{\hspace{1cm}} \div 8 = 1,000$	**21.** $2,500 \div \underline{\hspace{1cm}} = 500$
22. $\underline{\hspace{1cm}} \div 3 = 90$	**23.** $7,000 \div \underline{\hspace{1cm}} = 1,000$	**24.** $\underline{\hspace{1cm}} \div 5 = 500$
25. $60 \div \underline{\hspace{1cm}} = 6$	**26.** $\underline{\hspace{1cm}} \div 8 = 1,000$	**27.** $2,000 \div \underline{\hspace{1cm}} = 500$

Compare.

28. $70 \div 7 \bigcirc 7 \times 10$	**29.** $1,600 \div 10 \bigcirc 4 \times 40$	**30.** $900 \div 9 \bigcirc 3 \times 100$
31. $800 \div 4 \bigcirc 80 \times 4$	**32.** $8,000 \div 80 \bigcirc 8 \times 100$	**33.** $6,000 \div 6 \bigcirc 5 \times 100$

34. A choir has 240 students that are divided into 8 equal groups. How many students are in each group?

35. What is Newton's number?

When I divide my number by 4, I get 500. When I divide my number by 5, I get 400.

36. You walk 2,800 steps. This is 4 times as many as your friend. How many steps does your friend walk?

Name_____

You can use place value and basic division facts to divide tens, hundreds, or thousands by one-digit numbers.

Example Find $240 \div 4$.

Think: $24 \div 4 = 6$ Division fact

$240 \div 4 = 24$ tens $\div 4$ Use place value.

     $= 6$ tens   Divide.

     $= 60$

So, $240 \div 4 = 60$.

6	6	6	6
├──── 24 ────┤

60	60	60	60
├──── 240 ────┤

Example Find $8{,}100 \div 9$.

Think: $81 \div 9 = 9$ Division fact

$8{,}100 \div 9 = 81$ hundreds $\div 9$ Use place value.

     $= 9$ hundreds   Divide.

     $= 900$

So, $8{,}100 \div 9 = 900$.

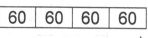

Multiply 900 by 9 to check your answer.

---

1. Find $720 \div 6$.

   Think: _____ ÷ _____ = _____

   $720 \div 6 = $ _____ tens $\div 6$

        $= $ _____ tens

        $= $ _____

   So, $720 \div 6 = $ _____.

2. Find each quotient.

   $32 \div 4 = $ _____

   $320 \div 4 = $ _____

   $3{,}200 \div 4 = $ _____

Name _____

Enrichment and Extension

The table shows the numbers of seats and equal sections in a stadium.

	Number of Seats	Number of Sections
North stands	840	4
South stands	1,600	4
East stands	3,400	8
West stands	4,200	8

1. How many seats are in each section of the north stands?

_____

2. How many seats are in each section of the south stands?

_____

3. A row has 25 seats. How many rows are in the east stands?

_____

4. Which stands have the greatest number of rows? Explain.

Lesson 5.2 Daily Skills Practice
For use before Lesson 5.2

Find the product.

1. $60 \times 78 =$ _____

2. $58 \times 60 =$ _____

Lesson 5.2 Vocabulary Practice
For use before Lesson 5.2

1. Write what you know about this word. Give an example.

estimate

Prerequisite Skills Practice

For use before Lesson 5.2

Find the quotient.

1. $2,000 \div 4 =$ _____

2. $6,000 \div 3 =$ _____

Name_____

Lesson 5.2 Extra Practice

Estimate the quotient.

1. $34 \div 5$

2. $71 \div 8$

2. $315 \div 8$

4. $207 \div 4$

5. $158 \div 5$

6. $802 \div 9$

Find two estimates that the quotient is between.

7. $205 \div 3$

8. $626 \div 8$

9. $1,292 \div 2$

10. $6,998 \div 9$

Estimate to compare.

11. $88 \div 3 \bigcirc 50$

12. $189 \div 4 \bigcirc 60$

13. $30 \bigcirc 116 \div 6$

14. $70 \bigcirc 158 \div 2$

15. $381 \div 5 \bigcirc 283 \div 4$

16. $627 \div 6 \bigcirc 798 \div 9$

17. $198 \div 3 \bigcirc 457 \div 8$

18. $460 \div 7 \bigcirc 263 \div 3$

19. Five friends want to share 272 tokens equally. They want to determine whether they can each have at least 52 tokens. Can they use an estimate, or is an exact answer required? Explain.

20. Explain how to find a better estimate for $658 \div 7$ than the one shown.

Round 658 to 700. Estimate $700 \div 100$. $700 \div 7 = 100$, so $658 \div 7$ is about 100.

21. A machine that makes boxes is in operation for 6 hours each day. The machine makes 7,405 boxes in 1 day. About how many boxes does the machine make each hour?

22. There are 3,782 fans at a basketball game. This was 3 times as many fans as the previous game. About how many fans were at the previous game?

23. A company sold 4,233 light bulbs this year. This was 3 times as many light bulbs as the company sold last year. About how many light bulbs did the company sell last year?

Name_____

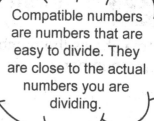

Compatible numbers are numbers that are easy to divide. They are close to the actual numbers you are dividing.

You can use division facts and compatible numbers to estimate a quotient.

Example Estimate $190 \div 3$.

Look at the first two digits of the dividend and use basic division facts.

Think: What number close to 190 is easily divided by 3?

Try 180. $18 \div 3 = 6$, so $180 \div 3 = 60$.

Try 210. $21 \div 3 = 7$, so $210 \div 3 = 70$.

Choose 180 because 190 is closer to 180.

So, $190 \div 3$ is about 60.

When solving division problems, you can check whether an answer is reasonable by finding two estimates that a quotient is between.

Look at the first two digits of the dividend and use basic division facts.

Example Find two estimates that the quotient $5,123 \div 8$ is between.

Think: What numbers close to 5,123 are easily divided by 8?

Use 4,800. $48 \div 8 = 6$, so $4,800 \div 8 = 600$.

Use 5,600. $56 \div 8 = 7$, so $5,600 \div 8 = 700$.

5,123 is between 4,800 and 5,600.

So, the quotient $5,123 \div 8$ is between 600 and 700.

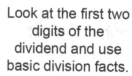

Estimate the quotient.

1. $87 \div 4$	**2.** $43 \div 7$
3. $653 \div 9$	**4.** $395 \div 5$

Find two estimates that the quotient is between.

5. $201 \div 3$	**6.** $153 \div 8$
7. $5,203 \div 6$	**8.** $2,360 \div 5$

Lesson 5.2 Enrichment and Extension

The table shows the number of miles biked by different people. Each person biked the same number of miles each day.

Person	Miles	Days
A	325	6
B	264	4

1. To estimate the number of miles Person A biked each day, find two numbers that the quotient is between.

_____

2. Which is the better estimate for the number of miles Person A biked each day?

_____

3. To estimate the number of miles Person B biked each day, find two numbers that the quotient is between.

_____

4. Which is the better estimate for the number of miles Person B biked each day?

1. Write an equation for the comparison sentence.

   12 is 3 times as many as 4.

   12 = _____ × _____

1. Write what you know about this phrase. Give an example.

   Distributive Property

Prerequisite Skills Practice
For use before Lesson 5.3

Estimate the quotient.

1. $78 \div 4 =$ _____

2. $290 \div 7 =$ _____

Name_____

Use a model to find the quotient and the remainder.

1. $9 \div 2 =$ _____ R _____

2. $11 \div 4 =$ _____ R _____

3. $16 \div 6 =$ _____ R _____

4. $17 \div 2 =$ _____ R _____

5. $43 \div 8 =$ _____ R _____

6. $17 \div 5 =$ _____ R _____

7. $14 \div 3 =$ _____ R _____

8. $29 \div 6 =$ _____ R _____

Use a model to find the quotient and the remainder.

9. $59 \div 9 =$ _____ R _____

10. $86 \div 9 =$ _____ R _____

11. $74 \div 8 =$ _____ R _____

12. $57 \div 7 =$ _____ R _____

13. A number divided by 3 has a remainder. What numbers might the remainder be? Explain.

14. A number divided by 5 has a remainder. What numbers might the remainder be? Explain.

15. Each car on a carnival ride can have no more than 8 riders. There are 78 riders in line.

    - How many cars can be filled?
    - How many cars are needed?
    - How many riders are in the last car when all the others have 8 riders?

16. You need 4 boards to make a shelf. You have 32 boards. How many shelves can you make?

17. There are 79 songs in your playlist. You listen to 9 songs each day. How many days will it take you to listen to all the songs in your playlist?

18. Thirty-four students attend tryouts for a debate league. Each team can have 5 students. How many students will *not* be on a team?

Name_____

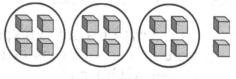

Lesson 5.3 Reteach

Sometimes you cannot divide a number evenly and there is an amount left over.

The amount left over is called the **remainder**.

Use an R to represent the remainder.

$14 \div 3 = 4$ with 2 left over

$14 \div 3 = 4$ R2

$$\begin{array}{r} 4 \ \text{R}2 \\ 3\overline{)14} \end{array}$$

Example Find $26 \div 5$.

Divide 26 into 5 equal groups.

You need to regroup 2 tens as 20 ones.

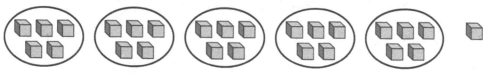

Number of units in each group: 5

Number of units left over: 1

So, $26 \div 5 = 5$ R 1.

Use a model to find the quotient and the remainder.

1. $16 \div 5 =$ _____ R _____

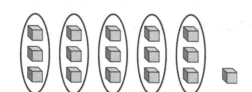

2. $20 \div 3 =$ _____ R _____

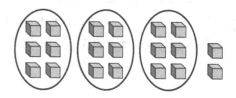

3. $39 \div 6 =$ _____ R _____

4. $41 \div 8 =$ _____ R _____

Name _____

Lesson 5.3   Enrichment and Extension

There are 28 red marbles and 14 blue marbles.

1. The red marbles are to be put into large boxes. Each box can hold 9 marbles. How many boxes will be full? How many red marbles will be left?

2. The blue marbles are to be put into small boxes. Each box can hold 3 marbles. How many boxes will be full? How many blue marbles will be left?

3. Instead of boxes, you fill bags with 7 marbles in each bag. Can all the marbles be placed into the bags? Explain.

4. If you fill bags with 8 marbles in each bag, can all the marbles be placed into the bags? Explain.

1. Find each product.

    $3 \times 4 =$ _____

    $3 \times 40 =$ _____

    $3 \times 400 =$ _____

    $3 \times 4,000 =$ _____

Lesson 5.4 **Vocabulary Practice**
For use before Lesson 5.4

1. Write what you know about this phrase. Give an example.

    partial products

Prerequisite Skills Practice
For use before Lesson 5.4

Use a model to find the quotient and the remainder.

1. $22 \div 4 =$ _____ R _____

2. $19 \div 8 =$ _____ R _____

Name_____

Use an area model and partial quotients to divide.

1. $228 \div 4$

$4\overline{)228}$

$-\boxed{} = 4 \times \underline{}$

$\boxed{}$

$-\boxed{} = 4 \times \underline{}$

$\boxed{}$

$\boxed{}$

$+\boxed{}$

$\boxed{}$

2. $141 \div 3$

$3\overline{)141}$

$-\boxed{} = 3 \times \underline{}$

$\boxed{}$

$-\boxed{} = 3 \times \underline{}$

$\boxed{}$

$\boxed{}$

$+\boxed{}$

$\boxed{}$

Use partial quotients to divide.

3. $3\overline{)51}$

4. $6\overline{)84}$

5. $4\overline{)84}$

6. $5\overline{)85}$

7. $4\overline{)112}$

8. $3\overline{)108}$

Use partial quotients to divide.

9. 7)378	**10.** 4)248	**11.** 7)259
12. 6)246	**13.** 8)424	**14.** 9)639
15. 5)240	**16.** 7)385	**17.** 7)511

18. Newton finds $791 \div 7$. Is he correct? Explain.

```
  7)791
 -  700  = 7 × 100        100
     91

 -   70  = 7 × 10          10

     21

 -   21  = 7 × 3        +    3
      0                   113
```

19. Explain how you can use an area model and partial quotients to divide.

20. Each gift bag gets 4 stickers. How many gift bags are there?

Gift Bag Items	
Item	**Number**
Pencils	149
Pens	102
Erasers	268
Stickers	160
Crayons	97

Name_____

To divide using **partial quotients**, subtract a multiple of the divisor that is less than the dividend. Continue to subtract multiples until the remainder is less than the divisor. The factors that are multiplied by the divisor are called partial quotients. Their sum is the quotient.

Example Use an area model and partial quotients to find 224 ÷ 4.

One Way:		**Partial Quotients**	**Another Way:**		**Partial Quotients**

One Way:

$$4\overline{)224}$$
$$-\ 100 = 4 \times 25$$
$$\overline{\quad 124}$$

$$-\ 100 = 4 \times 25$$
$$\overline{\quad 24}$$

$$-\ \ 24 = 4 \times 6$$
$$\overline{\quad\ \ 0}$$

Partial Quotients
25
25
+ 6
56

So, 224 ÷ 4 = 56.

		25	6
4	100	100	24

Area = 224 square units

Another Way:

$$4\overline{)224}$$
$$-\ 200 = 4 \times 50$$
$$\overline{\quad 24}$$

$$-\ \ 24 = 4 \times 6$$
$$\overline{\quad\ \ 0}$$

Partial Quotients
50
+ 6
56

So, 224 ÷ 4 = 56.

	50	6
4	200	24

Area = 224 square units

Use an area model and partial quotients to divide.

1. 84 ÷ 3 = _____

$$3\overline{)84}$$
$$-\ \boxed{60} = 3 \times \underline{\quad} \qquad \boxed{\ }$$
$$\overline{\boxed{\ }}$$
$$-\ \boxed{24} = 3 \times \underline{\quad} \qquad +\boxed{\ }$$
$$\overline{\boxed{\ }}$$
$$\overline{\underline{\quad}}$$

3	60	24

2. 144 ÷ 8 = _____

$$8\overline{)144}$$
$$-\ \boxed{\ } = 8 \times \underline{\quad} \qquad \boxed{\ }$$
$$\overline{\boxed{\ }}$$
$$-\ \boxed{\ } = 8 \times \underline{\quad} \qquad +\boxed{\ }$$
$$\overline{\boxed{\ }}$$
$$\overline{\underline{\quad}}$$

8	80	___

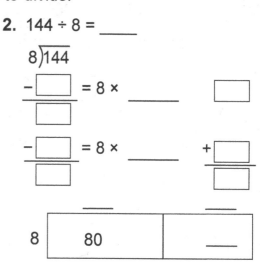

Name _____

Enrichment and Extension

Write the division problem that is represented by the model.

1.

	10	1
5	50	5

2.

	50	6
6	300	36

Complete the model. Then write the division problem that is represented by the model.

3.

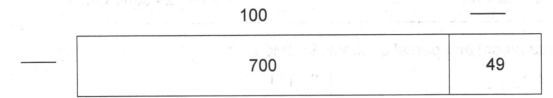

	100	___
___	700	49

Daily Skills Practice
For use before Lesson 5.5

1. Write two comparison sentences for 16 = 8 × 2.

   16 is _____ times as many as _____.

   16 is _____ times as many as _____.

Vocabulary Practice
For use before Lesson 5.5

1. Write what you know about this phrase. Give an example.

   fact family

Prerequisite Skills Practice
For use before Lesson 5.5

Use partial quotients to divide.

1. $6\overline{)348}$

2. $7\overline{)553}$

Name_____

Extra Practice

Use partial quotients to divide.

1. $2\overline{)63}$

2. $3\overline{)91}$

3. $4\overline{)70}$

4. $5\overline{)68}$

5. $6\overline{)319}$

6. $3\overline{)277}$

7. $8\overline{)423}$

8. $5\overline{)616}$

9. $7\overline{)523}$

10. $4\overline{)729}$

11. $3\overline{)418}$

12. $9\overline{)804}$

Use partial quotients to divide.

13. $2\overline{)799}$

14. $2\overline{)1{,}091}$

15. $6\overline{)677}$

16. $4\overline{)4{,}253}$

17. $5\overline{)2{,}016}$

18. $3\overline{)4{,}159}$

19. Show how to use the least number of partial quotients to find $4{,}136 \div 6$.

20. Show how to use the least number of partial quotients to find $5{,}287 \div 8$.

21. There are 263 volunteers for an event. Each group needs 6 volunteers. How many full groups can there be?

22. There are 1,325 ounces of water. A cup can hold up to 6 fluid ounces of the water. How many cups can hold all the water?

23. You have 230 stamps. You place 8 stamps on each page of a stamp book. Your friend has 278 stamps. He places 5 stamps on each page of a stamp book. Who uses more pages? Explain.

Name_____

Lesson 5.5 Reteach

Example Use partial quotients to find $3{,}504 \div 9$.

Remember to continue to divide until the remainder is less than the divisor.

$$
\begin{array}{r}
9)\overline{3{,}504} \\
-\,2{,}700 = 9 \times 300 \quad 300 \\
\hline
804 \\
-\,720 = 9 \times 80 \quad\;\; 80 \\
\hline
84 \\
-\,81 = 9 \times 9 \quad +\;9 \\
\hline
3 \qquad\qquad 389\ \text{R}\ 3
\end{array}
$$

The remainder, 3, is
less than the divisor, 9. $\longrightarrow$

So, $3{,}504 \div 9 = 389\ \text{R}\ 3$.

Use partial quotients to divide.

1. $98 \div 5 =$ _____

$$5)\overline{98}$$

$-\,50 = 5 \times$ ____ ☐

☐

$-\,45 = 5 \times$ ____ $+\dfrac{\square}{\square}$

☐ ☐ R ☐

2. $673 \div 7 =$ _____

$$7)\overline{673}$$

$-\,630 = 7 \times$ ____ ☐

☐

$-\,42 = 7 \times$ ____ $+\dfrac{\square}{\square}$

☐ ☐ R ☐

3. $6)\overline{359}$

4. $4)\overline{1{,}038}$

5. $3)\overline{1{,}199}$

Name _____

1. Write a division equation that has a two-digit dividend, a one-digit divisor, and a remainder of 4.

_____

2. Write a division equation that has a three-digit dividend, a one-digit divisor, and a remainder of 5.

_____

3. Write a division equation that has a four-digit dividend, a one-digit divisor, and a remainder of 6.

_____

4. A four-digit dividend is divided by 7. What are the possible remainders? Explain.

1. Compare the values of the underlined digits.

   5̲0,000 and 5̲00

   The value of the 5 in 50,000 is _____ times the value of the 5 in 500.

Lesson 5.6 **Vocabulary Practice**
For use before Lesson 5.6

1. Write what you know about this phrase. Give an example.

   square unit

Use partial quotients to divide.

1. 4)‾301‾

2. 5)‾2,043‾

Name_____

Find the quotient. Then check your answer.

1.
```
    □
  4)56
 -□↓
   □
  -□
 ────
   □
```

2.

```
    □
  7)84
 -□↓
   □
  -□
 ────
   □
```

3.
```
   □
 6)84
```

4.
```
   □
 6)72
```

5.
```
   □
 4)64
```

6.
```
   □ R ____
 6)93
```

7.
```
   □ R ____
 7)51
```

8.
```
   □ R ____
 5)73
```

9.
```
   □ R ____
 3)29
```

Find the quotient. Then check your answer.

10. $4\overline{)72}$

11. $5\overline{)39}$

12. $8\overline{)36}$

13. $9\overline{)93}$

14. $3\overline{)39}$

15. $2\overline{)71}$

16. $6\overline{)48}$

17. $7\overline{)63}$

18. $3\overline{)45}$

19. Which problem does *not* require regrouping to find the quotient?

$4\overline{)36}$ $3\overline{)48}$ $5\overline{)65}$ $7\overline{)97}$

20. A group of 4 people have 84 trading cards to share. How many trading cards does each person receive?

21. Admission to an amusement park is $95 for 5 people. The price is the same for each person. What is the cost of admission for each person?

22. You want to read 28 pages in 3 hours. You want to read about the same number of pages each hour. How many pages should you read each hour? How can you interpret the remainder?

Name_____

Example Find 92 ÷ 6.

Divide the tens.

Think: 92 is 9 tens and 2 ones.

Regroup.

```
  1
6)92
- 6
  3
```

Divide: 9 tens ÷ 6
Multiply: 1 ten × 6
Subtract: 9 tens − 6 tens
There are 3 tens left over.

```
  1
6)92
- 6↓
  32
```

Regroup 3 tens as 30 ones.
30 ones + 2 ones = 32 ones

Divide the ones.

```
  15  R  2
6)92
- 6 ↓
  32
- 30
   2
```

Divide: 32 ones ÷ 6
Multiply: 5 ones × 6
Subtract: 32 ones − 30 ones
There are 2 ones left over.

Check:
15 × 6 + 2 = 90 + 2 = 92

So, 92 ÷ 6 = 15 R 2.

Find the quotient. Then check your answer.

1.

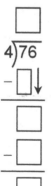

```
 □
4)76
-□↓
 □
-□
 □
```

2.

```
 □
5)65
```

3.

```
 □  R____
6)83
```

Name _____

Complete the division problem so that regrouping is *not* needed and the quotient is a two-digit quotient number without a remainder. Do not use 1 as the divisor.

1.

$\boxed{})\overline{96}$

2.

$\boxed{})\overline{55}$

3.

$\boxed{})\overline{84}$

4.

$\boxed{})\overline{63}$

Complete the division problem so that regrouping is needed and the quotient is a two-digit number without a remainder.

5.

$\boxed{})\overline{96}$

6.

$\boxed{})\overline{65}$

7.

$\boxed{})\overline{84}$

8.

$\boxed{})\overline{48}$

Lesson 5.7 · Daily Skills Practice

For use before Lesson 5.7

1. Write the number in two other forms.

   Word form: four hundred seventy-one thousand, nine hundred two

   Standard form: _____

   Expanded form: _____

Lesson 5.7 · Vocabulary Practice

For use before Lesson 5.7

1. Write what you know about this phrase. Give an example.

   inverse operations

Prerequisite Skills Practice
For use before Lesson 5.7

Find the quotient. Check your answer.

1. $3\overline{)84}$

2. $6\overline{)92}$

Lesson 5.7 **Extra Practice**

Find the quotient. Then check your answer.

1. $\square$ 6)474	**2.** $\square$ R _____ 7)538	**3.** $\square$ 2)1,904
4. $\square$ 3)2,523	**5.** $\square$ R _____ 5)5,138	**6.** $\square$ R _____ 4)8,349
7. 5)492	**8.** 2)394	**9.** 4)189
10. 7)847	**11.** 7)981	**12.** 9)840

Find the quotient. Then check your answer.

13.

$6\overline{)804}$

14.

$3\overline{)786}$

15.

$6\overline{)164}$

16.

$5\overline{)993}$

17.

$5\overline{)3,315}$

18.

$4\overline{)7,755}$

19.

$6\overline{)3,069}$

20.

$9\overline{)6,717}$

21.

$5\overline{)3,837}$

22. At a game, there are 1,705 fans in attendance. Every fifth fan receives a prize. How many fans receive a prize?

23. Which expression does *not* have a 3-digit quotient? Explain how you know without solving.

$795 \div 2$ $394 \div 3$

$605 \div 4$ $491 \div 5$

24. There are 1,728 seats in an auditorium. The seats are in 9 equal sections. How many seats are in each section?

Lesson 5.7 **Reteach**

Example Find 619 ÷ 4.

Estimate: 600 ÷ 4 = 150
Divide the hundreds.

$$\begin{array}{r} 1 \\ 4\overline{)619} \\ -4 \\ \hline 2 \end{array}$$

Divide: 6 hundreds ÷ 4
Multiply: 1 hundred × 4
Subtract: 6 hundreds – 4 hundreds
There are 2 hundreds left over.

Divide the tens.

$$\begin{array}{r} 15 \\ 4\overline{)619} \\ -4\downarrow \\ \hline 21 \\ -20 \\ \hline 1 \end{array}$$

Regroup 2 hundreds and 1 ten as
21 tens: 21 ÷ 4
5 tens × 4
21 tens – 20 tens
There is 1 ten left over.

Divide the ones.

$$\begin{array}{r} 154\ R\ 3 \\ 4\overline{)619} \\ -4 \\ \hline 21 \\ -20 \\ \hline 19 \\ -16 \\ \hline 3 \end{array}$$

Regroup 1 ten and 9 ones as
19 ones: 19 ÷ 4
4 ones × 4
19 ones – 16 ones
There are 3 ones left over.

So, 619 ÷ 4 = 154 R 3.

Check: Because 154 R 3 is close to the estimate, the answer is reasonable.

Find the quotient. Then check your answer.

1. ☐ R _____
   5)842

2. ☐ R _____
   7)7,304

3. ☐ R _____
   4)7,652

Name _____

Complete the division problem.

1.
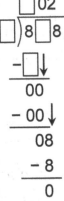

```
        13□
    □)6□5
    - 5↓
      16
    - 15↓
      15
    - 15
       0
```

2.
```
       □02
    □)8□8
    -□↓
     00
   - 00↓
     08
    - 8
      0
```

3. A company has 9,435 candles to put into boxes. There will be 8 candles in a box. How many boxes will be filled? Will there be any candles left over? Explain.

4. How can you tell if 4,603 ÷ 5 will have a remainder without completing the division? Explain.

1. You have 4,650 songs in your music library. You download 2,724 more songs. Then you delete 142 songs. How many songs do you have now?

   You have _____ songs now.

Lesson 5.8 **Vocabulary Practice**
For use before Lesson 5.8

1. Write what you know about this word. Give an example.

   round

Find the quotient. Check your answer.

1. $7\overline{)893}$

2. $8\overline{)8,079}$

Name_____

Find the quotient. Then check your answer.

1. R ____ 5)294	**2.** ☐ 7)336	**3.** ☐ R ____ 4)449
4. 4)212	**5.** 5)335	**6.** 6)512
7. 7)282	**8.** 6)831	**9.** 2)423
10. 8)408	**11.** 5)980	**12.** 9)906
13. 4)2,312	**14.** 5)7,505	**15.** 3)8,898

16. $3\overline{)9,607}$

17. $4\overline{)9,204}$

18. $5\overline{)6,923}$

19. $7\overline{)7,561}$

20. $8\overline{)3,390}$

21. $9\overline{)5,341}$

22. There are 729 apples to be put into bags. There will be 9 apples in each bag. How many bags are needed?

23. How could you change one digit in the dividend of 275 ÷ 3 so that there would be no remainder? Explain.

24. The table shows the number of volunteers in each of four schools. The Central volunteers are placed into groups of 8. Remaining Central volunteers are added to the groups, so some of the groups have 9 volunteers. How many groups have 8 Central volunteers? 9 Central volunteers?

School	Number of Volunteers
Southern	144
Central	169
Western	128
Eastern	95

Name_____

Example Find 3,651 ÷ 6.

3 thousands *cannot* be shared among 6 groups without regrouping.
So, regroup 3 thousands as 30 hundreds and combine with 6 hundreds.

Divide the hundreds.	$\begin{array}{r} 6 \\ 6\overline{)3,651} \\ -36 \\ \hline 0 \end{array}$	36 hundreds ÷ 6 6 hundreds × 6 Subtract: 36 hundreds – 36 hundreds There are 0 hundreds left over.
Divide the tens.	$\begin{array}{r} 60 \\ 6\overline{)3,651} \\ -36 \\ \hline 05 \\ -00 \\ \hline 5 \end{array}$	5 tens *cannot* be shared among 6 groups without regrouping. So, place a zero in the quotient. 0 tens × 6 5 tens – 0 tens There are 5 tens left over.
Divide the ones.	$\begin{array}{r} 608 \text{ R } 3 \\ 6\overline{)3,651} \\ -36 \\ \hline 05 \\ -00 \\ \hline 51 \\ -48 \\ \hline 3 \end{array}$	Regroup 5 tens as 50 ones and combine with 1 one. 51 ones ÷ 6 8 ones × 6 51 ones – 48 ones There are 3 ones left over.

So, 3,651 ÷ 6 = 608 R 3.

Find the quotient. Then check your answer.

1.

$8\overline{)864}$

2.
$4\overline{)832}$

3.
$5\overline{)5,469}$ R _____

Name _____

Enrichment and Extension

Change the divisor so the quotient has no remainder. Write the new division problem.

1.　　　338 R 1
　　　3)1,015

_____

2.　　　679 R 1
　　　3)2,038

_____

3.　　　354 R 1
　　　5)1,771

_____

Complete the division problem so that the quotient has a remainder of 1.

4.
　　　□
　□)4,045

_____

5.
　　　□
　□)1,831

Daily Skills Practice
For use before Lesson 5.9

Find the product.

1. 65
      × 8

2. 16
      × 6

Vocabulary Practice
For use before Lesson 5.9

1. Write what you know about this phrase. Give an example.

unit fraction

Find the quotient. Check your answer.

1. $4\overline{)1,442}$

2. $7\overline{)7,231}$

Name_____

Lesson 5.9 Extra Practice

Understand the problem. Then make a plan. How will you solve? Explain.

1. You need to read a 325-page book before the end of summer. You have read 221 pages. There are 4 weeks left in summer. You want to read the same number of pages each week to finish the book. How many pages should you read each week?

2. There are 18 adults and 36 children at a museum. If 6 people can go on a tour, how many tours are needed?

Solve.

3. A teacher has 6 boxes of pens. Each box has 24 pens. The teacher wants to give 5 pens to each student. What is the greatest number of students that can receive 5 pens?

4. There are 1,842 red candles, 1,842 white candles, and 1,842 blue candles. The candles are put into boxes with 14 candles in each box. How many candles are left over?

5. A teacher has 106 students. One class has 16 students. Each of the other 5 classes have the same number of students. How many students are in each of the other classes?

6. You have 270 minutes of activities this week. Outside of basketball, you divide your activity time equally among 3 other activities. How many minutes do you spend on each of the other 3 activities?

   M: basketball 45 min
   W: basketball 45 min
   F: basketball 45 min

7. You want to run 80 miles this month. You have run 62 miles. There are 6 days left in the month. You want to run the same number of miles each day to reach your goal. How many miles should you run each day?

8. There are 24 third graders and 32 fourth graders on a field trip. If the students need to be placed in groups of 8, how many groups will there be?

9. A librarian has 8 boxes of new books. Each box has 18 books. The librarian wants to put 6 books on each shelf. How many shelves are needed?

10. There are 452 red apples, 452 green apples, and 452 yellow apples. The apples are put into crates with 18 apples in each crate. How many apples are left over?

11. There are 6 bags of golf balls. Each bag has 24 golf balls. The golf balls are put in boxes with 3 golf balls in each box. How many boxes are needed?

12. There are 48 goldfish and 64 catfish in a pet store. The fish need to be put into fish bowls with 4 fish in each bowl. How many bowls are needed?

13. A drone takes a picture every 3 seconds. How many pictures does the drone take in 45 minutes?

Name_____

Example Your family traveled 1,242 miles last summer. This is 120 more than 3 times as many miles as your friend's family traveled last summer. How many miles did your friend's family travel last summer?

Understand the Problem

What do you know?	What do you need to find?
• Your family traveled 1,242 miles last summer. • This is 120 more than 3 times as many miles as your friend's family traveled last summer.	• You need to find the number of miles your friend's family traveled last summer.

Make a Plan

How will you solve?

• Subtract 120 from 1,242 to find 3 times the number of miles your friend's family traveled last summer.

• Then divide the difference by 3 to find the number of miles your friend's family traveled last summer.

Solve

Step 1: $1,242 - 120 = b$

b is the unknown difference.

$$\begin{array}{r} 1,242 \\ -\ 120 \\ \hline 1,122 \end{array} \quad b = 1,122$$

Step 2: $b \div 3 = c$

c is the unknown quotient.

$$3\overline{)1,122} \quad c = 374$$
$$374$$

Your friend's family traveled 374 miles last summer.

1. Explain how you can check if your answer is reasonable.

Name _____

Enrichment and Extension

1. Your family traveled 2,306 miles last summer. This is 1,200 more than 2 times as many miles as your friend's family traveled last summer. How many miles did your friend's family travel last summer?

2. You read 124 pages this week. This is 35 less than 3 times as many pages as your friend read. How many pages did your friend read?

3. You walk 145 steps from your door to the mailbox. This is 35 less than one-half as many steps as you walk to your friend's home. How many steps do you walk to your friend's home?

Name _____

Chapter Self-Assessment

Use the scale below to rate your understanding of the learning target and the success criteria.

1	**2**	**3**	**4**
I do not understand.	I can do it with help.	I can do it on my own.	I can teach someone else.

	Rating
5.1 Divide Tens, Hundreds, and Thousands	
Learning Target: Use place value to divide tens, hundreds, or thousands.	1 2 3 4
I can divide a multiply of ten, one hundred, or one thousand by a one-digit number.	1 2 3 4
I can explain how to use place value and division facts to divide tens, hundreds, or thousands.	1 2 3 4
5.2 Estimate Quotients	
Learning Target: Use division facts and compatible numbers to estimate quotients.	1 2 3 4
I can use division facts and compatible numbers to estimate a quotient.	1 2 3 4
I can find two estimates that a quotient is between.	1 2 3 4
5.3 Understand Division and Remainders	
Learning Target: Use models to find quotients and remainders.	1 2 3 4
I can use models to divide numbers that do not divide evenly.	1 2 3 4
I can find a quotient and a remainder.	1 2 3 4
I can interpret the quotient and the remainder in a division problem.	1 2 3 4
5.4 Use Partial Quotients	
Learning Target: Use partial quotients to divide.	1 2 3 4
I can explain how to use an area model to divide.	1 2 3 4
I can write partial quotients for a division problem.	1 2 3 4
I can add the partial quotients to find a quotient.	1 2 3 4

Name _____

	Rating			
5.5 Use Partial Quotients with a Remainder				
Learning Target: Use partial quotients to divide and find remainders.	1	2	3	4
I can use partial quotients to divide.	1	2	3	4
I can find a remainder.	1	2	3	4
5.6 Divide Two-Digit Numbers by One-Digit Numbers				
Learning Target: Divide two-digit numbers by one-digit numbers.	1	2	3	4
I can divide to find the partial quotients.	1	2	3	4
I can show how to regroup 1 or more tens.	1	2	3	4
I can use place value to record the partial quotients.	1	2	3	4
5.7 Divide Multi-Digit Numbers by One-Digit Numbers				
Learning Target: Divide multi-digit numbers by one-digit numbers.	1	2	3	4
I can use place value to divide.	1	2	3	4
I can show how to regroup thousands, hundreds, or tens.	1	2	3	4
I can find a quotient and a remainder.	1	2	3	4
5.8 Divide by One-Digit Numbers				
Learning Target: Divide by one-digit numbers.	1	2	3	4
I can use place value to divide.	1	2	3	4
I can explain why there might by a 0 in the quotient.	1	2	3	4
I can find a quotient and a remainder.	1	2	3	4
5.9 Problem Solving: Division				
Learning Target: Solve multi-step word problems involving division.	1	2	3	4
I can understand a problem.	1	2	3	4
I can make a plan to solve using letters to represent the unknown numbers.	1	2	3	4
I can solve a problem using an equation.	1	2	3	4

Chapter 6

Name _____

Factors, Multiples, and Patterns

Dear Family,

In this chapter, your student is learning about factors, multiples, prime and composite numbers, and patterns. The vocabulary terms for this chapter are: factor pair, divisible, multiple, prime number, composite number, and rule.

Your student can practice identifying factors, multiples, and patterns using coins!

- Show your student a dime and ask, "How much is this coin worth? What are the factors of 10? What are some multiples of 10?" Repeat the questions with other coins and combinations of coins. Ask your student to explain how he or she found the factors of each number.

- Display a set of coins and ask your student to determine their value. Then ask your student if the value is divisible by several numbers. For example, if the value is 27 cents, ask, "Is 27 divisible by 2? Why not? Is 27 divisible by 3? How do you know?" Continue asking if the value is divisible by 5, 6, 9, and 10.

- Display a set of coins and ask your student to determine their value. Then ask your student whether a given number is a factor or multiple of the value. For example, display coins with a value of 15 cents. Ask, "Is 15 a multiple or factor of 5? Is 15 a multiple or factor of 45?" You can also review prime and composite numbers. Ask, "Is 15 a prime number or a composite number? How do you know?"

- Have your student use coins to create a pattern. Then ask, "What would be the 20th coin? What would be the 75th coin? How do you know?"

By the end of this chapter, your student should feel confident with the learning targets and success criteria. Encourage your student to practice these skills in other contexts, such as page numbers, speed limit signs, and addresses.

Have a great time practicing factors, multiples, and patterns!

Big Ideas Math: Modeling Real Life Grade 4   **257**
Resources by Chapter

Lesson	Learning Target	Success Criteria
6.1 Understand Factors	Use models to find factor pairs.	• I can draw area models that show a product. • I can find the factors of a number. • I can find the factor pairs for a number.
6.2 Factors and Divisibility	Use division to find factor pairs.	• I can divide to find factor pairs. • I can use divisibility rules to find factor pairs.
6.3 Relate Factors and Multiples	Understand the relationship between factors and multiples.	• I can tell whether a number is a multiple of another number. • I can tell whether a number is a factor of another number. • I can explain the relationship between factors and multiples.
6.4 Identify Prime and Composite Numbers	Tell whether a given number is prime or composite.	• I can explain what prime and composite numbers are. • I can identify prime and composite numbers.
6.5 Number Patterns	Create and describe number patterns.	• I can create a number pattern given a number rule. • I can describe features of a number pattern.
6.6 Shape Patterns	Create and describe shape patterns.	• I can create a shape pattern given a rule. • I can find the shape at a given position in a pattern. • I can describe features of a shape pattern.

Capítulo 6 — Factores, múltiplos y patrones

Querida familia:

En este capítulo, su estudiante está aprendiendo sobre factores, múltiplos, números primos y compuestos, y patrones. Palabras de vocabulario asociadas con este capítulo: par de factores, divisible, múltiplo, número primo, número compuesto y regla.

¡Su estudiante puede practicar con monedas para identificar factores, múltiplos y patrones!

- Muestre a su estudiante una moneda de diez centavos y pregunte, "¿Cuánto vale esta moneda? ¿Cuántos factores de 10 representa? ¿Cuántos múltiples de 10?". Repita la pregunta con otras monedas y combinaciones de monedas. Pregunte a su estudiante cómo encontró el factor de cada número.

- Escoja un grupo de monedas y pida a su estudiante que determine su valor. Luego pregunte a su estudiante si su valor es divisible entre varios números. Por ejemplo, si el valor es 27 centavos, pregunte, "¿27 es divisible entre 2? ¿Por qué no? ¿27 es divisible entre 3? ¿Cómo lo puedes saber?". Continúe preguntando si el valor es divisible entre 5, 6, 9 y 10.

- Escoja un grupo de monedas y pida a su estudiante que determine su valor. Luego pregunte a su estudiante si un número dado es un factor o múltiplo de ese valor. Por ejemplo, muestre monedas con un valor de 15 centavos. Pregunte, "¿15 es un múltiplo o factor de 5? ¿15 es un múltiplo o factor de 45?". También pueden revisar acerca de primos y números compuestos. Pregunte, "15 es un número primo o un número compuesto? ¿Cómo lo puedes saber?".

- Haga que su estudiante use monedas para crear un patrón. Luego pregunte, "¿Cuál sería la vigésima moneda? ¿Cuál sería la moneda 75? ¿Cómo lo puedes saber?".

Al final de este capítulo, su estudiante debe sentirse seguro sobre los objetivos de aprendizaje y criterios de éxito que se indican en la siguiente página. Anime a su estudiante a practicar estas habilidades en otros contextos, como los números de las páginas, señales de límite de velocidad y direcciones.

¡Disfruten juntos practicando con factores, múltiplos y patrones!

Capítulo 6 Factores, múltiplos y patrones

Lección	Objetivo de aprendizaje	Criterios de éxito
6.1 Entender factores	Usar modelos para hallar pares de factores.	• Sé dibujar modelos de áreas para mostrar un producto. • Sé hallar los factores de un número. • Sé hallar pares de factores de un número.
6.2 Factores y divisibilidad	Usar división para hallar pares de factores.	• Sé dividir para hallar pares de factores. • Sé usar reglas de divisibilidad para hallar pares de factores.
6.3 Relacionar factores y múltiplos	Entender la relación entre factores y múltiplos.	• Sé decir si un número es un múltiplo de otro número. • Sé decir si un número es un factor de otro número. • Sé explicar la relación entre factores y múltiplos.
6.4 Identificar números primos y compuestos	Decir si un número dado es primo o compuesto.	• Sé explicar que son números primos y compuestos. • Sé identificar números primos y compuestos.
6.5 Patrones de números	Crear y describir patrones de números.	• Sé crear un patrón de números dada una regla de número. • Sé describir características de un patrón de número.
6.6 Tipos de patrones	Crear y describir tipos de patrones.	• Sé crear un tipo de patrón según una regla dada. • Sé hallar el elemento de una posición dada en un patrón. • Sé describir las características de un tipo de patrón.

Lesson 6.1 Daily Skills Practice
For use before Lesson 6.1

1. Write an equation for the comparison sentence.

   24 is 4 times as many as 6.

   24 = _____ × _____

Lesson 6.1 Vocabulary Practice
For use before Lesson 6.1

1. Write what you know about this word. Give an example.

   remainder

Find the area of the shape.

1.

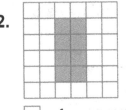

☐ = 1 square inch

Area = _____

2.

☐ = 1 square meter

Area = _____

Name _____

1. Use the rectangles to find the factor pairs for 10.

    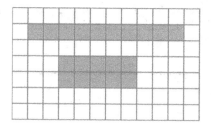

2. Draw rectangles to find the factor pairs for 18.

    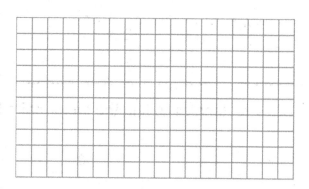

3. Draw rectangles to find the factor pairs for 6.

    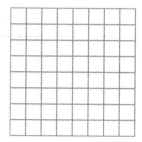

4. Draw rectangles to find the factor pairs for 22.

    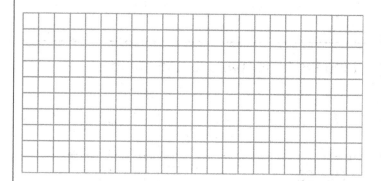

5. Draw rectangles to find the factor pairs for 36.

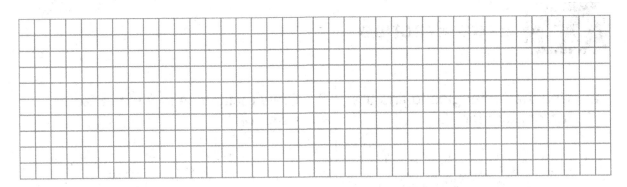

6. Draw rectangles to find the factor pairs for 30.

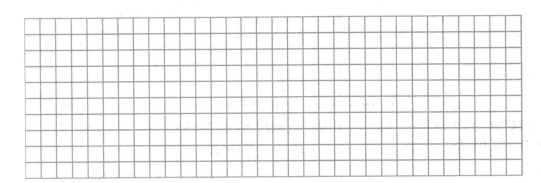

Find the factor pairs for the number.

7. 17	**8.** 32	**9.** 15
10. 56	**11.** 48	**12.** 27

13. Newton says there are 3 factor pairs for 12. Descartes says there are 6 factor pairs for 12. Who is correct? Explain.

14. A teacher has 24 desks. He wants to arrange the desks into a rectangular array. How many different arrays can he make?

Name _____

You can write whole numbers as products of two factors. The factors are called a **factor pair** for the number.

Example Find the factor pairs for 18.

- Draw rectangles with an area of 18 square units.

- Find the side lengths of the rectangles.

factor pair

$$2 \times 3 = 6$$

factor factor

2 and 3 are a factor pair of 6.

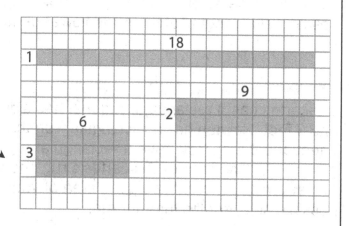

A 3 × 6 rectangle has the same area as a 6 × 3 rectangle. Both give the factor pair 3 and 6.

The side lengths of each rectangle are a factor pair.

So, the factor pairs for 18 are 1 and 18, 2 and 9, and 3 and 6.

---

1. Use the rectangles to find the factor pairs for 15.

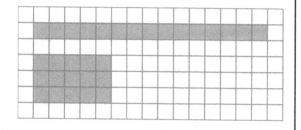

2. Draw rectangles to find the factor pairs for 9.

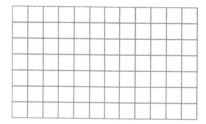

Name _____

Enrichment and Extension

1. You draw a rectangle that has side lengths of 6 and 10. Newton and Descartes each draw a rectangle that has the same area but different side lengths. What are the possible side lengths of Newton's and Descartes's rectangles?

_____

2. Newton plants a rectangular flower bed that has side lengths of 36 feet and 2 feet. You and your friend each plant a flower bed that has the same area but different side lengths. What are the possible side lengths of the other flower beds?

_____

3. Descartes has a rectangular rug that has side lengths of 4 feet and 9 feet. Newton has a rectangular rug that has side lengths of 7 feet and 8 feet. You have a rectangular rug with an area that is greater than the area of Descartes's rug and less than the area of Newton's rug. What could the area of your rug be? Name two possible side lengths for your rug.

_____

4. You have a square game board that has side lengths of 7 inches. Newton has a game board that has side lengths of 12 inches and 5 inches. Descartes has a game board with an area that is greater than the area of your game board and less than the area of Newton's game board. What could the area of Descartes's game board be? Name two possible side lengths for Descartes's game board.

1. Find each product.

   2 × 9 = _____

   2 × 90 = _____

   2 × 900 = _____

   2 × 9,000 = _____

Lesson 6.2 Vocabulary Practice
For use before Lesson 6.2

1. Write what you know about this phrase. Give an example.

   factor pair

Prerequisite Skills Practice

For use before Lesson 6.2

Find the factor pairs for the number.

1. 12

2. 60

Name _____

Find the factor pairs for the number.

1. 21	**2.** 40	**3.** 62
4. 81	**5.** 16	**6.** 36
7. 57	**8.** 95	**9.** 20
10. 32	**11.** 53	**12.** 49
13. 76	**14.** 66	**15.** 17
16. 85	**17.** 96	**18.** 23

List the factors of the number.

19. 27	20. 70	21. 18
22. 52	23. 65	24. 34

25. Why does a number that has 6 as a factor also have 2 as a factor?

26. The number below has 5 as a factor. What could the unknown digit be?

    67_____

27. Which numbers have 3 as a factor?

    21   43   326   1,275   600   35

28. Which numbers have 2 as a factor?

    30   78   2,485   500   29   283

29. You have 2 pages of stickers with 25 stickers on each page. Can you share the stickers equally between yourself and two friends?

30. A gardener has 48 plants. He wants to put the same number of plants in each row of the garden without any left over. Should he put 6, 9, or 10 plants in each row? Explain.

Name _____

A number is **divisible** by another number when the quotient is a whole number and the remainder is 0.

Some numbers have divisibility rules. These help you determine whether the numbers are factors of other numbers.

> The sum of the digits in 27 is 9 because 2 + 7 = 9. So, 27 is divisible by 3. 27 is also divisible by 9.

Divisor	Divisibility Rule
2	The number is even.
3	The sum of the digits is divisible by 3.
5	The ones digit is 0 or 5.
6	The number is even and divisible by 3.
9	The sum of the digits is divisible by 9.
10	The ones digit is 0.

Example Find the factor pairs for 24.

Use divisibility rules and division to find the factors of 24.

> A number is divisible by its factors.

Divisor	Is the number a factor of 24?	Multiplication Equation
1	Yes, 1 is a factor of every number.	$1 \times 24 = 24$
2	Yes, 24 is even.	$2 \times 12 = 24$
3	Yes, 2 + 4 = 6 is divisible by 3.	$3 \times 8 = 24$
4	Yes, $24 \div 4 = 6$ R0	$4 \times 6 = 24$
5	No, the ones digit is not 0 or 5.	
6	Yes, 24 is even and divisible by 3.	$6 \times 4 = 24$

You can stop checking after 6 because the factor pairs start to repeat.

The equations show the factors and factor pairs.

The factors of 24 are 1, 2, 3, 4, 6, 8, 12, and 24.

The factor pairs for 24 are 1 and 24, 2 and 12, 3 and 8, and 4 and 6.

Find the factor pairs for the number.

1. 18

2. 45

Name _____

Enrichment and Extension

Use what you know about divisibility rules and factors to answer each riddle.

1. I am a number between 40 and 60. I am divisible by 2, 3, 6, and 9. What number am I?

_____

2. I am a number between 60 and 100. I am divisible by 2, 4, 5, 8, and 10. What number am I?

_____

3. I am an even number between 25 and 75. I am divisible by 4 and 5. What numbers could I be?

_____

4. I am an odd number between 40 and 100. I am divisible by 3 and 5. What numbers could I be?

_____

5. I am a two-digit odd number between 0 and 40. I am divisible by 9. What number am I? What are my factors?

_____

6. I am a number between 50 and 80. I am divisible by 12 but not divisible by 10. What number am I? What are my factors?

Lesson 6.3 Daily Skills Practice
For use before Lesson 6.3

1. A teacher buys 7 cases of bottled water and spends $56. Each case has 24 bottles. During a field trip, students drink 76 bottles. How many bottles are left?

There are _____ bottles left.

Lesson 6.3 Vocabulary Practice
For use before Lesson 6.3

1. Write what you know about this word. Give an example.

divisible

List the factors of the number.

1. 32

2. 72

Name _____

1. Is 18 a multiple of 4? Explain.

2. Is 48 a multiple of 6? Explain.

3. Is 30 a multiple of 5? Explain.

4. Is 70 a multiple of 8? Explain.

5. Is 6 a factor of 28? Explain.

6. Is 9 a factor of 81? Explain.

7. Is 4 a factor of 62? Explain.

8. Is 7 a factor of 35? Explain.

Tell whether 20 is a multiple or a factor of the number. Write *multiple*, *factor*, or *both*.

9. 5

10. 20

11. 60

Tell whether 40 is a multiple or a factor of the number. Write *multiple*, *factor*, or *both*.

12. 20

13. 80

14. 40

Tell whether 12 is a multiple or a factor of the number. Write *multiple*, *factor*, or *both*.

15. 12

16. 4

17. 48

18. Name two numbers that are each a multiple of both 2 and 5. What do you notice about the multiples?

19. Is Descartes correct? Explain.

All numbers that are multiples of 9 have 3 as a factor.

20. A quotient is a multiple of 2. The dividend is a multiple of 4. The divisor is a factor of 10. Write one possible equation for the problem.

21. Your friend wants to ride her bike a total of 75 miles. She wants to ride the same number of miles each day. Which numbers of miles can she ride each day: 2, 3, 4, or 5?

22. Newton goes to the library every 4 days and visits his grandparents every 3 days. You want to go with him on a day when he does both. What other date in April will this happen?

April						
Sun	Mon	Tue	Wed	Thu	Fri	Sat
						1
2	3	4	5	6	7	8
9	10	11	(12)	13	14	15
16	17	18	19	20	21	22
23	24	25	26	27	28	29
30						

◯ Go to the Library
☐ Visit Grandparents

Name _____

Lesson 6.3 Reteach

A whole number is a multiple of each of its factors.

15 is a multiple of 1, 3, 5, and 15.

$1 \times 15 = 15$

$3 \times 5 = 15$

Example Is 30 a multiple of 6?

One Way: List multiples of 6.

$1 \times 6 = 6$
$2 \times 6 = 12$
$3 \times 6 = 18$
$4 \times 6 = 24$
$5 \times 6 = 30$

Multiples of 6 include: 6, 12, 18, 24, 30.

So, 30 is a multiple of 6.

Another Way: Use division to determine whether 6 is a factor of 30.

$30 \div 6 = 5$

6 is a factor of 30.

So, 30 is a multiple of 6.

Example Is 3 a factor of 24?

One Way: Use divisibility rules.

3 is a factor of 24 because $2 + 4 = 6$ is divisible by 3.

Another Way: List multiples of 3.

Multiples of 3 include: 3, 6, 9, 12, 15, 18, 21, 24.

24 is a multiple of 3.

So, 3 is a factor of 24.

1. Is 26 a multiple of 4? Explain.

2. Is 9 a factor of 36? Explain.

Name _____

Enrichment and Extension

Use the numbers to complete each sentence.

1. _____ and _____ are factors of _____.

   _____ and _____ are multiples of _____.

63	17	7	68	34	9

2. _____ and _____ are factors of _____.

   _____ and _____ are multiples of _____.

6	32	8	60	15	40

3. _____ and _____ are factors of _____.

   _____ and _____ are multiples of _____.

75	15	36	12	96	25

4. _____, _____, and _____ are factors of _____.

   _____, _____, and _____ are multiples of _____.

28	18	7	42	84	81	9	45

5. _____, _____, and _____ are factors of _____.

   _____, _____, and _____ are multiples of _____.

3	78	35	21	7	26	84	39

Lesson 6.4 Daily Skills Practice
For use before Lesson 6.4

1. Divide.

$243 \div 2 =$ _____ R _____

Lesson 6.4 Vocabulary Practice
For use before Lesson 6.4

1. Write what you know about this word. Give an example.

multiple

Prerequisite Skills Practice

For use before Lesson 6.4

Tell whether 12 is a multiple or a factor of the number. Write *multiple*, *factor*, or *both*.

1. 4

2. 60

Name _____

Tell whether the number is prime or composite. Explain.

1. 65	**2.** 98	**3.** 13
4. 33	**5.** 49	**6.** 80
7. 73	**8.** 24	**9.** 52
10. 84	**11.** 59	**12.** 97
13. 51	**14.** 36	**15.** 61
16. 78	**17.** 57	**18.** 21

19. Explain why a number cannot be both prime and composite.

20. Newton is thinking of a prime number between 70 and 100. The tens digit is one less than the ones digit. What is the number?

Write *true* or *false* for the statement. If false, provide an example to support your answer.

21. All one-digit odd numbers are prime. _____

---

22. Even numbers less than 10 are prime. _____

---

23. A prime number has exactly two factors. _____

---

24. There are 39 students in the school choir. Can the director separate the students into equal rows for a performance? Explain.

---

25. There are 47 paintings in an art show. Can the paintings be separated into equal groups to be displayed? Explain.

---

26. In which month was the number of inches of snowfall a prime number?

Snowfall (in inches)	
November	❄ ❄
December	❄ ❄ ❄ ❄ ❄
January	❄ ❄ ❄ ❄
February	❄ ❄

Each ❄ = 2 inches

Name _____

A **prime number** is a whole number greater than 1 with exactly two factors, 1 and itself. A **composite number** is a whole number greater than 1 with more than two factors.

Example Tell whether 15 is *prime* or *composite*.

Use divisibility rules.

- 15 is odd, so it is not divisible by 2 or any other even number.
- 1 + 5 = 6 is divisible by 3, so 15 is divisible by 3.

Odd numbers are not divisible by even numbers.

15 has factors in addition to 1 and itself.

So, 15 is composite.

Example Tell whether 37 is *prime* or *composite*.

Use divisibility rules.

- 37 is odd, so it is not divisible by 2 or any other even number.
- 3 + 7 = 10 is not divisible by 3 or 9, so 37 is not divisible by 3 or 9.
- The ones digit is not 0 or 5, so 37 is not divisible by 5.

37 has exactly two factors, 1 and itself.

So, 37 is prime.

Tell whether the number is *prime* or *composite*. Explain.

1. 5	2. 25	3. 18
4. 64	5. 87	6. 71

Name _____

Enrichment and Extension

1. What factor pair for 35 includes two prime numbers?

_____

2. What factor pair for 22 includes two prime numbers?

_____

3. What factor pair for 24 includes two composite numbers?

_____

4. What factor pair for 54 includes two composite numbers?

_____

5. What factor pair for 60 includes one prime number and one composite number?

_____

6. What factor pair for 78 includes one prime number and one composite number?

_____

7. What factors of 63 are prime numbers?

_____

8. What factors of 70 are composite numbers?

1. Find the product.

$$
\begin{array}{r}
538 \\
\times \quad 8 \\
\hline
\end{array}
$$

Lesson 6.5 **Vocabulary Practice**
For use before Lesson 6.5

1. Write what you know about this phrase. Give an example.

prime number

Big Ideas Math: Modeling Real Life Grade 4 **285**
Resources by Chapter

Tell whether the number is *prime* or *composite*. Explain.

1. 21

2. 17

Name _____

Write the first six numbers in the pattern. Then describe another feature of the pattern.

1. Rule: Add 6.

First number: 15

15, ___, ___, ___, ___, ___

2. Rule: Divide by 3.

First number: 1,458

1,458, ___, ___, ___, ___, ___

3. Rule: Subtract 4.

First number: 80

80, ___, ___, ___, ___, ___

4. Rule: Multiply by 6.

First number: 2

2, ___, ___, ___, ___, ___

5. Rule: Divide by 4.

First number: 4,096

6. Rule: Subtract 9.

First number: 100

7. Rule: Multiply by 3.

First number: 4

8. Rule: Add 10.

First number: 25

9. Rule: Subtract 7.

First number: 70

10. Rule: Multiply by 2.

First number: 6

Use the rule to generate a pattern of four numbers.

11. Rule: Multiply by 7.

12. Rule: Subtract 10.

13. Rule: Add 5.

14. Rule: Divide by 2.

15. Rule: Multiply by 4.

16. Rule: Add 9.

17. List the first ten multiples of 5. What patterns do you notice with the digits in the ones place? in the tens place?

    Does this pattern continue beyond the tenth number in the pattern?

18. Your friend gets his hair cut every 35 days. How many times will your friend get his hair cut in 1 year?

19. There are 350 students enrolled in your friend's school at the beginning of the school year. Each month, 7 new students enroll and 2 students leave. How many students will be enrolled in the school after 7 months?

Name _____

A **rule** tells how numbers or shapes in a pattern are related.

Example Use the rule "Add 2" to create a number pattern. The first number in the pattern is 5. Then describe another feature of the pattern.

Create the pattern.

| The rule is "Add 2." | → | +2 +2 +2 +2 +2 |
| The first number is 5. | → | 5, 7, 9, 11, 13, 15, ... |

Think: What is another feature of the pattern?

The numbers in the pattern are all odd.

Example Use the rule "Multiply by 2."
The first number in the pattern is 3.
Then describe another feature of the pattern.

Create the pattern.

×2   ×2   ×2   ×2   ×2

3,   6,   12,   24,   48,   96, ...

Think: What is another feature of the pattern?

The numbers in the pattern are multiples of 3.

Look at the ones or tens digits to find another feature of the pattern.

Write the first six numbers in the pattern. Describe another feature of the pattern.

1. Rule: Add 4.

First number: 8

8, ___, ___, ___, ___, ___

2. Rule: Subtract 10.

First number: 100

100, ___, ___, ___, ___, ___

Name _____

Choose a rule to match each pattern.

Subtract 3, then multiply by 3.	Add 5, then multiply by 2.	Multiply by 2, then add 1.
Multiply by 2, then subtract 5.	Divide by 3, then add 3.	Divide by 2, then add 2.

1. 288, 99, 36, 15, 8

   Rule: _____

_____

2. 10, 21, 43, 87, 175

   Rule: _____

_____

3. 15, 25, 45, 85, 165

   Rule: _____

_____

4. 5, 6, 9, 18, 45

   Rule: _____

_____

5. 1, 12, 34, 78, 166

   Rule: _____

_____

6. 100, 52, 28, 16, 10

   Rule: _____

Lesson 6.6 **Daily Skills Practice**
For use before Lesson 6.6

1. Divide.

    $19 \div 2 =$ _____ R _____

Lesson 6.6 **Vocabulary Practice**
For use before Lesson 6.6

1. Write what you know about this phrase. Give an example.

    composite number

Prerequisite Skills Practice
For use before Lesson 6.6

Write the first six numbers in the pattern. Then describe another feature of the pattern.

1. Rule: Add 7
First number: 14

2. Rule: Multiply by 3
First number: 2

Name _____

1. Extend the pattern of shapes by repeating the rule "triangle, star, heart, square." What is the 45th shape in the pattern?

2. Extend the pattern of shapes by repeating the rule "circle, hexagon, trapezoid." What is the 79th shape in the pattern?

3. Extend the pattern of symbols by repeating the rule "add, subtract." What is the 15th symbol in the pattern?

4. Extend the pattern of shapes by repeating the rule "parallelogram, circle, pentagon, circle, octagon." What is the 37th shape in the pattern?

5. Describe the dot pattern. How many dots are in the 120th figure?

Figure 1   Figure 2   Figure 3

---

6. Describe the dot pattern. How many dots are in the 50th figure?

Figure 1   Figure 2   Figure 3

---

7. You and your friend each create a shape pattern with 100 shapes. Your friend says both patterns will have the same number of stars. Is your friend correct? Explain.

You

Friend

---

8. Draw the missing figure in the pattern. Explain the pattern.

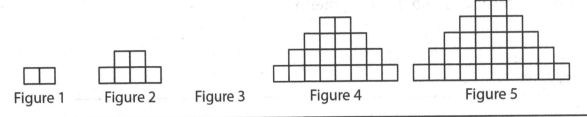

Figure 1   Figure 2   Figure 3   Figure 4   Figure 5

---

9. Descartes uses the rule "fish, heart, fish" to make a shape pattern. He wants the pattern to repeat 5 times. How many fish will be in Descartes's pattern?

10. The pattern on Newton's wallpaper is "three blue stripes, four red stripes." There are 80 stripes on the wall. How many times does the entire pattern repeat?

Name _____

Lesson 6.6 **Reteach**

Example Create a shape pattern by repeating the rule "circle, star, square." What is the 20th shape in the pattern?

Create the pattern.

You divide by 3 because there are three shapes in the rule.

Find the 20th shape in the pattern.

20 ÷ 3 is 6 R2, so the pattern repeats 6 times.

After repeating 6 times, there are 18 shapes because 6 × 3 = 18. The last shape in the pattern is a square. So, the 18th shape is a square, the 19th shape is a circle, and the 20th shape is a star.

Example Describe the dot pattern.

How many dots are in the 10th figure?

Figure 1   Figure 2   Figure 3

Figure 1 has 1 column of 2 dots, so it has 1 × 2 = 2 dots.

Figure 2 has 2 columns of 2 dots, so it has 2 × 2 = 4 dots.

Figure 3 has 3 columns of 2 dots, so it has 3 × 2 = 6 dots.

The 10th figure has 10 columns of 2 dots, so it has 10 × 2 = 20 dots.

1. Extend the pattern of shapes by repeating the rule "triangle, square, hexagon" What is the 40th shape in the pattern?

 _____ _____ _____ _____ _____ ...

_____

2. Describe the dot pattern. How many dots are in the 40th figure?

Figure 1   Figure 2   Figure 3

Name _____

1. Newton says the 75th shape in the pattern is a triangle.
Descartes says the 80th shape in the pattern is a square.
Are either of them correct? Explain.

_____

2. Newton says the 100th shape in the pattern is a heart.
Descartes says the 112th shape in the pattern is a star.
Are either of them correct? Explain.

_____

3. Newton says the 82nd shape in the pattern is a hexagon.
Descartes says the 135th shape in the pattern is an oval.
Are either of them correct? Explain.

_____

4. Newton creates a shape pattern. The 24th shape is a circle and
the 34th shape is a triangle. What could the rule for Newton's
pattern be?

_____

5. Descartes creates a shape pattern. The 53rd shape is a star and
the 72nd shape is a heart. What could the rule for Descartes's
pattern be?

Name _____

Chapter Self-Assessment

Use the scale below to rate your understanding of the learning target and the success criteria.

1	*2*	*3*	*4*
I do not understand.	I can do it with help.	I can do it on my own.	I can teach someone else.

	Rating
6.1 Understand Factors	
Learning Target: Use models to find factor pairs.	1 2 3 4
I can draw area models that show a product.	1 2 3 4
I can find the factors of a number.	1 2 3 4
I can find the factor pairs for a number.	1 2 3 4
6.2 Factors and Divisibility	
Learning Target: Use division to find factor pairs.	1 2 3 4
I can divide to find factor pairs.	1 2 3 4
I can use divisibility rules to find factor pairs.	1 2 3 4
6.3 Relate Factors and Multiples	
Learning Target: Understand the relationship between factors and multiples.	1 2 3 4
I can tell whether a number is a multiple of another number.	1 2 3 4
I can tell whether a number is a factor of another number.	1 2 3 4
I can explain the relationship between factors and multiples.	1 2 3 4
6.4 Identify Prime and Composite Numbers	
Learning Target: Tell whether a given number is prime or composite.	1 2 3 4
I can explain what prime and composite numbers are.	1 2 3 4
I can identify prime and composite numbers.	1 2 3 4

Name _____

	Rating			
6.5 Number Patterns				
Learning Target: Create and describe number patterns.	1	2	3	4
I can create a number pattern given a number rule.	1	2	3	4
I can describe features of a number pattern.	1	2	3	4
6.6 Shape Patterns				
Learning Target: Create and describe shape patterns.	1	2	3	4
I can create a shape pattern given a rule.	1	2	3	4
I can find the shape at a given position in a pattern.	1	2	3	4
I can describe features of a shape pattern.	1	2	3	4

Chapter 7

Name _____

Chapter 7 Understand Fraction Equivalence and Comparison

Dear Family,

In this chapter, your student is learning different strategies for writing equivalent fractions and comparing fractions. The lessons address how to use multiplication and division to find equivalent fractions, as well as how to compare fractions using benchmarks and equivalent fractions. The vocabulary words for this chapter are: benchmark, common factor, equivalent, and equivalent fractions.

You can help your student practice with fractions during your next cooking hour!

- Pull out your recipe book and look for meal recipes with a variety of fraction sizes, like a soup that requires various seasonings. Before you and your student start cooking, change some of the ingredient quantities to familiarize your student with a variety of fractions. For example, you can change 1 cup to $\frac{3}{3}$ cup, or $\frac{1}{4}$ teaspoon to $\frac{2}{8}$ teaspoon to give more "fraction flavor" to your recipe!

- Invite your student to be your recipe reader. Choose a fraction from your recipe's ingredient list, and then ask your student, "What is an equivalent fraction for [$\frac{3}{4}$ cup]?" Encourage him or her to use multiplication to find an equivalent fraction. Next, choose a fraction with a numerator and denominator that are both divisible by the same one-digit number, such as $\frac{6}{12}$. (You may need to add this fraction to your recipe!) Continue by asking, "What are two equivalent fractions for [$\frac{6}{12}$ cup]? How can you use division to find equivalent fractions?"

- Then, help your student compare two fractions from a recipe by comparing them to a commonly used benchmark number, such as $\frac{1}{2}$ or 1. (For example, $\frac{3}{8} < \frac{1}{2}$ and $\frac{2}{3} > \frac{1}{2}$, so $\frac{3}{8} < \frac{2}{3}$.)

- Challenge your student to compare two fractions by rewriting one of them with either the same numerator or denominator as the other fraction, and have him or her explain how to identify which fraction is greater.

- As a final challenge, choose three fractions from your recipe list for your student. Then, ask your student to order them from least to greatest!

By the end of this chapter, your student should feel confident with the learning targets and success criteria on the next page.

Have a great time cooking with fractions!

Lesson	Learning Target	Success Criteria
7.1 Model Equivalent Fractions	Model and write equivalent fractions.	• I can use an area model to find equivalent fractions. • I can use a number line to find equivalent fractions. • I can write equivalent fractions.
7.2 Generate Equivalent Fractions by Multiplying	Use multiplication to find equivalent fractions.	• I can multiply a numerator and a denominator by a chosen number. • I can multiply to find equivalent fractions. • I can explain why multiplication can be used to find equivalent fractions.
7.3 Generate Equivalent Fractions by Dividing	Use division to find equivalent fractions.	• I can find the factors of a number. • I can find the common factors of a numerator and denominator. • I can divide to find equivalent fractions.
7.4 Compare Fractions Using Benchmarks	Compare fractions using benchmarks.	• I can compare a fraction to a benchmark of $\frac{1}{2}$ or 1. • I can use a benchmark to compare two fractions.
7.5 Compare Fractions	Compare fractions using equivalent fractions.	• I can compare numerators and denominators of two fractions. • I can make the numerators or the denominators of two fractions the same. • I can compare fractions with like numerators or like denominators.

Nombre _____

Capítulo 7 · Entender la equivalencia y comparación de fracciones

Querida familia:

En este capítulo, su estudiante está aprendiendo diferentes estrategias para escribir la equivalencia y comparación de fracciones. Las lecciones se centran en cómo usar multiplicación y división para hallar fracciones equivalentes, también cómo comparar fracciones usando fracciones de referencias y equivalentes. Las palabras de vocabulario asociadas con este capítulo son: referencia, factor común, equivalente y fracciones equivalentes.

¡Puede ayudar a su estudiante a practicar con fracciones la próxima vez que vaya a cocinar!

- Saque su libro de recetas y busque alguna que muestre una variedad de tamaños de fracciones, como una sopa que requiere varios condimentos. Antes que empiece a cocinar junto a su estudiante, cambie algunas cantidades de los ingredientes para familiarizar a su estudiante con la variedad de fracciones. Por ejemplo, ¡puede cambiar 1 taza por $\frac{3}{3}$ de taza, o $\frac{1}{4}$ de cucharita a $\frac{2}{8}$ de cucharita para darle más "sabor de fracción" a su receta!

- Invite a su estudiante a que sea re-lector de la receta. Escoja una fracción de su lista de ingredientes y luego pregunte a su estudiante, "¿Cuál es la fracción equivalente para [$\frac{3}{4}$ de taza]?". Anímelos a que use multiplicación para hallar una fracción equivalente. A continuación, escoja una fracción con un numerador y denominador que ambos sean divisibles por el mismo número de un dígito, así como $\frac{6}{12}$. (¡Podría añadir esta fracción a su receta!) Continúe preguntando, "¿Cuáles son dos fracciones equivalentes para [$\frac{6}{12}$ de taza]? ¿Cómo podrías usar división para hallar fracciones equivalentes?".

- Luego, ayude a su estudiante a comparar dos fracciones de una receta comparándolas a un número de referencia común, así como $\frac{1}{2}$ o 1. (Por ejemplo: $\frac{3}{8} < \frac{1}{2}$ y $\frac{2}{3} > \frac{1}{2}$, por lo tanto $\frac{3}{8} < \frac{2}{3}$.)

- Rete a su estudiante a comparar dos fracciones rescribiendo una de ellas con el mismo numerador o el denominador de la otra y haga que explique cómo identicar cuál fracción es más grande.

- Como un reto final, escoja para su estudiante tres fracciones de la lista de su receta. Luego, ¡pida a su estudiante que las ordene de menor a mayor!

Al final de este capítulo, su estudiante debe sentirse seguro sobre los objetivos de aprendizaje y criterios de éxito que se indican en la siguiente página.

¡Disfruten juntos cocinando con fracciones!

Lección	Objetivo de aprendizaje	Criterios de éxito
7.1 Modelar fracciones equivalentes	Modelar y escribir fracciones equivalentes.	• Sé usar un modelo de área para hallar fracciones equivalentes. • Sé usar una línea numerada para hallar fracciones equivalentes. • Sé escribir fracciones equivalentes.
7.2 Generar fracciones equivalentes por multiplicación	Usar multiplicación para hallar fracciones equivalentes.	• Sé multiplicar un numerador y un denominador por un número escogido. • Sé multiplicar para hallar fracciones equivalentes. • Sé explicar por qué multiplicación puede ser usada para hallar fracciones equivalentes.
7.3 Generar fracciones equivalentes por división	Usar división para hallar fracciones equivalentes.	• Sé hallar factores de un número. • Sé hallar los factores comunes de un numerador y denominador. • Sé dividir para hallar fracciones equivalentes.
7.4 Comparar fracciones usando referencias	Comparar fracciones usando referencias.	• Sé comprara una fracción con la referencia de $\frac{1}{2}$ o 1. • Sé usar una referencia para comparar dos fracciones.
7.5 Comparar fracciones	Comparar fracciones usando fracciones equivalentes.	• Sé comparar numeradores y denominadores de dos fracciones. • Sé hacer iguales a los numeradores o denominadores de dos fracciones. • Sé comparar fracciones con iguales numeradores o denominadores.

1. Find the product.

```
   58
 × 99
 ____
```

Lesson 7.1 **Vocabulary Practice**
For use before Lesson 7.1

1. Write what you know about this word. Give an example.

rule

Prerequisite Skills Practice

For use before Lesson 7.1

Use models to find an equivalent fraction. Both models show the same whole.

1.

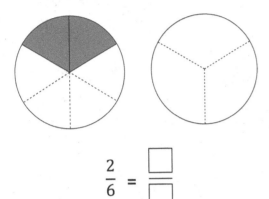

$$\frac{2}{6} = \frac{\square}{\square}$$

2.

$$\frac{2}{4} = \frac{\square}{\square}$$

Name _____

Use the model to find an equivalent fraction.

1. $\frac{2}{6}$

2. $\frac{3}{4}$

3. $\frac{2}{3}$

4. $\frac{1}{2}$

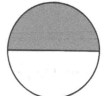

5. $\frac{6}{8}$

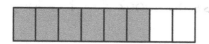

6. $\frac{4}{12}$

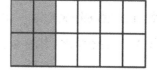

Use the number line to find an equivalent fraction.

7. $\frac{2}{5}$

8. $\frac{1}{4}$

Find the equivalent fraction.

9. $\frac{2}{3} = \dfrac{\Box}{6}$

10. $\frac{6}{8} = \dfrac{\Box}{4}$

11. $\frac{2}{4} = \dfrac{\Box}{12}$

12. $\frac{6}{10} = \dfrac{\Box}{5}$

13. Which model does *not* belong with the other three? Explain.

   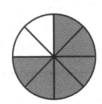

14. Newton's notebook is $\frac{2}{3}$ foot long. Descartes's notebook is $\frac{8}{12}$ foot long. Are the notebooks the same length?

Name_____

Two or more numbers that have the same value are **equivalent**. Two or more fractions that name the same part of a whole are **equivalent fractions**. Equivalent fractions name the same point on a number line.

Example Use models to find an equivalent fraction for $\frac{3}{4}$.

One Way: Draw models that show the same whole divided into different numbers of parts.

$\frac{3}{4}$ and $\frac{6}{8}$ are equivalent fractions. So, $\frac{3}{4} = \frac{6}{8}$.

Another Way: Use a number line.

Step 1: Plot $\frac{3}{4}$ on the number line.

Step 2: Divide the number line into eighths and label the tick marks.

Step 3: Find the fraction that names the same point as $\frac{3}{4}$.

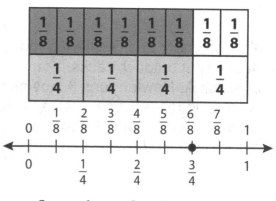

The fractions that name the same point are $\frac{3}{4}$ and $\frac{6}{8}$. So, $\frac{3}{4} = \frac{6}{8}$.

1. Use the model to find an equivalent fraction for $\frac{2}{3}$.

2. Use the number line to find an equivalent fraction for $\frac{1}{4}$.

Lesson 7.1 Enrichment and Extension

1. You, Newton, and Descartes swim laps at different swimming pools. You swim 4 laps at Pool A, Newton swims 2 laps at Pool B, and Descartes swims 8 laps at Pool C. Do you, Newton, and Descartes swim the same distance? Explain.

Pool A	6 laps = 1 mile
Pool B	3 laps = 1 mile
Pool C	12 laps = 1 mile

2. You, Newton, and Descartes run laps at different outdoor tracks. You run 5 laps at Track A, Newton runs 3 laps at Track B, and Descartes runs 1 lap at Track C. Do you, Newton, and Descartes run the same distance? Explain.

Track A	10 laps = 1 mile
Track B	5 laps = 1 mile
Track C	2 laps = 1 mile

Lesson 7.2 Daily Skills Practice

For use before Lesson 7.2

1. Is 96 a multiple of 8?

Lesson 7.2 Vocabulary Practice

For use before Lesson 7.2

1. Write what you know about this word. Give an example.

equivalent

Use the model to find an equivalent fraction.

1. $\dfrac{4}{5}$

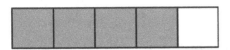

2. $\dfrac{2}{3}$

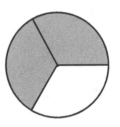

Name _____

Find an equivalent fraction.

1. $\dfrac{1}{4} = \dfrac{1 \times \boxed{}}{4 \times \boxed{}} = \dfrac{\boxed{}}{\boxed{}}$

2. $\dfrac{6}{5} = \dfrac{6 \times \boxed{}}{5 \times \boxed{}} = \dfrac{\boxed{}}{\boxed{}}$

Find the equivalent fraction.

3. $\dfrac{1}{3} = \dfrac{\boxed{}}{12}$

4. $\dfrac{2}{4} = \dfrac{4}{\boxed{}}$

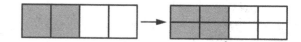

5. $\dfrac{5}{6} = \dfrac{\boxed{}}{12}$

6. $\dfrac{10}{6} = \dfrac{100}{\boxed{}}$

Find an equivalent fraction.

7. $\dfrac{2}{10}$

8. $\dfrac{6}{3}$

9. $\dfrac{4}{8}$

Find two equivalent fractions.

10. $\frac{2}{2}$

11. $\frac{9}{6}$

12. $\frac{3}{4}$

13. What is Newton's fraction?

My fraction is equivalent to $\frac{4}{5}$ and has a denominator that is 2 more than its numerator.

14. Your friend says she can write a fraction equivalent to $\frac{3}{6}$ that has a denominator of 8 and a whole number in the numerator. Is your friend correct? Explain.

15. A recipe calls for 1 teaspoon of basil. You only have a $\frac{1}{4}$ teaspoon measuring spoon. What fraction of a teaspoon of basil, in fourths, do you need?

16. A family lives in Canada for $\frac{1}{4}$ of the year. Each year has 12 months. What fraction of the year, in twelfths, does the family *not* live in Canada?

Name _____

You can find an equivalent fraction by multiplying the numerator and denominator by the same number.

Example Find an equivalent fraction for $\frac{1}{4}$.

Step 1: Choose a number.

Step 2: Multiply both the numerator and denominator by that number.

$$\frac{1}{4} = \frac{1 \times \boxed{2}}{4 \times \boxed{2}} = \frac{2}{8}$$

$\frac{1}{4}$ is equivalent to $\frac{2}{8}$.

Find an equivalent fraction.

1. $\frac{1}{2} = \dfrac{1 \times \boxed{}}{2 \times \boxed{}} = \dfrac{\boxed{}}{\boxed{}}$

2. $\frac{4}{3} = \dfrac{4 \times \boxed{}}{3 \times \boxed{}} = \dfrac{\boxed{}}{\boxed{}}$

Find the equivalent fraction.

3. $\frac{1}{3} = \dfrac{\boxed{}}{6}$

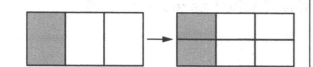

4. $\frac{3}{6} = \dfrac{6}{\boxed{}}$

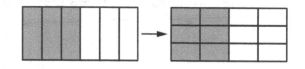

Lesson 7.2 Enrichment and Extension

1. A recipe calls for $\frac{3}{4}$ teaspoon of ginger and $\frac{1}{2}$ teaspoon of nutmeg. You only have a $\frac{1}{8}$ teaspoon measuring spoon. What fraction of a teaspoon of ginger, in eighths, do you need? What fraction of a teaspoon of nutmeg, in eighths, do you need? Does the recipe call for more ginger or more nutmeg?

2. You eat $\frac{5}{6}$ of a cheese pizza. Your friend eats $\frac{2}{3}$ of a vegetarian pizza. Each pizza has 12 slices. What fraction of the cheese pizza, in twelfths, do you eat? What fraction of the vegetarian pizza, in twelfths, does your friend eat? Who eats more pizza?

3. Newton has $\frac{7}{10}$ of a dollar in coins. Descartes has $\frac{4}{5}$ of a dollar in coins. What fraction of a dollar, in hundreths, does Newton have? What fraction of a dollar, in hundreths, does Descartes have? Who has more money?

1. Find the factor pairs for 72. Select all that apply.

    a. 2 and 36

    b. 5 and 14

    c. 7 and 10

    d. 8 and 9

Lesson 7.3 **Vocabulary Practice**
For use before Lesson 7.3

1. Write what you know about this phrase. Give an example.

equivalent fractions

Prerequisite Skills Practice

For use before Lesson 7.3

Find an equivalent fraction.

1. $\dfrac{2}{3} = \dfrac{2 \times \boxed{}}{3 \times \boxed{}} = \dfrac{\boxed{}}{\boxed{}}$

2. $\dfrac{9}{4} = \dfrac{9 \times \boxed{}}{4 \times \boxed{}} = \dfrac{\boxed{}}{\boxed{}}$

Name _____

Lesson 7.3 **Extra Practice**

Find an equivalent fraction.

1. $\dfrac{4}{6} = \dfrac{4 \div \boxed{}}{6 \div \boxed{}} = \dfrac{\boxed{}}{\boxed{}}$

2. $\dfrac{12}{9} = \dfrac{12 \div \boxed{}}{9 \div \boxed{}} = \dfrac{\boxed{}}{\boxed{}}$

Find the equivalent fraction.

3. $\dfrac{32}{8} = \dfrac{\boxed{}}{1}$

4. $\dfrac{5}{15} = \dfrac{1}{\boxed{}}$

5. $\dfrac{70}{100} = \dfrac{\boxed{}}{10}$

6. $\dfrac{6}{18} = \dfrac{2}{\boxed{}}$

Find an equivalent fraction for the point on the number line.

7.

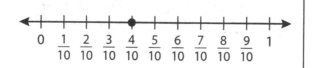

8.

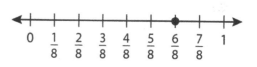

Find an equivalent fraction.

9. $\dfrac{8}{12}$

10. $\dfrac{8}{8}$

11. $\dfrac{20}{4}$

Find two equivalent fractions.

12. $\dfrac{30}{60}$

13. $\dfrac{18}{9}$

14. $\dfrac{100}{80}$

15. Explain how to use a common factor to find an equivalent fraction.

16. Describe and complete the pattern.

$$\dfrac{4{,}800}{80} , \dfrac{2{,}400}{40} , \dfrac{1{,}200}{20} , \dfrac{\square}{\square} , \dfrac{\square}{\square}$$

17. A book shows 100 hieroglyphic symbols. You have learned the meanings of 80 of them. What fraction of the symbols' meanings, in tenths, have you learned?

18. There are 56 players in an indoor soccer club. Seven of the players cannot attend a game night. The coach needs to make even teams with the players who are there. What fraction of players, in eighths, are at the game night?

Name _____

A factor that is shared by two or more given numbers is a **common factor**. You can find an equivalent fraction by dividing the numerator and denominator by a common factor.

Example Find an equivalent fraction for $\frac{4}{12}$.

Step 1: Find the common factors of 4 and 12.

- The factors of 4 are ①, ②, and ④.

- The factors of 12 are ①, ②, 3, ④, 6, and 12.

So, the common factors of 4 and 12 are 1, 2, and 4.

You can also divide the numerator and denominator by 4 to find the equivalent fraction, $\frac{1}{3}$.

Step 2: Divide both the numerator and denominator

by a common factor greater than 1.

$$\frac{4}{12} = \frac{4 \div 2}{12 \div 2} = \frac{2}{6}$$

$\frac{4}{12}$ is equivalent to $\frac{2}{6}$.

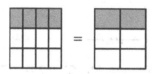

Find an equivalent fraction.

1. $\frac{4}{8} = \frac{4 \div \boxed{}}{8 \div \boxed{}} = \frac{\boxed{}}{\boxed{}}$

2. $\frac{10}{2} = \frac{10 \div \boxed{}}{2 \div \boxed{}} = \frac{\boxed{}}{\boxed{}}$

Find the equivalent fraction.

3. $\frac{60}{100} = \frac{\boxed{}}{10}$

4. $\frac{12}{8} = \frac{6}{\boxed{}}$

5. $\frac{15}{5} = \frac{\boxed{}}{1}$

Name _____

1. Newton has two nickels and two dimes. What fraction of a dollar, in tenths, does Newton have?

_____

2. Descartes has eight nickels and eight dimes. What fraction of a dollar, in tenths, does Descartes have?

_____

3. Newton has ten pennies, six nickels, and two dimes. What fraction of a dollar, in fifths, does Newton have?

_____

4. Descartes has twenty pennies, ten nickels, and seven dimes. What fraction of a dollar, in fifths, does Descartes have?

1. A pet store receives a shipment of 7 boxes of cat treats. Each box is 18 inches high and has 28 bags of cats treats. Each bag has 42 ounces of cat treats. How many ounces of cat treats does the pet store receive in the shipment?

   The pet store receives _____ ounces of cat treats.

1. Write what you know about this phrase. Give an example.

   common factor

Big Ideas Math: Modeling Real Life Grade 4   **323**
Resources by Chapter

Find an equivalent fraction.

1. $\dfrac{4}{16} = \dfrac{4 \div \boxed{}}{16 \div \boxed{}} = \dfrac{\boxed{}}{\boxed{}}$

2. $\dfrac{15}{5} = \dfrac{15 \div \boxed{}}{5 \div \boxed{}} = \dfrac{\boxed{}}{\boxed{}}$

Name _____

Compare. Use a model to help.

1. $\frac{4}{6}$ ◯ $\frac{4}{8}$

2. $\frac{3}{12}$ ◯ $\frac{5}{6}$

3. $\frac{30}{100}$ ◯ $\frac{8}{8}$

4. $\frac{2}{3}$ ◯ $\frac{3}{4}$

5. $\frac{2}{10}$ ◯ $\frac{5}{12}$

6. $\frac{3}{9}$ ◯ $\frac{5}{15}$

7. $\frac{6}{8}$ ◯ $\frac{10}{20}$

8. $\frac{8}{4}$ ◯ $\frac{5}{3}$

9. $\frac{1}{4}$ ◯ $\frac{2}{10}$

10. $\frac{5}{1}$ ◯ $\frac{5}{5}$

11. $\frac{4}{3}$ ◯ $\frac{2}{2}$

12. $\frac{25}{100}$ ◯ $\frac{1}{4}$

13. In a litter of kittens, $\frac{4}{12}$ are white and $\frac{2}{3}$ are tan. Are there more white or more tan kittens?

Complete the statement.

14. $\frac{2}{3} < \frac{\square}{\square}$

15. $\frac{4}{5} > \frac{\square}{\square}$

16. $\frac{7}{10} < \frac{\square}{\square}$

---

17. Which statements are true?

$\frac{7}{8} \overset{?}{>} \frac{3}{2}$

$\frac{3}{6} \overset{?}{>} \frac{50}{100}$

$\frac{3}{4} \overset{?}{<} \frac{11}{12}$

$\frac{1}{5} \overset{?}{<} \frac{5}{12}$

---

18. You have $\frac{5}{6}$ cup of blueberries and $\frac{2}{3}$ cup of raspberries. Do you have enough of each ingredient to make the smoothie? Explain.

Smoothie Recipe
$\frac{5}{8}$ cup of blueberries
$\frac{5}{4}$ cups of raspberries

19. Newton and Descartes are picking cherries at a farm. Newton's bag of cherries weighs $\frac{2}{3}$ pound. Descartes's bag weighs $\frac{5}{4}$ pounds. How much money will Newton and Descartes each pay for their bag of cherries?

Cherry Prices
Less than $\frac{1}{2}$ pound: 75¢
$\frac{1}{2}$ pound – 1 pound: $1
Over 1 pound: $1.25

Name _____

You can use the benchmarks $\frac{1}{2}$ and 1 to help you compare fractions.

A **benchmark** is a commonly used number that you can use to compare other numbers.

Example Use fraction strips to compare $\frac{4}{6}$ and $\frac{3}{8}$.

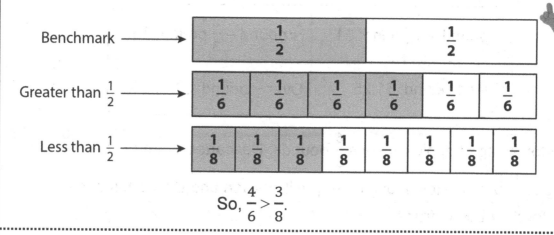

Benchmark

Greater than $\frac{1}{2}$

Less than $\frac{1}{2}$

So, $\frac{4}{6} > \frac{3}{8}$.

Example Use a number line to compare $\frac{3}{6}$ and $\frac{10}{8}$.

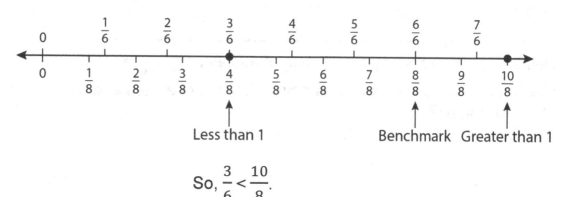

So, $\frac{3}{6} < \frac{10}{8}$.

Compare. Use a model to help.

1. $\frac{1}{8} \bigcirc \frac{5}{6}$

2. $\frac{2}{4} \bigcirc \frac{3}{6}$

3. $\frac{5}{4} \bigcirc \frac{2}{3}$

Name _____

Enrichment and Extension

Newton and Descartes are picking apples and cherries at a farm.

Apple Prices	Cherry Prices
Less than $\frac{1}{2}$ pound: 75¢	Less than $\frac{1}{3}$ pound: 50¢
$\frac{1}{2}$ pound – 1 pound: \$1	$\frac{1}{3}$ pound – $\frac{2}{3}$ pound: 75¢
Over 1 pound: \$1.25	Over $\frac{2}{3}$ pound: \$1

1. Newton's bag of apples weighs $\frac{6}{5}$ pounds. Descartes's bag of cherries weighs $\frac{1}{2}$ pound. How much money will Newton and Descartes each pay for their bag of fruit?

2. Descartes also picks apples. His bag of apples weighs $\frac{3}{8}$ pound. How much money will Descartes pay for his bag of apples and bag of cherries in all?

3. Newton also picks cherries. His bag of cherries weighs $\frac{3}{4}$ pound. How much money will Newton pay for his bag of apples and bag of cherries in all?

Lesson 7.5 **Daily Skills Practice**
For use before Lesson 7.5

1. Divide.

    $54 \div 6 = $ _____

Lesson 7.5 **Vocabulary Practice**
For use before Lesson 7.5

1. Write what you know about this word. Give an example.

    benchmark

Compare. Use a model to help.

1. $\dfrac{2}{4}$ ◯ $\dfrac{6}{8}$

2. $\dfrac{5}{3}$ ◯ $\dfrac{3}{4}$

Name _____

Compare. Use a model to help.

1. $\frac{8}{10}$ ◯ $\frac{2}{5}$

2. $\frac{1}{3}$ ◯ $\frac{3}{4}$

3. $\frac{17}{100}$ ◯ $\frac{2}{10}$

4. $\frac{4}{8}$ ◯ $\frac{8}{12}$

5. $\frac{3}{5}$ ◯ $\frac{6}{8}$

6. $\frac{5}{3}$ ◯ $\frac{7}{6}$

7. $\frac{3}{4}$ ◯ $\frac{2}{6}$

8. $\frac{3}{1}$ ◯ $\frac{6}{3}$

9. $\frac{2}{5}$ ◯ $\frac{40}{100}$

Compare. Use a model to help.

10. $\frac{5}{8}$ ◯ $\frac{6}{6}$

11. $\frac{2}{4}$ ◯ $\frac{5}{6}$

12. $\frac{6}{8}$ ◯ $\frac{4}{6}$

13. $\frac{4}{6}$ ◯ $\frac{8}{12}$

14. $\frac{2}{10}$ ◯ $\frac{8}{12}$

15. $\frac{5}{6}$ ◯ $\frac{2}{5}$

16. Compare $\frac{2}{3}$ and $\frac{1}{6}$ two different ways.

17. A sailor is making a ship in a bottle. The last thing she needs to do is seal the bottle with a cork stopper. She tries a $\frac{5}{8}$-inch cork stopper, but it is too big. Should she try a $\frac{3}{4}$-inch cork stopper or a $\frac{1}{3}$-inch cork stopper next? Explain.

18. Order the lengths of hair donated from greatest to least.

Student	Hair Length Donated (feet)
Student A	$\frac{10}{12}$
Student B	$\frac{2}{4}$
Student C	$\frac{5}{8}$

Name _____

Lesson 7.5 Reteach

Example Compare $\frac{1}{3}$ and $\frac{4}{6}$.

One Way: Use a like denominator.	**Another Way:** Use a like numerator.

One Way: Use a like denominator.

Step 1: Find an equivalent fraction for $\frac{1}{3}$ that has a denominator of 6.

Think: 3 times what number equals 6?

Step 2: Multiply the numerator and the denominator of $\frac{1}{3}$ by 2.

$$\frac{1}{3} = \frac{1 \times 2}{3 \times 2} = \frac{2}{6}$$

Step 3: Compare $\frac{2}{6}$ and $\frac{4}{6}$.

$\frac{2}{6}$ is less than $\frac{4}{6}$. So, $\frac{1}{3} < \frac{4}{6}$.

$$\frac{1}{3} = \frac{2}{6} \qquad \frac{4}{6}$$

Another Way: Use a like numerator.

Step 1: Find an equivalent fraction for $\frac{1}{3}$ that has a numerator of 4.

Think: 1 times what number equals 4?

Step 2: Multiply the numerator and the denominator of $\frac{1}{3}$ by 4.

$$\frac{1}{3} = \frac{1 \times 4}{3 \times 4} = \frac{4}{12}$$

Step 3: Compare $\frac{4}{12}$ and $\frac{4}{6}$.

$\frac{4}{12}$ is less than $\frac{4}{6}$. So, $\frac{1}{3} < \frac{4}{6}$.

$$\frac{1}{3} = \frac{4}{12} \qquad \frac{4}{6}$$

Compare. Use a model to help.

1. $\frac{1}{2} \bigcirc \frac{3}{4}$

2. $\frac{5}{6} \bigcirc \frac{2}{3}$

3. $\frac{5}{10} \bigcirc \frac{1}{8}$

Name _____

1. Order the heights of sunflowers from least to greatest.

Sunflower	Height (feet)
Sunflower A	$\frac{4}{4}$
Sunflower B	$\frac{6}{5}$
Sunflower C	$\frac{5}{6}$
Sunflower D	$\frac{2}{3}$
Sunflower E	$\frac{3}{2}$

2. Order the heights of corn stalks from greatest to least.

Corn Stalk	Height (feet)
Stalk A	$\frac{7}{12}$
Stalk B	$\frac{3}{2}$
Stalk C	$\frac{1}{8}$
Stalk D	$\frac{6}{3}$
Stalk E	$\frac{3}{4}$

Name _____

Chapter Self-Assessment

Use the scale below to rate your understanding of the learning target and the success criteria.

1	2	3	4
I do not understand.	I can do it with help.	I can do it on my own.	I can teach someone else.

	Rating
7.1 Model Equivalent Fractions	
Learning Target: Model and write equivalent fractions.	1 2 3 4
I can use an area model to find equivalent fractions.	1 2 3 4
I can use a number line to find equivalent fractions.	1 2 3 4
I can write equivalent fractions.	1 2 3 4
7.2 Generate Equivalent Fractions by Multiplying	
Learning Target: Use multiplication to find equivalent fractions.	1 2 3 4
I can multiply a numerator and a denominator by a chosen number.	1 2 3 4
I can multiply to find equivalent fractions.	1 2 3 4
I can explain why multiplication can be used to find equivalent fractions.	1 2 3 4
7.3 Generate Equivalent Fractions by Dividing	
Learning Target: Use division to find equivalent fractions.	1 2 3 4
I can find the factors of a number.	1 2 3 4
I can find the common factors of a numerator and a denominator.	1 2 3 4
I can divide to find equivalent fractions.	1 2 3 4
7.4 Compare Fractions Using Benchmarks	
Learning Target: Compare fractions using benchmarks.	1 2 3 4
I can compare a fraction to a benchmark of $\frac{1}{2}$ or 1.	1 2 3 4
I can use a benchmark to compare two fractions.	1 2 3 4

Name _____

	Rating
7.5 Compare Fractions	
Learning Target: Compare fractions using equivalent fractions.	1 2 3 4
I can compare the numerators and denominators of two fractions.	1 2 3 4
I can make the numerators or the denominators of two fractions the same.	1 2 3 4
I can compare fractions with like numerators or like denominators.	1 2 3 4

Answers

Chapter 1

1.1 Daily Skills Practice
1. Check students' work; 12

1.1 Vocabulary Practice
1. *Sample answer:* a number written in numeral form; 412 is in standard form.

1.1 Prerequisite Skills Practice
1. 7
2. 500

1.1 Extra Practice
1. 700
2. 2,000
3. 9
4. 60,000
5. 10
6. 900,000
7. 20,000
8. 4,000
9. 200
10. 500,000
11. 70
12. 6,000
13. The 4 in 4,037 is 10 times greater than the 4 in 425.
14. The 3 in 341,095 is 100 times the value of the 3 in 3,715.
15. The 7 in 17,525 is 100 times the value of the 7 in 970.
16. The value of the 2 in 8,325 is 10 times the value of the 2 in 6,542.
17. 10 times
18. 100 times
19. No; *Sample answer:* because there are different digits in each place value. The thousands digit has a value of 5,000 and the hundreds digit has a value of 800.
20. Greatest; 876,542; Least: 245,678
21. no; *Sample answer:* the value in the ten thousands place is 100 times the value in the hundreds place.
22. Greatest: 9,831; Least: 1,389
23. South Carolina
24. 9,000; 900; The value of the digit 9 in the land area of Georgia is 10 times the value of the digit 9 in Hawaii.
25. The 3 in the ten thousands place is 1,000 times the value of the 3 in the tens place.

1.1 Reteach
1. 6,000
2. 50,000
3. 400
4. 700,000
5. The 3 in 300 is 10 times the value of the 3 in 30.

6. The 8 in 8,000 is 10 times the value of the 8 in 800.

1.1 Enrichment and Extension
1. 73,449
2. 85,050
3. 703,309
4. 65,494

1.2 Daily Skills Practice
1. 0

1.2 Vocabulary Practice
1. *Sample answer:* a group of three place values, consisting of hundreds, tens, and ones;

period

Ones Period		
Hundreds	**Tens**	**Ones**
0	0	0

1.2 Prerequisite Skills Practice
1. 300
2. 60,000

1.2 Extra Practice
1. 254,397; two hundred fifty-four thousand, three hundred ninety-seven
2. 35,047; $30,000 + 5,000 + 40 + 7$
3. nine hundred twenty-three thousand, seven hundred six; $900,000 + 20,000 + 3,000 + 700 + 6$
4. 61,315; $60,000 + 1,000 + 300 + 10 + 5$
5.

Standard Form	Word Form	Expanded Form
5,426	five thousand, four hundred twenty-six	$5,000 + 400 + 20 + 6$
72,013	seventy-two thousand, thirteen	$70,000 + 2,000 + 10 + 3$
407,023	four hundred seven thousand, twenty-three	$400,000 + 7,000 + 20 + 3$
803,012	eight hundred three thousand, twelve	$800,000 + 3,000 + 10 + 2$

6. Student A; Student B wrote four hundred as four thousand.
7. 510,098
8. 45,391; forty-five thousand, three hundred ninety-one; $40,000 + 5,000 + 300 + 90 + 1$
9. 16,820; sixteen thousand, eight hundred twenty; $10,000 + 6,000 + 800 + 20$
10. 7,203; seven thousand, two hundred three

Answers

1.2 Reteach
1. twenty-four thousand, five hundred twenty; $20,000 + 4,000 + 500 + 20$

2. $302,400; 300,000 + 2,000 + 400$

1.2 Enrichment and Extension
1. Check students' work; *Sample answer:* 1,234; one thousand, two hundred thirty-four; $1,000 + 200 + 30 + 4$

2. Check students' work; *Sample answer:* 67,890; sixty-seven thousand, eight hundred ninety; $60,000 + 7,000 + 800 + 90$

3. Check students' work; *Sample answer:* 357,246; three hundred fifty-seven thousand, two hundred forty-six; $300,000 + 50,000 + 7,000 + 200 + 40 + 6$

1.3 Daily Skills Practice
1. Check students' work; 5

1.3 Vocabulary Practice
1. *Sample answer:* two or more numbers having the same value; $\frac{4}{4} = 1$

1.3 Prerequisite Skills Practice
1. $475 < 481$ 2. $305 > 35$

1.3 Extra Practice
1. hundreds
2. ten thousands
3. thousands
4. tens
5. hundred thousands
6. thousands
7. ten thousands
8. thousands
9. hundreds
10. $4,521 < 4,530$
11. $48,250 < 49,123$
12. $613,426 > 612,578$
13. $300,000 > 30,000$
14. $2,237 < 3,136$
15. $73,841 < 80,950$
16. $917,333 < 917,421$
17. $940,713 > 876,924$
18. $55,328 > 55,327$
19. $6,358 < 6,361$
20. $92,605 > 92,506$
21. $7,000 < 600,000$
22. $36,431 > 36,413$
23. $8,830 > 8,645$
24. $521,984 > 507,699$
25. $24,650 > 20,000 + 4,000 + 600 + 5$
26. thirty-five thousand $< 350,000$
27. seven hundred thousand, twenty-six $< 726,000$
28. four hundred ten thousand, sixty-five $< 410,605$
29. $675,419 = 600,000 + 70,000 + 5,000 + 400 + 10 + 9$
30. $307,982 < 300,000 + 70,000 + 900 + 80 + 2$

31. $2,075

32. *Sample answer:* The greater number is the number with more digits. If the number of digits is the same, start at the left and compare the digits in each place value until the digits differ.

33. Compare the leftmost digits. If they have the same value, compare the digits to the right.

34. Charlotte, Fort Worth; Baltimore, Detroit

1.3 Reteach
1. hundreds
2. thousands
3. tens
4. $6,348 < 6,572$
5. $8,270 < 8,291$
6. $57,011 > 56,123$

1.3 Enrichment and Extension
1. *Sample answer:* $68,143 > 67,427$

2. *Sample answer:* $543,837 < 543,912$

3. *Sample answer:* $352,896 > 325,896$

1.4 Daily Skills Practice
1.
$$\begin{array}{r} 500 \\ -130 \\ \hline 370 \end{array}$$

1.4 Vocabulary Practice
1. *Sample answer:* the value of the place of a digit in a number; In 241, 2 has a place value of 100 because it is in the hundreds place.

1.4 Prerequisite Skills Practice
1. 350   2. 600

1.4 Extra Practice
1. 7,930
2. 4,200
3. 10,000
4. 31,000
5. 70,000
6. 13,600
7. 73,850
8. 110,000
9. 500,000
10. 524,330
11. 925,700
12. 400,000
13. 2,000
14. 55,000
15. 47,000
16. 9,000
17. 210,000
18. 780,000
19. 870,000
20. 130,000
21. 500,000
22. 100,000
23. 100,000
24. 700,000
25. 5,000; 10,000

Answers

26. 526,725; 548,900; 453,215

27. *Sample answer:* Round to the nearest ten because the price is probably not more than $100.

28. no; *Sample answer:* When a 9 rounds to the next number, the digit to the left also changes, so the answer is 30,000.

29. $24,395; $23,590; $24,499

1.4 Reteach

1. 4,000   **2.** 54,000   **3.** 40,000

4. 270,000   **5.** 700,000   **6.** 8,000

1.4 Enrichment and Extension

1. Check students' work: any number from 6,450 to 6,499

2. Check students' work: any number from 45,000 to 45,499

3. 749,999; 750,000; 750,000; 750,000

4. 350,001; 350,000; 350,000; 350,000

Answers

Chapter 2

2.1 Daily Skills Practice
1. 6

2.1 Vocabulary Practice
1. *Sample answer:* the third digit from the right that tells how many hundreds are in a number; In 1,438, 4 is in the hundreds place.

2.1 Prerequisite Skills Practice
1. 4,000   2. 620,000

2.1 Extra Practice
1. *Sample answer:* 9,000 + 5,000 = 14,000

2. *Sample answer:* 20,000 + 30,000 = 50,000

3. *Sample answer:* 8,000 − 3,000 = 5,000

4. *Sample answer:* 70,000 − 30,000 = 40,000

5. *Sample answer:* 20,000

6. *Sample answer:* 140,000

7. *Sample answer:* 30,000

8. *Sample answer:* 100,000

9. *Sample answer:* 500,000

10. *Sample answer:* 600,000

11. *Sample answer:* 500,000

12. *Sample answer:* 900,000

13. *Sample answer:* 400,000

14. *Sample answer:* 100,000

15. *Sample answer:* 580,000

16. *Sample answer:* 800,000

17. *Sample answer:* 600,000

18. 437,964 − 85,376; 476,208 − 183,115

19. *Sample answer:* when you need more accuracy; when you need less accuracy

20. *Sample answer:* 100,000 people

21. *Sample answer:* 8,000 pages

22. *Sample answer:* 50,000 books

23. *Sample answer:* 15,000 points

2.1 Reteach
1. *Sample answer:* 50,000 + 40,000 = 90,000

2. *Sample answer:* 6,000 − 4,000 = 2,000

2.1 Enrichment and Extension
1. 8,800

2. 63,000; 63,400

3. 47,000; 46,200; 100,000; 47,300

4. 300,000; 236,000

5. 458,000; 400,000; 450,000

2.2 Daily Skills Practice
1. $\frac{2}{3} = \frac{4}{6}$

2.2 Vocabulary Practice
1. *Sample answer:* a number that is being added to another number; In 4 + 1 = 5, 4 and 1 are the addends.

2.2 Prerequisite Skills Practice
1. *Sample answer:* 400,000 + 400,000 = 800,000

2. *Sample answer:* 700,000 − 300,000 = 400,000

2.2 Extra Practice
1. *Sample answer:* 13,000; 7,436 + 5,815 = 13,251

2. *Sample answer:* 16,000; 9,238 + 6,572 = 15,810

3. *Sample answer:* 65,000; 62,482 + 2,941= 65,423

4. *Sample answer:* 29,000; 24,175 + 4,537 = 28,712

5. *Sample answer:* 90,000; 53,810 + 38,726 = 92,536

6. *Sample answer:* 120,000;
   43,804 + 76,318 = 120,122

7. *Sample answer:* 180,000;
   85,436 + 92,775 = 178,211

8. *Sample answer:* 700,000;
   625,319 + 73,742 = 699,061

9. *Sample answer:* 870,000;
   817,856 + 45,390 = 863,246

10. *Sample answer:* 900,000;
    228,363 + 704,683 = 933,046

11. *Sample answer:* 900,000;
    385,712 + 532,184 = 917,896

12. *Sample answer:* 600,000;
    447,650 + 176,351 = 624,001

Answers

13. *Sample answer:* 926,000;
921,934 + 3,581 = 925,515

14. *Sample answer:* 830,000;
764,325 + 68,903 = 833,228

15. *Sample answer:* 170,000;
138,463 + 29,648 = 168,111

16. *Sample answer:* 900,000;
658,103 + 215,899 = 874,002

17. *Sample answer:* The regrouped thousand was not included; 371,046

18. *Sample answer:* A museum sold 34,781 tickets in April and 48,227 in May. How many tickets were sold in all?

19. yes   **20.** 407,611 points

2.2 Reteach
1. *Sample answer:* 98,000; 98,009

2. *Sample answer:* 473,000; 472,908

2.2 Enrichment and Extension
1. no; *Sample answer:* He did not align the digits by place value.

2. yes   **3.** yes

4. no; *Sample answer:* He did not regroup the 14 tens as 1 hundred and 4 tens.

2.3 Daily Skills Practice
1. 421

2.3 Vocabulary Practice
1. *Sample answer:* the answer to a subtraction problem; In 8 – 2 = 6, 6 is the difference.

2.3 Prerequisite Skills Practice
1. *Sample answer:* 550,000; 550,354

2. *Sample answer:* 350,000; 349,836

2.3 Extra Practice
1. 7,235 – 2,940 = 4,295

2. 5,612 – 3,621 = 1,991

3. 82,705 – 6,432 = 76,273

4. 45,143 – 4,089 = 41,054

5. 70,381 – 14,203 = 56,178

6. 92,175 – 35,698 = 56,477

7. 38,206 – 24,715 = 13,491

8. 67,112 – 39,018 = 28,094

9. 725,300 – 52,225 = 673,075

10. 146,375 – 72,193 = 74,182

11. 536,041 – 172,131 = 363,910

12. 974,215 – 882,042 = 92,173

13. 215,871 – 203,184 = 12,687

14. 495,307 – 186,573 = 308,734

15. 600,395 – 227,608 = 372,787

16. 875,419 – 9,325 = 866,094

17. 603,200 – 8,535 = 594,665

18. 328,416 – 31,605 = 296,811

19. 455,866- 48,783 = 407,083

20. *Sample answer:* There were 27,305 people at a football game. 9,413 people left during half-time. How many people were left? 17,892 people

21. 48 years   **22.** 107 years

2.3 Reteach
1. 2,085   **2.** 27,769

2.3 Enrichment and Extension
1. *Sample answer:* 15,375 – 5,275 = 10,100; 20,480 – 8,500 = 11,980

2. *Sample answer:* 37,415 – 19,300 = 18,115; 45,250 – 25,750 = 19,500

3. *Sample answer:* 350,795 – 45,850 = 304,945; 365,225 – 48,750 = 316,475

2.4 Daily Skills Practice
1. 12

2.4 Vocabulary Practice
1. *Sample answer:* the answer in an addition problem; In 8 + 2 = 10, 10 is the sum.

2.4 Prerequisite Skills Practice
1. 8,325 – 2,746 = 5,579

2. 54,106 – 7,342 = 46,764

2.4 Extra Practice
1. 8,419 + 3,725 = 12,144

Answers

2. $9,543 - 6,213 = 3,330$

3. $6,782 + 7,009 = 13,791$

4. $7,582 - 1,483 = 6,099$

5. $16,315 + 8,527 = 24,842$

6. $6,300 - 4,275 = 2,025$

7. $19,345 - 3,721 = 15,624$

8. $245,860 + 36,173 = 282,033$

9. $428,330 + 54,281 = 482,611$

10. $634,726 - 45,218 = 589,508$

11. $827,306 + 62,813 = 890,119$

12. $325,090 + 127,305 = 452,395$

13. $731,062 - 534,713 = 196,349$

14. $902,470 - 410,625 = 491,845$

15. $186,304 + 326,278 = 512,582$

16. no; *Sample answer:* The 2 in 35,204 has a value of 200, not 20.

17. yes; *Sample answer:* He subtracted 36 at the beginning, then added it back in.

18. *Sample answer:* I would use compensation and add 25 to 7,075.

19. 610,700 students   20. $20,375

2.4 Reteach

1. $8,300 + 7,435 = 15,735$

2. $6,510 - 4,105 = 2,405$

2.4 Enrichment and Extension

1.

5,275	3,200	1,525
4,000	5,380	3,120
7,425	4,270	3,305

2. *Sample answer:* The top row and left column were only missing one number so I completed those rows first. I added the given numbers and subtracted from the sum. After those numbers were filled in, other rows were only missing one number, so I did the same.

3. *Sample answer:* $15,000 = 5,250 + 3,695 + 6,055$

2.5 Daily Skills Practice

1. <

2.5 Vocabulary Practice

1. *Sample answer:* a strategy of adding to or subtracting from a number to make it easier to work with, but making up for the change somewhere else; In $23 + 38$, you can add 2 to 38 and subtract 2 from 23 to make it easier to solve; $21 + 40$.

2.5 Prerequisite Skills Practice

1. $7,425 + 6,810 = 14,235$

2. $34,609 - 8,243 = 26,366$

2.5 Extra Practice

1. *Sample answer:* Subtract how many were left after the first day to find how many were sold, then add this to the number sold the second day. 111,622 CDs were sold in all.

2. *Sample answer:* Add $182 + 182$, then subtract the sum from 2,400. An elephant eats 2,036 more pounds of food.

3. *Sample answer:* Add the numbers of tickets, then subtract the sum from 52,000. The park sold 9,976 more tickets.

4. *Sample answer:* Add the gallons of water used by the golf course and car wash, then subtract the total from 18,000. The water park uses 13,786 more gallons of water per day.

5. *Sample answer:* Subtract how many pounds were left after selling to the restaurant to find how many pounds were sold, then add this to the pounds sold at the market. He sold 700 pounds of vegetables.

6. *Sample answer:* Add $376 + 1,468$ to find the number of students at Oak Hill School. Then, add the sum to 1,468 to find the total. There are 3,312 students in all.

7. *Sample answer:* Add to find the total number of visitors in May and June, then subtract 215,378 from the sum to find how many visitors in July. There were 546,797 visitors in July.

8. *Sample answer:* I have 725 baseball cards and 515 football cards. My friend has 630 sports cards. How many more cards do I have than my friend? 610 cards

9. *Sample answer:* Subtract both president's birth year from the year they died to find their ages, then subtract how many years they lived to find the difference. Washington lived 11 years longer.

Answers

10. *Sample answer:* Multiply the number of adult tickets by 7, then multiply the number of children's tickets by 5. Add the products and subtract the sum from 1,200. The class needs to raise $380 more.

11. *Sample answer:* Add to find the total number of miles my family traveled. Then add to find the number of miles my uncle traveled. Then, subtract to find the difference. My uncle travels 13,107 more miles.

12. *Sample answer:* Find the total miles traveled in question 11, then add the miles traveled back home; 22,881 miles.

2.5 Reteach

1. *Sample answer:* Add 4,900 + 350 to find the total, subtract 730 to find how many are at the zoo now; 4,520 people.

2.5 Enrichment and Extension

1. 17,258 people

2. The most people chose green; 11,547 in all

3. Sample answer: One way: Add to find the number of glass bottles, then add the number of aluminum cans and glass bottles, and subtract the sum from 12,725; Another way: Subtract the number of aluminum cans from 12,725. Then, subtract the number of glass bottles from the difference; The class collected 3,172 plastic items.

Answers

Chapter 3

3.1 Daily Skills Practice
1. 10

3.1 Vocabulary Practice
1. *Sample answer:* to find a number that is close to the actual number; The sum of 997 and 1,011 is about 2,000.

3.1 Prerequisite Skills Practice
1. *Sample answer:* $7 \times 5 = 5 \times 7$; $9 \times 3 = 3 \times 9$

3.1 Extra Practice
1. 35 is 5 times as many as 7; 35 is 7 times as many as 5.

2. 16 is 2 times as many as 8; 16 is 8 times as many as 2.

3. 72 is 8 times as many as 9; 72 is 9 times as many as 8.

4. 54 is 9 times as many as 6; 54 is 6 times as many as 9.

5. 28 is 7 times as many as 4; 28 is 4 times as many as 7.

6. 45 is 5 times as many as 9; 45 is 9 times as many as 5.

7. $24 = 6 \times 4$
8. $14 = 9 + 5$
9. $9 = 3 \times 3$
10. $21 = 7 \times 3$
11. $13 = 6 + 7$
12. $40 = 8 \times 5$
13. 575 students
14. 24 students

15. *Sample answer:* Using the Commutative Property of Multiplication, $560 = 70 \times 8$ and $560 = 8 \times 70$.

16. *Sample answer:* The giraffe is 6 times as tall as the tiger. The giraffe is 15 feet taller than the tiger.

17. *Sample answer:* 36 is 16 more than 20.

18. 4 boys
19. 12 hours

20. 72 cents

21. *Sample answer:* 24 is 10 more than 14.

22. 20 hours

3.1 Reteach
1. 56 is 7 times as many as 8; 56 is 8 times as many as 7.

2. 36 is 4 times as many as 9; 36 is 9 times as many as 4.

3. Check students' work; $16 = 12 + 4$

4. Check students' work; $30 = 5 \times 6$

3.1 Enrichment and Extension
1. 24 is 18 more than 6. 24 is 4 times as many as 6.

2. 35 is 15 more than 20. 35 is 5 times as many as 7.

3. *Sample answer:* 15 is 4 more than 11. 15 is 5 times as many as 3.

4. *Sample answer:* 12 is 4 more than 8. 12 is 2 times as many as 6.

3.2 Daily Skills Practice
1. 111,398

3.2 Vocabulary Practice
1. *Sample answer:* the value of a digit in a number; In 364, the 6 has a place value of 10 because it is in the tens place.

3.2 Prerequisite Skills Practice
1. 20 is 4 times as many as 5; 20 is 5 times as many as 4.

2. 12 is 2 times as many as 6; 12 is 6 times as many as 2.

3.2 Extra Practice
1. 28; 280; 2,800; 28,000
2. 12; 120; 1,200; 12,000
3. 27; 270; 2,700; 27,000
4. 40; 400; 4,000; 40,000
5. 120
6. 18,000
7. 3,500
8. 8,000
9. 2,400
10. 60
11. 2,000
12. 480
13. 21,000
14. 7
15. 4,000
16. 1
17. 800
18. 3
19. 400
20. <
21. =
22. >

Answers

23. $=$ **24.** $<$ **25.** $>$

26. $1 \times 5 = 5$; $2 \times 50 = 100$; $3 \times 500 = 1,500$;
$4 \times 5,000 = 20,000$; $5 \times 50,000 = 250,000$;
$6 \times 500,000 = 3,000,000$; *Sample answer:* The first
factors are 1 more. The second factors are 10 times
as much.

27. *Sample answer:* The product of 6 and 7,000 is
greater because 7,000 is greater than 700.

28. *Sample answer:* Find the product of 2 and 9, then
add 3 zeros to show thousands.

29. *Sample answer:* $9 \times 40 = 360$

30. 11,100 minutes

31. 475 pounds

3.2 Reteach

1. 16; 160; 1,600; 16,000

2. 30; 300; 3,000; 30,000

3.2 Enrichment and Extension

1. $2 \times 7 = 14$; $2 \times 70 = 140$; $2 \times 700 = 1,400$;
$2 \times 7,000 = 14,000$; $2 \times 70,000 = 140,000$;
$2 \times 700,000 = 1,400,000$

2. $9 \times 4 = 36$; $9 \times 40 = 360$; $9 \times 400 = 3,600$;
$9 \times 4,000 = 36,000$; $9 \times 40,000 = 360,000$;
$9 \times 400,000 = 3,600,000$

3. $8 \times 3 = 24$; $8 \times 30 = 240$; $8 \times 300 = 2,400$;
$8 \times 3,000 = 24,000$; $8 \times 30,000 = 240,000$;
$8 \times 300,000 = 2,400,000$

4. $9 \times 5 = 45$; $9 \times 50 = 450$; $9 \times 500 = 4,500$;
$9 \times 5,000 = 45,000$; $9 \times 50,000 = 450,000$;
$9 \times 500,000 = 4,500,000$

5. *Sample answer:* $3 \times 6 = 18$; $3 \times 60 = 180$;
$3 \times 600 = 1,800$; $3 \times 6,000 = 18,000$; $9 \times 2 = 18$;
$9 \times 20 = 180$; $9 \times 200 = 1,800$; $9 \times 2,000 = 18,000$

3.3 Daily Skills Practice

1. 2,248

3.3 Vocabulary Practice

1. *Sample answer:* to find the ten, hundred, or
thousand that a number is closest to; 478 rounded
to the nearest ten is 480.

3.3 Prerequisite Skills Practice

1. 2,000   **2.** 56,000

3.3 Extra Practice

1. *Sample answer:* 200

2. *Sample answer:* 560

3. *Sample answer:* 3,600

4. *Sample answer:* 1,800

5. *Sample answer:* 14,000

6. *Sample answer:* 54,000

7. *Sample answer:* 2,800

8. *Sample answer:* 4,000

9. *Sample answer:* 540   **10.** 200 and 240

11. *Sample answer:* 540 and 630

12. *Sample answer:* 2,100 and 2,800

13. *Sample answer:* 1,000 and 1,200

14. *Sample answer:* 2,400 and 3,000

15. *Sample answer:* 6,400 and 7,200

16. *Sample answer:* 2,400 and 2,700

17. *Sample answer:* 30,000 and 35,000

18. *Sample answer:* 27,000 and 36,000

19. exact answer; *Sample answer:* An estimate of 8×60 is close to 500, but you need an exact answer to know there will be 500 books.

20. yes; $4 \times 6,000 = 24,000$

21. greater than; *Sample answer:* The estimate
multiplies 6 months by $3,000 per month and the
actual rent is higher than $3,000 per month.

22. *Sample answer:* Rounding lets me multiply easier
numbers to get an estimate. If my answer is too
different from the estimate, I know to check for a
mistake.

23. Douglas Fir

24. between 120 feet and 160 feet

25. about 350 feet

3.3 Reteach

1. *Sample answer:* 180

2. *Sample answer:* 4,200

Answers

3. *Sample answer:* 32,000

4. *Sample answer:* 180 and 210

5. *Sample answer:* 4,500 and 5,400

6. *Sample answer:* 28,000 and 32,000

3.3 Enrichment and Extension

1. 5 skateboards

2. golf club set

3. *Sample answer:* Round each price, or add the prices and then round; 320 + 40 = 360, 4 × 360 = $1,440; (319 + 37) = 356, so an estimate is 4 × 360 = $1,440; rounding each price first; Both ways give the same estimate.

3.4 Daily Skills Practice

1. 95,000

3.4 Vocabulary Practice

1. *Sample answer:* the group of place values that includes thousands, ten thousands, and hundred thousands; The thousands period of 3,463,111 consists of the digits 463 which represent 463 thousands.

3.4 Prerequisite Skills Practice

1. *Sample answer:* 240

2. *Sample answer:* 54,000

3.4 Extra Practice

1. Check students' work; 60

2. Check students' work; 102

3. Check students' work; 60

4. Check students' work; 42

5. Check students' work; 175

6. Check students' work; 96

7. 376   8. 130   9. 747

10. 212   11. 370   12. 234

13. *Sample answer:* You can break one factor apart to have easier numbers to multiply.

14. *Sample answer:*
8 × (20 + 9) = 232; 8 × (30 − 1) = 232

15. *Sample answer:* I would rather use 20 + 4 because it is easier to multiply by a decade number.

16. yes; 38 × 5 = 190, so 190 feet of fence are needed.

17. yes; The dog needs 144 ounces in 4 days.

18. *Sample answer:* 3 × (20 + 5) = 75; 3 × (30 − 5) = 75

3.4 Reteach

1. Check students' work; 4 × 13 = 52

2. Check students' work; 6 × 17 = 102

3.4 Enrichment and Extension

1. Check students' work; *Sample answer:* 5(10 + 15) = 125

2. Check students' work; *Sample answer:* 5(5 + 20) = 125

3. Check students' work; *Sample answer:* 5(30 − 5) = 125

4. *Sample answer:* The answers are represented by the same number of squares; the parts used for the answer are different.

5. *Sample answer:* yes; 25 × (4 + 1) = 100 + 25

3.5 Daily Skills Practice

1. 6,157

3.5 Vocabulary Practice

1. *Sample answer:* the product of a number and a sum equals the sum of the products of the number and each addend; 3(4 + 1) = 3(4) + 3(1)

3.5 Prerequisite Skills Practice

1. 190   2. 496

3.5 Extra Practice

1. 3,248   2. 2,703

3. 9,232   4. 18,450

5. 56 × 7 = (50 + 6) × 7
         = (50 × 7) + (6 × 7)
         = 350 + 42
         = 392

6. 2 × 594 = 2 × (500 + 90 + 4)
          = (2 × 500) + (2 × 90) + (2 × 4)
          = 1,000 + 180 + 8
          = 1,188

7. 5,607   8. 37,405

9. 1,422 tulips   10. 1,650 miles

11. 4,602 × 7

Answers

12. *Sample answer:* First, write 6,075 in expanded form: $6,000 + 70 + 5$. Then, multiply each number by 9 and add the products.

13. 135 more rows   **14.** no

15. 526×8 **16.** 144 more pencils

3.5 Reteach

1. $7 \times 204 = 7 \times (200 + 4)$
$\qquad\qquad = (7 \times 200) + (7 \times 4)$
$\qquad\qquad = 1,400 + 28$
$\qquad\qquad = 1,428$

2. 2,992

3.5 Enrichment and Extension

1. no; The first box should include 500 rather than 50. The correct product is 2,092.

2. no; The second box should include 30 rather than 300. The correct product is 1,888.

3. yes

4. no; 3,605 has 0 tens, so the third box does not belong. The correct answer is 25,235.

3.6 Daily Skills Practice

1. 56,305; $50,000 + 6,000 + 300 + 5$

3.6 Vocabulary Practice

1. *Sample answer:* In a multiplication equation, the numbers that are multiplied are called factors; In the equation $3 \times 6 = 18$, 3 and 6 are factors.

3.6 Prerequisite Skills Practice

1. 462   **2.** 36,911

3.6 Extra Practice

1.
```
        43
  ×      6
  ┌──────────┐
  │   240    │
+ │    18    │
  └──────────┘
       258
```

2.
```
        75
  ×      9
  ┌──────────┐
  │   630    │
+ │    45    │
  └──────────┘
       675
```

3.
```
       358
  ×      4
  ┌──────────┐
  │  1,200   │
  │   200    │
+ │    32    │
  └──────────┘
      1,432
```

4.
```
       726
  ×      8
  ┌──────────┐
  │  5,600   │
  │   160    │
+ │    48    │
  └──────────┘
      5,808
```

5.
```
      6,289
  ×       5
  ┌──────────┐
  │  30,000  │
  │   1,000  │
  │    400   │
+ │     45   │
  └──────────┘
      31,445
```

6.
```
      8,903
  ×       7
  ┌──────────┐
  │  56,000  │
  │   6,300  │
  │      0   │
+ │     21   │
  └──────────┘
      62,321
```

7. 741   **8.** 192   **9.** 30,328

10. 5,136   **11.** 4,419   **12.** 25,736

13. 16,455   **14.** 18,874   **15.** 10,490

16. 28,000; 6,300; 210; 35   **17.** 8 and 634

18. 4,345 miles   **19.** 7,848 miles

3.6 Reteach

1.
```
        58
  ×      3
  ┌──────────┐
  │   150    │
+ │    24    │
  └──────────┘
       174
```

2.
```
       215
  ×      9
  ┌──────────┐
  │  1,800   │
  │    90    │
+ │    45    │
  └──────────┘
      1,935
```

3.
```
      7,163
  ×       8
  ┌──────────┐
  │  56,000  │
  │    800   │
  │    480   │
+ │     24   │
  └──────────┘
      57,304
```

3.6 Enrichment and Extension

1.
```
        45              52
  ×      3        ×      8
  ┌──────────┐    ┌──────────┐
  │   120    │    │   400    │
+ │    15    │  + │    16    │
  └──────────┘    └──────────┘
  │   135    │    │   416    │
  └──────────┘    └──────────┘
```

2.
```
       419              283
  ×      5        ×      7
  ┌──────────┐    ┌──────────┐
  │  2,000   │    │  1,400   │
  │    50    │    │    560   │
+ │    45    │  + │     21   │
  └──────────┘    └──────────┘
  │  2,095   │    │  1,981   │
  └──────────┘    └──────────┘
```

Answers

3.7 Daily Skills Practice
1. $<$

3.7 Vocabulary Practice
1. *Sample answer:* the products formed by breaking apart a factor into ones, tens, hundreds, and so on, and multiplying each of these by the other factor;

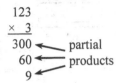

```
   123
 ×   3
   300  ◄——— partial
    60  ◄——— products
     9  ◄———
```

3.7 Prerequisite Skills Practice

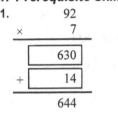

1.
```
        92
     ×   7
   ┌─────────┐
   │     630 │
   ├─────────┤
 + │      14 │
   └─────────┘
       644
```

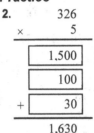

2.
```
       326
    ×    5
  ┌─────────┐
  │   1,500 │
  ├─────────┤
  │     100 │
  ├─────────┤
+ │      30 │
  └─────────┘
     1,630
```

3.7 Extra Practice
1. 115
2. 140
3. 70; $7 \times 14 = 98$
4. 450; $9 \times 48 = 432$
5. 420; $6 \times 72 = 432$
6. 270; $3 \times 86 = 258$
7. 140; $2 \times 67 = 134$
8. 480; $8 \times 59 = 472$
9. 150; $45 \times 3 = 135$
10. 240; $8 \times 27 = 216$
11. 80; $19 \times 4 = 76$
12. 350; $7 \times 53 = 371$
13. 180; $85 \times 2 = 170$
14. 240; $8 \times 32 = 256$
15. 72 checkers
16. 4 and 22
17. 84 students
18. 3 and 12
19. no; *Sample answer:* An *estimate* is $90 \times 5 = 450$.
20. 23; *Sample answer:* $9 \times 23 = 8 \times 23 + 1 \times 23$
21. the principal
22. 232 miles

3.7 Reteach
1. 100; $5 \times 23 = 115$

3.7 Enrichment and Extension
1. 3,024 apples
2. 2,368 miles
3. 3,375 feet
4. 7,350 beads
5. 8,544 ounces

3.8 Daily Skills Practice
1. 22,237

3.8 Vocabulary Practice
1. *Sample answer:* the answer to a multiplication problem; the product of 4×6 is 24.

3.8 Prerequisite Skills Practice
1. 180; $58 \times 3 = 174$
2. 420; $6 \times 74 = 444$

3.8 Extra Practice
1. 1,800; $6 \times 295 = 1,770$
2. 4,000; $4 \times 953 = 3,812$
3. 1,200; $2 \times 578 = 1,156$
4. 36,000; $9 \times 4,276 = 38,484$
5. 6,000; $3 \times 2,485 = 7,455$
6. 56,000; $8 \times 7,049 = 56,392$
7. 1,500; $5 \times 317 = 1,585$
8. 63,000; $7 \times 9,264 = 64,848$
9. 10,000; $2 \times 4,791 = 9,582$
10. 12,000; $6 \times 1,532 = 9,192$
11. 7,200; $8 \times 913 = 7,304$
12. 1,400; $7 \times 237 = 1,659$
13. 18,000; $3 \times 6,403 = 19,209$
14. 900; $9 \times 147 = 1,323$
15. 12,000; $4 \times 2,790 = 11,160$
16. 2,400; $427 \times 6 = 2,562$
17. 30,000; $5 \times 6,215 = 31,075$
18. 800; $439 \times 2 = 878$
19. 3,000; $1,442 \times 3 = 4,326$
20. 21,000; $2,760 \times 7 = 19,320$

Answers

21. 800; 4 × 168 = 672   **22.** <

23. <   **24.** 8,580 tickets   **25.** 54,427

26. no; *Sample answer:* If the product of the thousands digit and the one-digit number is greater than 9, the product will have 5 digits.

27. Newton

3.8 Reteach
1. 3,200; 415 × 8 = 3,320   **2.** 1,500; 276 × 5 = 1,380

3. 16,000; 3,693 × 4 = 14,772

3.8 Enrichment and Extension
1. no; *Sample answer:* He will add 2 tens to the product of the tens. Then, he will have to regroup 11 tens as 1 hundred and 1 ten.

2. no; *Sample answer:* He will regroup the ones because the product of 5 and 2 is 10.

3. *Sample answer:* 3 × 132 = 396

4. *Sample answer:* 2 × 3,267 = 6,534

5. *Sample answer:* 5 × 1,173 = 5,865

3.9 Daily Skills Practice
1. 8,000

3.9 Vocabulary Practice
1. *Sample answer:* a mathematical sentence that uses an equal sign, =, to show that two expressions are equal; 3 = 5 − 2

3.9 Prerequisite Skills Practice
1. 5,600; 715 × 8 = 5,720

2. 12,000; 4 × 3,276 = 13,104

3.9 Extra Practice
1. 7 × 295 = 2,065; *Sample answer:* Distributive Property: I multiplied 7 and 300, then subtracted 7 times 5.

2. 43 × 6 = 258; *Sample answer:* Distributive Property: I multiplied 40 and 6, then added the product of 3 and 6.

3. 4 × 630 = 2,520; *Sample answer:* Distributive Property: I multiplied 4 by 600, then multiplied 4 by 30 and added the products.

4. 8 × 76 = 608; *Sample answer:* Distributive Property: I multiplied 8 and 70, then added the product of 8 and 6.

5. 6 × 450 = 2,700; *Sample answer:* Associative Property of Multiplication: I multiplied 3 × (2 × 450).

6. 9 × 507 = 4,563; *Sample answer:* Distributive Property: I multiplied 9 and 500, then added the product of 9 and 7.

7. 4 × 3 × 25 = 300; *Sample answer:* Commutative Property of Multiplication: I multiplied 4 and 25 because I know the product is 100. Then I multiplied 3 and 100.

8. 899 × 2 = 1,798; *Sample answer:* Distributive Property: I multiplied 900 and 2, then subtracted the product of 1 and 2 because 899 is 1 less than 900.

9. 6 × 392 = 2,352; *Sample answer:* Distributive Property: I multiplied 6 and 400, then subtracted the product of 6 and 8 because 392 is 8 less than 400.

10. 8 × 503 = 4,024; *Sample answer:* Distributive Property: I multiplied 8 and 500, then added the product of 8 and 3.

11. 50 × 9 × 2 = 900; *Sample answer:* Commutative Property of Multiplication: I multiplied 2 and 50 because I know the product is 100, then multiplied 100 and 9.

12. 5 × 197 = 985; *Sample answer:* Distributive Property: I multiplied 5 and 200, then subtracted the product of 5 and 3 because 197 is 3 less than 200.

13. 7 × 604 = 4,228; *Sample answer:* Distributive Property: I multiplied 7 and 600, then added the product of 7 and 4.

14. 15 × 6 × 2 = 180; *Sample answer:* Commutative Property of Multiplication: I multiplied 15 and 2 because I know the product is 30, then multiplied 30 and 6.

15. 3 × 2,995 = 8,985; *Sample answer:* Distributive Property: I multiplied 3 and 3,000, then subtracted the product of 3 and 5 because 2,995 is 5 less than 3,000.

16. 2 × 83 × 5 = 830; *Sample answer:* Commutative Property of Multiplication: I multiplied 2 and 5 because I know the product is 10, then multiplied 10 and 83.

Answers

17. $6,005 \times 9 = 54,045$; *Sample answer:* Distributive Property: I multiplied 9 and 6,000, then added the product of 9 and 5.

18. $4 \times 396 = 1,584$; *Sample answer:* Distributive Property: I multiplied 4 and 400, then subtracted the product of 4 and 4 because 396 is 4 less than 400.

19. yes; *Sample answer:* He multiplied 6 by 400 and 6 by 3, then added; This is the same as multiplying 6 by 403.

20.

3	200	3
300	3	2
2	3	300

21. 1,454 feet

22. 240 feet

23. 61 mph

24. 576 cans

3.9 Reteach

1. $6 \times 250 = 1,500$; *Sample answer:* Associative Property of Multiplication: I multiplied $3 \times (2 \times 250)$.

2. $8 \times 296 = 2,368$; *Sample answer:* Distributive Property: I multiplied 8 and 300, then subtracted the product of 8 and 4 because 296 is 4 less than 300.

3. $25 \times 3 \times 4 = 300$; *Sample answer:* Commutative Property of Multiplication: I multiplied 4 and 25 because the product is 100, then I multiplied by 3.

3.9 Enrichment and Extension

1. $8 \times 450 = 3,600$; *Sample answer:* There are 450 sheets of paper in a package. How many sheets are in 8 packages?

2. $9 \times 692 = 6,228$; *Sample answer:* There are 692 seats in a theater. The theater is filled for 9 shows. How many people attend the shows in all?

3. $2 \times 84 \times 50 = 8,400$; *Sample answer:* A store sells packages of 50 plastic cups. They receive a shipment of 84 packages twice each week. How many cups does the store receive each week?

4. $16 \times 25 = 400$; *Sample answer:* 16 people donate $25 each to charity. How much do they donate in all?

3.10 Daily Skills Practice

1. 132,704

3.10 Vocabulary Practice

1. *Sample answer:* an operation that gives the total number of objects when you combine equal groups; $4 \times 3 = 12$

3.10 Prerequisite Skills Practice

1. $36 = 4 \times 9$

2. $56 = 7 \times 8$

3.10 Extra Practice

1. *Sample answer:* Multiply the number of tickets sold on Thursday by 4, then subtract 362 from the product.

2. *Sample answer:* Multiply 45 minutes each day by 7 days. Then add 185 to the product.

3. *Sample answer:* Multiply the number of adult tickets by 9, and multiply the number of children's tickets by 6. Then add to find the sum of the products.

4. *Sample answer:* Multiply the number of pages by the number of photos that fit on each page. Then, subtract 135.

5. *Sample answer:* Multiply 9 and 24, then subtract the product from 275.

6. *Sample answer:* Add 65 and 82 to find the total number of candles she made, then subtract the number that did not sell. Multiply the difference by 8.

7. 23 cards

8. no; There are 450 straws. This is less than 460.

9. 252 paint brushes

10. yes; He has practiced for 225 minutes.

11. *Sample answer:* There are 8 baskets of green apples with 20 apples in each basket. There are also 50 red apples. How many apples are there in all? 210 apples

12. $623

13. 268 miles

14. $160

3.10 Reteach

1. 81 glitter pens

3.10 Enrichment and Extension

1. 444 students

2. $6,168

3. 440 miles

4. 2,320 minutes

5. 8,680 miles

Answers

Chapter 4

4.1 Daily Skills Practice
1. A. and B.

4.1 Vocabulary Practice
1. *Sample answer:* the first period in a number. In 123,456, 456 is in the ones period.

4.1 Prerequisite Skills Practice
1. 90   2. 200

4.1 Extra Practice
1. 700   2. 2,400   3. 2,400   4. 1,100

5. 760   6. 4,340   7. 1,350   8. 1,520

9. 2,250   10. 4,860   11. 370   12. 1,530

13. 40   14. 20   15. 60   16. 80

17. 30   18. 80   19. >   20. <

21. =   22. <   23. =   24. <

25. 880 miles   26. 1,050 students

27. $60 \times 12 = 720$ 28. $80 \times 11 = 880$

29. *Sample answer:* Add on 2 more 30s to 600 to find $30 \times 22 = 660$.

30. 30 and 90   31. 88 guests   32. 470 wrestlers

4.1 Reteach
1. 2,700   2. 3,500   3. 1,380   4. 2,340

4.1 Enrichment and Extension
1. $30 \times 12 = 360$ muffins   2. $24 \times 20 = 480$ scones

3. $12 \times 30 = 360$ bagels   4. $30 \times 18 = 540$ muffins

5. $24 \times 40 = 960$ scones   6. $12 \times 20 = 240$ bagels

7. $30 \times 11 = 330$ muffins   8. $24 \times 10 = 240$ scones

9. $12 \times 10 = 120$ bagels

4.2 Daily Skills Practice
1. 6   2. 3

4.2 Vocabulary Practice
1. *Sample answer:* to replace a number with the nearest multiple of ten or hundred. 37 rounded to the nearest ten is 40.

4.2 Prerequisite Skills Practice
1. 2,400   2. 2,220

4.2 Extra Practice
1–19. Sample answers are given.

1. 500   2. 2,400   3. 2,000   4. 4,800

5. 1,600   6. 2,100   7. 1,750   8. 4,000

9. 3,000   10. 2,000   11. 2,000   12. 2,500

13. 5,600   14. 6,300   15. 5,600

16. 81×61; $80 \times 60 = 4,800$

17. 22×71; $20 \times 70 = 1,400$

18. 41×52; $40 \times 50 = 2,000$

19. 51×92; $50 \times 90 = 4,500$

20. greater than; *Sample answer:* 70 is greater than 67 and 80 is greater than 79.

21. greater than; *Sample answer:* 80 is greater than 78 and 90 is greater than 88.

22. *Sample answer:* about 500 candles

4.2 Reteach
1–6. Sample answers are given.

1. 600   2. 1,200   3. 5,600   4. 1,500

5. 2,500   6. 2,000

4.2 Enrichment and Extension
1–9. Sample answers are given.

1. $20 \times 30 = 600$ volunteers

2. $25 \times 30 = 750$ volunteers

3. $20 \times 30 = 600$ volunteers

4. $20 \times 25 = 500$ volunteers

5. $30 \times 30 = 900$ volunteers

6. $25 \times 30 = 750$ volunteers

7. $40 \times 30 = 1,200$ volunteers

8. $50 \times 30 = 1,500$ volunteers

9. Check students' work.

4.3 Daily Skills Practice
1. 28

Answers

4.3 Vocabulary Practice

1. *Sample answer:* the amount of surface a shape covers;

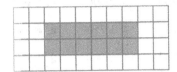

   Area: 12 square units

4.3 Prerequisite Skills Practice

1. *Sample answer:* 3,500   2. *Sample answer:* 5,400

4.3 Extra Practice

1. 770;

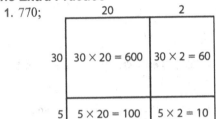

   $600 + 60 + 100 + 10 = 770$

2. 288;

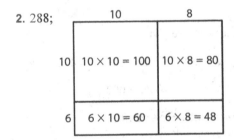

   $100 + 80 + 60 + 48 = 288$

3. 627;

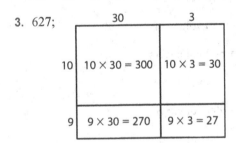

   $300 + 30 + 270 + 27 = 627$

4. 984;

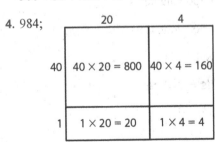

   $800 + 160 + 20 + 4 = 984$

5. 459;

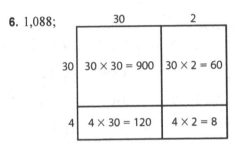

   $200 + 140 + 70 + 49 = 459$

6. 1,088;

   $900 + 60 + 120 + 8 = 1,088$

7. Check students' work; 198

8. Check students' work; 320

9. Check students' work; 325

10. Check students' work; 1,312

11. no; *Sample answer:* Your friend added 10 to 2 and 3 to 2 instead of multiplying. $13 \times 32 = 300 + 20 + 90 + 6 = 416$.

12. *Sample answer:* Break apart 14 into 10 and 4. Write 10 and 4 on the left side of the area model. Break apart 23 into 20 and 3. Write 20 and 3 above the area model. Find the area of each rectangle (the partial products). Add the partial products.

13. 156 tomato plants

14. Check students' work; 378 bagged snacks

4.3 Reteach

1. $31 \times 25 = 775$

   $30 \times 20 = 600$; $30 \times 5 = 150$; $1 \times 20 = 20$; $1 \times 5 = 5$;

   $600 + 150 + 20 + 5 = 775$

2. $53 \times 42 = 2,226$

   $50 \times 40 = 2,000$; $50 \times 2 = 100$; $3 \times 40 = 120$; $3 \times 2 = 6$; $2,000 + 100 + 120 + 6 = 2,226$

4.3 Enrichment and Extension

1. $28 \times 42 = 1,176$ 2. $29 \times 33 = 957$

3. $56 \times 62 = 3,472$ 4. $44 \times 44 = 1,936$

Answers

5. $31 \times 51 = 1{,}581$ **6.** $71 \times 65 = 4{,}615$

4.4 Daily Skills Practice
1. 6

4.4 Vocabulary Practice
1. *Sample answer:*

$3 \times (10 + 2) = (3 \times 10) + (3 \times 2)$

4.4 Prerequisite Skills Practice
1. 1,292; *Sample answer:*

	30	4
30	30×30	30×4
8	8×30	8×4

2. 3,172; *Sample answer:*

	50	2
60	60×50	60×2
1	1×50	1×2

4.4 Extra Practice
1. $32 \times 47 = 1{,}504$;
Line 3: 40; 7   Line 4: 40; 40; 7; 7
Line 5: 1,200; 80; 210; 14   Line 6: 1,504

2. $53 \times 38 = 2{,}014$;
Line 3: 30; 8   Line 4: 30; 30; 8; 8
Line 5: 1,500; 90; 400; 24   Line 6: 2,014

3. $64 \times 55 = 3{,}520$;
Line 3: 50; 5   Line 4: 50; 50; 5; 5
Line 5: 3,000; 200; 300; 20   Line 6: 3,520

4. 2,279   **5.** 1,407   **6.** 1,003   **7.** 1,862

8. 4,686   **9.** 2,185   **10.** 3,596   **11.** 5,632

12. 6,225   **13.** 6,808   **14.** 7,644   **15.** 6,650

16. $67 \times (30 + 4)$
$(67 \times 30) + (67 \times 4) = 2{,}010 + 268 = 2{,}278$

17. no; *Sample answer:* Three dogs need 6,600 square feet, and the area of the lot is only 6,450 square feet.

18. yes; *Sample answer:* There are 5,780 towels available and only 5,678 fans are attending.

19. yes; *Sample answer:* The first hour had ticket sales of $2,116.

4.4 Reteach
1. $34 \times 46 = 1{,}564$;
Line 3: 40; 6   Line 4: 40; 40; 6; 6
Line 5: 1,200; 160; 180; 24   Line 6: 1,564

4.4 Enrichment and Extension
1. $26 \times 36 = 936$;
Line 1: 26; 26   Line 2: 26; 26
Line 3: 6; 6

2. $81 \times 71 = 5{,}751$;   Line 1: 71; 81; 70
Line 2: 70; 1   Line 3: 80; 80
Line 4: 80; 80   Line 5: 5,600

3. $75 \times 92 = 6{,}900$;
Line 1: 75; 92; 75; 2   Line 2: 75; 75
Line 3: 5; 5   Line 4: 90; 90; 2; 2
Line 5: 6,300; 450; 140; 10   Line 6: 6,900

4.5 Daily Skills Practice
1. A.

4.5 Vocabulary Practice
1. *Sample answer:* The digits of a whole number from right to left have the place values 1, 10, 100, and so on; In the number 325, the 2 is in the tens place, and the value is 2 times 10, or 20.

4.5 Prerequisite Skills Practice
1. 888   **2.** 2,242

4.5 Extra Practice
1. *Sample answer:* Estimate: $25 \times 20 = 500$; 24, 160, 30, 200; 414

2. *Sample answer:* Estimate: $30 \times 25 = 750$; 14, 210, 40, 600; 864

3. *Sample answer:* Estimate: $45 \times 45 = 2{,}025$; 21, 280, 120, 1,600; 2,021

4. *Sample answer:* Estimate: $30 \times 60 = 1{,}800$; 18, 40, 540, 1,200; 1,798

Answers

5. *Sample answer:* Estimate: $55 \times 70 = 3,850$; 3, 50, 210, 3,500; 3,763

6. *Sample answer:* Estimate: $40 \times 95 = 3,800$; 24, 90, 720, 2,700; 3,534

7. *Sample answer:* Estimate: $30 \times 40 = 1,200$; 1,353

8. *Sample answer:* Estimate: $30 \times 40 = 1,200$; 1,232

9. *Sample answer:* Estimate: $50 \times 60 = 3,000$; 3,016

10. *Sample answer:* Estimate: $90 \times 25 = 2,250$; 2,116

11. *Sample answer:* Estimate: $60 \times 30 = 1,800$; 2,048

12. *Sample answer:* Estimate: $60 \times 50 = 3,000$; 2,610

13. *Sample answer:* Estimate: $50 \times 75 = 3,750$; 3,577

14. *Sample answer:* Estimate: $40 \times 90 = 3,600$; 3,458

15. *Sample answer:* Estimate: $50 \times 50 = 2,500$; 2,756

16. 18×14; 252

17. 192 miles

18. 24 miles

4.5 Reteach

1. *Sample answer:* Estimate: $40 \times 20 = 800$; 16, 320, 20, 400; 756

2. *Sample answer:* Estimate: $30 \times 50 = 1,500$; 6, 60, 150, 1,500; 1,716

3. *Sample answer:* Estimate: $75 \times 50 = 3,750$; 54, 630, 240, 2,800; 3,724

4.5 Enrichment and Extension

1. 3,008 seats

2. 2,322 seats

3. 1,968 seats

4. 1,425 seats

5. 1,156 seats

6. 648 seats

7. 10,527 seats

8. $47 \times 83 = 3,901$

9. $61 \times 59 = 3,599$

10. $87 \times 72 = 6,264$

11. $94 \times 58 = 5,452$

12. $63 \times 97 = 6,111$

13. $88 \times 77 = 6,776$

4.6 Daily Skills Practice

1. 600; 100; 500

4.6 Vocabulary Practice

1. *Sample answer:* the distance around a figure; The perimeter of a square with a side length of 4 units is 16 units.

4.6 Prerequisite Skills Practice

1. 1,960

2. 4,368

4.6 Extra Practice

1. *Sample answer:* Estimate: $40 \times 30 = 1,200$; 1,302

2. *Sample answer:* Estimate: $70 \times 80 = 5,600$; 5,751

3. *Sample answer:* Estimate: $50 \times 40 = 2,000$; 1,961

4. *Sample answer:* Estimate: $80 \times 30 = 2,400$; 2,352

5. *Sample answer:* Estimate: $50 \times 50 = 2,500$; 2,538

6. *Sample answer:* Estimate: $90 \times 40 = 3,600$; 3,354

7. *Sample answer:* Estimate: $70 \times 40 = 2,800$; 2,736

8. *Sample answer:* Estimate: $40 \times 60 = 2,400$; 2,240

9. *Sample answer:* Estimate: $60 \times 60 = 3,600$; 3,477

10. *Sample answer:* Estimate: $20 \times 80 = 1,600$; 1,558

11. *Sample answer:* Estimate: $30 \times 70 = 2,100$; 2,376

12. *Sample answer:* Estimate: $80 \times 50 = 4,000$; 4,056

13. *Sample answer:* Estimate: $20 \times 20 = 400$; 399

14. *Sample answer:* Estimate: $30 \times 40 = 1,200$; 1,428

15. *Sample answer:* Estimate: $50 \times 25 = 1,250$; 1,260

16. *Sample answer:* Estimate: $50 \times 25 = 1,250$; 1,377

17. *Sample answer:* Estimate: $60 \times 40 = 2,400$; 2,294

18. *Sample answer:* Estimate: $40 \times 30 = 1,200$; 1,248

19. $336

20. no; *Sample answer:* When the digits are 3 or less, the most the product of any two digits can be is 9.

21. Line 1: 3; Line 3: 2; Line 4: 5, 0; Line 5: 2

22. the office building

4.6 Reteach

1. *Sample answer:* Estimate: $20 \times 40 = 800$; 946

2. *Sample answer:* Estimate: $50 \times 10 = 500$; 598

3. *Sample answer:* Estimate: $80 \times 60 = 4,800$; 4,731

Answers

4.6 Enrichment and Extension

1. *Sample answer:* $78 \times 64 = 4,992$

2. *Sample answer:* $89 \times 67 = 5,963$

3. *Sample answer:* $89 \times 76 = 6,764$

4. *Sample answer:* $94 \times 85 = 7,990$

5. *Sample answer:* $96 \times 87 = 8,352$

4.7 Daily Skills Practice
1. A.

4.7 Vocabulary Practice
1. *Sample answer:* a parallelogram with four equal sides; A square is a rhombus.

4.7 Prerequisite Skills Practice

1. *Sample answer:* Estimate: $80 \times 75 = 6,000$; 5,986

2. *Sample answer:* Estimate: $60 \times 70 = 4,200$; 4,544

4.7 Extra Practice
1. 1,148	2. 1,674	3. 5,248	4. 3,380
5. 1,144	6. 648	7. 448	8. 779
9. 5,472	10. 3,072	11. 2,135	12. 3,450
13. 3,066	14. 4,872	15. 7,056	16. 9,025

17. Multiply by 10 pounds; 240; 300

18. 576 golf balls

4.7 Reteach
1. 264	2. 2,320	3. 858	4. 1,245
5. 2,624		6. 2,079	

4.7 Enrichment and Extension
1. 36	2. 54	3. 61	4. 83
5. 52	6. 44	7. 1	8. 4
9. 5	10. 9	11. 4	12. 3

4.8 Daily Skills Practice
1. $9

4.8 Vocabulary Practice
1. *Sample answer:* a unit of mass equal to 1,000 grams; 3 kilograms are equal to 3,000 grams.

4.8 Prerequisite Skills Practice
1. 3,154   2. 2,813

4.8 Extra Practice

1. *Sample answer:* Multiply the number of drivers by the number of tires and subtract the number of drivers; 396 tires

2. *Sample answer:* Multiply the number of two-packs of fig bars in one box by 2, and multiply by 15 boxes; 480 fig bars

3. *Sample answer:* Subtract the number of graded tests, then multiply the difference by 27; 567 questions

4. *Sample answer:* Multiply the number of bottles in each package by 3, then multiply by the number of fluid ounces in each bottle; 1,536 fluid ounces

5. *Sample answer:* Multiply the number of buses by the rows in each, then multiply the product by 2; 2,208 passengers

6. *Sample answer:* Multiply 28 and 44, then multiply 32 and 27. Add the products; 2,096 cars

7. 2,808 passengers

8. 1,332 miles

9. $2,097

10. 297 blocks

11. 1,952 seats

12. 175 inches

4.8 Reteach
1. 1,512 ounces

4.8 Enrichment and Extension

1. *Sample answer:* $275 - (10 \times 15)$; $275 - (15 \times 10)$

2. *Sample answer:* $21 \times (12 + 33)$; $21 \times (33 + 12)$

3. *Sample answer:* $12 \times (34 + 22)$; $12 \times (22 + 34)$

4. *Sample answer:* $(56 \times 25) + (84 \times 18)$; $(84 \times 18) + (56 \times 25)$

5. *Sample answer:* $50 \times (2 \times 8 + 2 \times 11)$; $50 \times (16 + 22)$

6. *Sample answer:* $14 \times (8 \times 8)$; $(8 \times 8) \times 14$

7. *Sample answer:* $1,423 - (46 \times 22)$; $1,423 - (22 \times 46)$

8. *Sample answer:* $18 \times (24 \times 3)$; $(24 \times 3) \times 18$

Answers

Chapter 5

5.1 Daily Skills Practice
1. 69,488 **2.** 63,192

5.1 Vocabulary Practice
1. *Sample answer:* the part of a fraction that represents how many equal parts are being counted; In $\frac{2}{3}$, 2 is in the numerator.

5.1 Prerequisite Skills Practice
1. 1,400 **2.** 600

5.1 Extra Practice
1. Think: $\underline{60} \div \underline{4} = \underline{15}$

$$\underline{600} \div \underline{4} = \underline{60} \text{ tens} \div 4$$

$$= \underline{15} \text{ tens}$$

$$= \underline{150}$$

So, $600 \div 4 = \underline{150}$.

2. Think: $\underline{72} \div \underline{9} = \underline{8}$

$$\underline{7,200} \div \underline{9} = \underline{72} \text{ hundreds} \div 9$$

$$= \underline{8} \text{ hundreds}$$

$$= \underline{800}$$

So, $7,200 \div 9 = \underline{800}$.

3. 4; 40; 400 **4.** 3; 30; 300

5. 8; 80; 800 **6.** 7; 70; 700

7. 40 **8.** 20 **9.** 1,000 **10.** 90

11. 200 **12.** 300 **13.** 200 **14.** 200

15. 100 **16.** 800 **17.** 100 **18.** 90

19. 10 **20.** 8,000 **21.** 5 **22.** 270

23. 7 **24.** 2,500 **25.** 10 **26.** 8,000

27. 4 **28.** < **29.** = **30.** <

31. < **32.** < **33.** >

34. 30 students

35. 2,000

36. 700 steps

5.1 Reteach
1. Think: $\underline{72} \div \underline{6} = \underline{12}$

$$720 \div 6 = \underline{72} \text{ tens} \div 6$$

$$= \underline{12} \text{ tens}$$

$$= \underline{120}$$

So, $720 \div 6 = \underline{120}$.

2. 8; 80; 800

5.1 Enrichment and Extension
1. 210 seats **2.** 400 seats

3. 136 rows

4. west stands; *Sample answer:* The west stands have the greatest number of seats, so when divided by 25, it will give the greatest quotient.

5.2 Daily Skills Practice
1. 4,680 **2.** 3,480

5.2 Vocabulary Practice
1. *Sample answer:* a number that is close to an exact number; 16,000 is an estimate for $5,946 + 9,724$.

5.2 Prerequisite Skills Practice
1. 500 **2.** 2,000

5.2 Extra Practice
1. *Sample answer:* 7 **2.** *Sample answer:* 9

3. *Sample answer:* 40 **4.** *Sample answer:* 50

5. *Sample answer:* 30 **6.** *Sample answer:* 90

7. 60 and 70 **8.** 70 and 80

9. 600 and 700 **10.** 700 and 800

11. < **12.** <

13. > **14.** <

15. > **16.** >

17. > **18.** <

19. *Sample answer:* exact answer; Each friend wants to share the 272 tokens equally.

20. *Sample answer:* 630 is a closer estimate for 658, than 700. $630 \div 7 = 90$, so $658 \div 7$ is about 90.

21. about 1,200 boxes

22. about 1,300 fans **23.** about 1,400 light bulbs

Answers

5.2 Reteach
1. *Sample answer:* 20   2. *Sample answer:* 6

3. *Sample answer:* 70   4. *Sample answer:* 80

5. 60 and 70   6. 10 and 20

7. 800 and 900   8. 400 and 500

5.2 Enrichment and Extension
1. 50 and 60   2. 50 miles

3. 60 and 70   4. 70 miles

5.3 Daily Skills Practice
1. 3; 4

5.3 Vocabulary Practice
1. *Sample answer:*

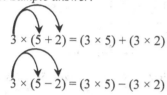

$3 \times (5 + 2) = (3 \times 5) + (3 \times 2)$

$3 \times (5 - 2) = (3 \times 5) - (3 \times 2)$

5.3 Prerequisite Skills Practice
1. *Sample answer:* 20   2. *Sample answer:* 40

5.3 Extra Practice
1. 4 R 1   2. 2 R 3   3. 2 R 4   4. 8 R 1

5. 5 R 3   6. 3 R 2   7. 4 R 2   8. 4 R 5

9. 6 R 5   10. 9 R 5   11. 9 R 2   12. 8 R 1

13. 1 or 2; *Sample answer:* The remainder is always less than the divisor.

14. 1, 2, 3, or 4; *Sample answer:* The remainder is always less than the divisor.

15. 9 cars; 10 cars; 6 riders

16. 8 shelves

17. 9 days   18. 4 students

5.3 Reteach
1. 3 R 1   2. 6 R 2   3. 6 R 3   4. 5 R 1

5.3 Enrichment and Extension
1. 3 boxes; 1 red marble   2. 4 boxes; 2 blue marbles

3. yes; *Sample answer:* $28 + 14 = 42$ and $42 \div 7 = 6$.

4. no; *Sample answer:* $28 + 14 = 42$ and $42 \div 8 = 5$ R 2.

5.4 Daily Skills Practice
1. 12; 120; 1,200; 12,000

5.4 Vocabulary Practice
1. *Sample answer:* the products found by breaking apart a factor into ones, tens, hundreds, and so on, and multiplying each of these by the other factor; For 39×7, 63 and 210 are partial products.

5.4 Prerequisite Skills Practice
1. 5 R 2   2. 2 R 3

5.4 Extra Practice
1. *Sample answers:*

$$
\begin{array}{r}
4\overline{)228} \\
-200 \\
\hline
28
\end{array}
\quad = 4 \times \underline{50} \;\boxed{50}
$$

$$
\begin{array}{r}
-\boxed{28} \\
\hline
\boxed{0}
\end{array}
\quad = 4 \times \underline{7} \;+\; \boxed{7} \quad \boxed{57}
$$

$$\underline{50}\;\underline{7}$$
$$4\;\boxed{200}\;\boxed{28}$$

2. *Sample answers:*

$$
\begin{array}{r}
3\overline{)141} \\
-\boxed{120} \\
\hline
\boxed{21}
\end{array}
\quad = 3 \times \underline{40}\;\boxed{40}
$$

$$
\begin{array}{r}
-\boxed{21} \\
\hline
\boxed{0}
\end{array}
\quad = 3 \times \underline{7}\;+\;\boxed{7}\quad\boxed{47}
$$

$$\underline{40}\;\underline{7}$$
$$3\;\boxed{120}\;\boxed{21}$$

3. 17   4. 14   5. 21   6. 17

7. 28   8. 36   9. 54   10. 62

11. 37   12. 41   13. 53   14. 71

15. 48   16. 55   17. 73

18. yes; *Sample answer:* Newton correctly used partial quotients.

19. *Sample answer:* Subtract to separate the dividend into smaller numbers that are easier to divide by the divisor. Use the related products to find the partial quotients. Add the partial quotients to find the original quotient. Use an area model to represent the new dividends and partial quotients.

20. 40 gift bags

Answers

5.4 Reteach

1. $84 \div 3 = \underline{28}$

$$3\overline{)84}$$
$\underline{-\ 60} = 3 \times \underline{20}$ $\boxed{20}$
$\boxed{24}$

$\underline{-\ 24} = 3 \times 8$ $\underline{+\ 8}$
$\boxed{0}$ $\boxed{28}$

    $\underline{20}$ $\underline{8}$
$3\ \boxed{60}\ \boxed{24}$

2. $144 \div 8 = \underline{18}$

$$8\overline{)144}$$
$\underline{-\ 80} = 8 \times \underline{10}$ $\boxed{10}$
$\boxed{64}$

$\underline{-\ 64} = 8 \times 8$ $\underline{+\ 8}$
$\boxed{0}$ $\boxed{18}$

    $\underline{10}$ $\underline{8}$
$8\ \boxed{80}\ \boxed{64}$

5.4 Enrichment and Extension

1. $55 \div 5 = 11$

2. $336 \div 6 = 56$

3.

	100	7
7	700	49

$749 \div 7 = 107$

5.5 Daily Skills Practice

1. 8, 2; 2, 8

5.5 Vocabulary Practice

1. *Sample answer:* a group of related facts that uses the same numbers; $3 \times 2 = 6$, $2 \times 3 = 6$, $6 \div 3 = 2$, $6 \div 2 = 3$

5.5 Prerequisite Skills Practice

1. 58   **2.** 79

5.5 Extra Practice

1. 31 R 1   **2.** 30 R 1   **3.** 17 R 2   **4.** 13 R 3

5. 53 R 1   **6.** 92 R 1   **7.** 52 R 7   **8.** 123 R 1

9. 74 R 5   **10.** 182 R 1   **11.** 139 R 1   **12.** 89 R 3

13. 399 R 1   **14.** 545 R 1   **15.** 112 R 5   **16.** 1,063 R 1

17. 403 R 1   **18.** 1,386 R 1

19. $6\overline{)4{,}136}$

$\underline{-3{,}600} = 6 \times 600$ 600
    536

$\underline{-480} = 6 \times 80$ 80
    56

$\underline{-54} = 6 \times 9$ $\underline{+9}$
   2   689 R 2

20. $8\overline{)5{,}287}$

$\underline{-4{,}800} = 8 \times 600$ 600
    487

$\underline{-480} = 8 \times 60$ +   60
    7

        $\boxed{660 \text{ R } 7}$

21. 43 groups   **22.** 221 cups

23. your friend; $8\overline{)230}$ is 28 R 6, or 29 pages. $5\overline{)278}$ is 55 R 3, or 56 pages.

5.5 Reteach

1. $98 \div 5 = 19 \text{ R } 3$

$$5\overline{)98}$$
$\underline{-\ 50} = 5 \times \underline{10}$ $\boxed{10}$
$\boxed{48}$

$\underline{-\ 45} = 5 \times 9$ $\underline{+\ 9}$
$\boxed{3}$ $\boxed{19}$ R $\boxed{3}$

2. $673 \div 7 = 96 \text{ R } 1$

$$7\overline{)673}$$
$\underline{-\ 630} = 7 \times \underline{90}$ $\boxed{90}$
$\boxed{43}$

$\underline{-\ 42} = 7 \times 6$ $\underline{+\ 6}$
$\boxed{1}$ $\boxed{96}$ R $\boxed{1}$

3. 59 R 5   **4.** 259 R 2   **5.** 399 R 2

5.5 Enrichment and Extension

1. *Sample answer:* $59 \div 5 = 11 \text{ R } 4$

2. *Sample answer:* $677 \div 6 = 112 \text{ R } 5$

3. *Sample answer:* $9{,}890 \div 7 = 1{,}412 \text{ R } 6$

4. 1, 2, 3, 4, 5, and 6; *Sample answer:* The remainder is always less than the divisor.

Answers

5.6 Daily Skills Practice
1. 100

5.6 Vocabulary Practice
1. *Sample answer:* a unit used to measure area; square centimeter

5.6 Prerequisite Skills Practice
1. 75 R 1   **2.** 408 R 3

5.6 Extra Practice

1. 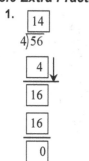   **2.**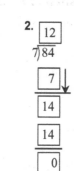

3. 14   **4.** 12   **5.** 16   **6.** 15 R 3

7. 7 R 2   **8.** 14 R 3   **9.** 9 R 2   **10.** 18

11. 7 R 4   **12.** 4 R 4   **13.** 10 R 3   **14.** 13

15. 35 R 1   **16.** 8   **17.** 9   **18.** 15

19. 4)‾36   **20.** 21 trading cards

21. $19

22. about 9 pages; *Sample answer:* The remainder of 1 means that you will need to read 10 pages one hour.

5.6 Reteach
1.
```
  19
4)76
  4
  36
  36
   0
```
2. 13

3. 13 R 5

5.6 Enrichment and Extension
1.
```
  32
3)96
```

2.
```
  11
5)55
```

3. *Sample answer:*
```
  21
4)84
```

4.
```
  21
3)63
```

5. *Sample answer:*
```
  16
6)96
```

6.
```
  13
5)65
```

7. *Sample answer:*
```
  14
6)84
```

8.
```
  16
3)48
```

5.7 Daily Skills Practice
1. 471,902; 400,000 + 70,000 + 1,000 + 900 + 2

5.7 Vocabulary Practice
1. *Sample answer:* operations that "undo" each other, such as addition and subtraction or multiplication and division

5.7 Prerequisite Skills Practice
1. 28   **2.** 15 R 2

5.7 Extra Practice
1. 79   **2.** 76 R 6   **3.** 952   **4.** 841

5. 1,027 R 3   **6.** 2,087 R 1   **7.** 98 R 2   **8.** 197

9. 47 R 1   **10.** 121   **11.** 140 R 1   **12.** 93 R 3

13. 134   **14.** 262   **15.** 27 R 2   **16.** 198 R 3

17. 663   **18.** 1,938 R 3

19. 511 R 3   **20.** 746 R 3

21. 767 R 2   **22.** 341 fans

23. 491 ÷ 5; *Sample answer:* 5 will not divide into 4.

24. 192 seats

5.7 Reteach
1. 168 R 2   **2.** 1,043 R 3

Answers

3. 1,913

5.7 Enrichment and Extension

1.
```
      13 3
   5 ) 66 5
    − 5 ↓
      16
    − 15 ↓
      15
    − 15
       0
```

2.
```
      2 02
   4 ) 80 8
   − 8 ↓
     00
   − 0 ↓
     08
   −  8
      0
```

3. 1,179 boxes will be filled; There will be 3 candles left over; 9,435 ÷ 8 = 1179 R 3.

4. *Sample answer:* Multiples of 5 have a 0 or 5 in the ones place. 4,603 does not have a 0 or 5 in the ones place, so 4,603 ÷ 5 will have a remainder.

5.8 Daily Skills Practice

1. 7,232

5.8 Vocabulary Practice

1. *Sample answer:* to replace a number with the nearest multiple of ten or hundred; 18 rounded to the nearest ten is 20.

5.8 Prerequisite Skills Practice

1. 127 R 4   2. 1,009 R 7

5.8 Extra Practice

1. 58 R 4   2. 48   3. 112 R 1   4. 53

5. 67   6. 85 R 2   7. 40 R 2   8. 138 R 3

9. 211 R 1   10. 51   11. 196   12. 100 R 6

13. 578   14. 1,501   15. 2,966   16. 3,202 R 1

17. 2,301   18. 1,384 R 3

19. 1080 R 1   20. 423 R 6

21. 593 R 4   22. 81 bags

23. *Sample answer:* Change the dividend to 273; 273 is a multiple of 3.

24. 20 groups; 1 group

5.8 Reteach

1. 108   2. 208

3. 1,093 R 4

5.8 Enrichment and Extension

1. *Sample answer:*
```
     203
  5 )1,015
```
2.
```
    1,019
  2 )2,038
```

3. *Sample answer:*
```
     253
  7 )1,771
```
4. *Sample answer:*
```
   1,011 R 1
  4 )4,045
```

5. *Sample answer:*
```
   305 R 1
  6 )1,831
```

5.9 Daily Skills Practice

1. 520   2. 96

5.9 Vocabulary Practice

1. *Sample answer:* fraction that represents 1 equal part of a whole; $\frac{1}{6}$

5.9 Prerequisite Skills Practice

1. 360 R 2   2. 1,033

5.9 Extra Practice

1. *Sample answer:* Subtract to find the number of pages left to read. Then divide the number of pages by 4.

2. *Sample answer:* Add to find how many people, and divide by 6 to find how many tours are needed.

3. 28 students   4. 10 candles   5. 18 students

6. 45 minutes   7. 3 miles   8. 7 groups

9. 24 shelves   10. 6 apples   11. 48 boxes

12. 28 bowls   13. 900 pictures

5.9 Reteach

1. *Sample answer:* You can check your answer by using inverse operations. Multiply the answer by 3, then add 120.

5.9 Enrichment and Extension

1. 553 miles   2. 53 pages   3. 360 steps

Answers

Chapter 6

6.1 Daily Skills Practice
1. 4; 6

6.1 Vocabulary Practice
1. *Sample answer:* the amount left over when a number cannot be divided evenly; 2 is the remainder in $14 \div 3$.

6.1 Prerequisite Skills Practice
1. 18 square inches   **2.** 8 square meters

6.1 Extra Practice
1. 1 and 10, 2 and 5

2. 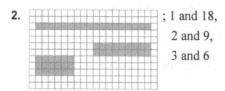 ; 1 and 18, 2 and 9, 3 and 6

3.  ; 1 and 6, 2 and 3

4.  ; 1 and 22, 2 and 11

5. 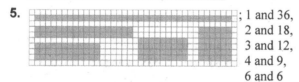 ; 1 and 36, 2 and 18, 3 and 12, 4 and 9, 6 and 6

6. 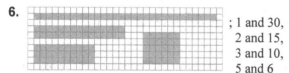 ; 1 and 30, 2 and 15, 3 and 10, 5 and 6

7. 1 and 17

8. 1 and 32, 2 and 16, 4 and 8

9. 1 and 15; 3 and 5

10. 1 and 56, 2 and 28, 4 and 14, 7 and 8

11. 1 and 48, 2 and 24, 3 and 16, 4 and 12, 6 and 8

12. 1 and 27, 3 and 9

13. Newton; The factor pairs are 1 and 12, 2 and 6, and 3 and 4.

14. 8 arrays

6.1 Reteach
1. 1 and 15, 3 and 5

2. 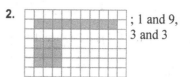 ; 1 and 9, 3 and 3

6.1 Enrichment and Extension
1. *Sample answer:* 3 and 20; 4 and 15

2. *Sample answer:* 9 ft and 8 ft, 24 ft and 3 ft

3. *Sample answer:* 40 square feet; 4 ft and 10 ft, 5 ft and 8 ft

4. *Sample answer:* 56 square inches; 4 in. and 14 in., 7 in. and 8 in.

6.2 Daily Skills Practice
1. 18; 180; 1,800; 18,000

6.2 Vocabulary Practice
1. *Sample answer:* two factors that, when multiplied, result in a given product; 2 and 4 are a factor pair for 8.

6.2 Prerequisite Skills Practice
1. 1 and 12, 2 and 6, 3 and 4

2. 1 and 60, 2 and 30, 3 and 20, 4 and 15, 5 and 12, 6 and 10

6.2 Extra Practice
1. 1 and 21, 3 and 7

2. 1 and 40, 2 and 20, 4 and 10, 5 and 8

3. 1 and 62, 2 and 31

4. 1 and 81, 3 and 27, 9 and 9

5. 1 and 16, 2 and 8, 4 and 4

6. 1 and 36, 2 and 18, 3 and 12, 4 and 9, 6 and 6

7. 1 and 57, 3 and 19

8. 1 and 95, 5 and 19

9. 1 and 20; 2 and 10; 4 and 5

10. 1 and 32, 2 and 16, 4 and 8

11. 1 and 53

12. 1 and 49, 7 and 7

13. 1 and 76, 2 and 38, 4 and 19

14. 1 and 66, 2 and 33, 3 and 22, 6 and 11

15. 1 and 17

Answers

16. 1 and 85, 5 and 17

17. 1 and 96, 2 and 48, 3 and 32, 4 and 24, 6 and 16, 8 and 12

18. 1 and 23

19. 1, 3, 9, 27

20. 1, 2, 5, 7, 10, 14, 35, 70

21. 1, 2, 3, 6, 9, 18

22. 1, 2, 4, 13, 26, 52

23. 1, 5, 13, 65

24. 1, 2, 17, 34

25. 2 is a factor of 6.

26. 0 or 5

27. 21; 1,275; 600

28. 30; 78; 500

29. no

30. 6 plants; *Sample answer:* 48 is divisible by 6 but not 9 or 10.

6.2 Reteach
1. 1 and 18, 2 and 9, 3 and 6

2. 1 and 45, 3 and 15, 5 and 9

6.2 Enrichment and Extension
1. 54

2. 80

3. 40 or 60

4. 45 or 75

5. 27; 1, 3, 9, 27

6. 72; 1, 2, 3, 4, 6, 8, 9, 12, 18, 24, 36, 72

6.3 Daily Skills Practice
1. 92

6.3 Vocabulary Practice
1. *Sample answer:* A number is divisible by another number when the quotient is a whole number and the remainder is 0; 48 is divisible by 4.

6.3 Prerequisite Skills Practice
1. 1, 2, 4, 8, 16, 32

2. 1, 2, 3, 4, 6, 8, 9, 12, 18, 24, 36, 72

6.3 Extra Practice
1. no; *Sample answer:* $18 \div 4 = 4$ R 2

2. yes; *Sample answer:* $6 \times 8 = 48$

3. yes; *Sample answer:* $5 \times 6 = 30$

4. no; *Sample answer:* $70 \div 8 = 8$ R 6

5. no; *Sample answer:* $28 \div 6 = 4$ R 4

6. yes; *Sample answer:* $81 \div 9 = 9$

7. no; *Sample answer:* $62 \div 4 = 15$ R 2

8. yes; *Sample answer:* $35 \div 7 = 5$

9. multiple

10. both

11. factor

12. multiple

13. factor

14. both

15. both

16. multiple

17. factor

18. *Sample answer:* 40 and 50; Both numbers are multiples of 10.

19. yes; *Sample answer:* 9 is a multiple of 3.

20. *Sample answer:* $40 \div 5 = 8$

21. 3 or 5 miles

22. April 24

6.3 Reteach
1. no; *Sample answer:* $26 \div 4 = 6$ R 2

2. yes; *Sample answer:* $9 \times 4 = 36$

6.3 Enrichment and Extension
1. 7 and 9 are factors of 63; 34 and 68 are multiples of 17.

2. 6 and 15 are factors of 60; 32 and 40 are multiples of 8.

3. 15 and 25 are factors of 75; 36 and 96 are multiples of 12.

4. 7, 28, and 42 are factors of 84; 18, 45, and 81 are multiples of 9.

5. 3, 26, and 39 are factors of 78; 21, 35, and 84 are multiples of 7.

6.4 Daily Skills Practice
1. 121 R 1

6.4 Vocabulary Practice
1. *Sample answer:* the product of a number and any other counting number; 18 is a multiple of 3.

6.4 Prerequisite Skills Practice
1. multiple

2. factor

Answers

6.4 Extra Practice

1. composite; 65 has more than two factors, 1, 5, 13, 65.

2. composite; 98 has more than two factors, 1, 2, 7, 14, 49, 98.

3. prime; 13 has only two factors, 1 and 13.

4. composite; 33 has more than two factors, 1, 3, 11, 33.

5. composite; 49 has more than two factors, 1, 7, 49.

6. composite; 80 has more than two factors, 1, 2, 4, 5, 8, 10, 16, 20, 40, 80.

7. prime; 73 has only two factors, 1 and 73.

8. composite; 24 has more than two factors, 1, 2, 3, 4, 6, 8, 12, 24.

9. composite; 52 has more than two factors, 1, 2, 4, 13, 26, 52.

10. composite; 84 has more than two factors, 1, 2, 3, 4, 6, 7, 12, 14, 21, 28, 42, 84.

11. prime; 59 has only two factors, 1 and 59.

12. prime; 97 has only two factors, 1 and 97.

13. composite; 51 has more than two factors, 1, 3, 17, 51.

14. composite; 36 has more than two factors, 1, 2, 3, 4, 6, 9, 12, 18, 36.

15. prime; 61 has only two factors, 1 and 61.

16. composite; 78 has more than two factors, 1, 2, 3, 6, 13, 26, 39, 78.

17. composite; 57 has more than two factors, 1, 3, 19, 57.

18. composite; 21 has more than two factors, 1, 3, 7, 21.

19. A number has either exactly 2 factors or more than 2 factors.

20. 89

21. false; *Sample answer:* 9 is a one-digit odd number but not prime. Its factors are 1, 3, 9.

22. false; *Sample answer:* 8 is a composite number.

23. true

24. yes; They can be in 3 rows of 13 students or 13 rows of 3 students.

25. no; 47 is a prime number.

26. January

6.4 Reteach

1. prime; 5 has only two factors, 1 and 5.

2. composite; 25 has more than two factors, 1, 5, 25.

3. composite; 18 has more than two factors, 1, 2, 3, 6, 9, 18.

4. composite; 64 has more than two factors, 1, 2, 4, 8, 16, 32, 64.

5. composite; 87 has more than two factors, 1, 3, 29, 87.

6. prime; 71 has only two factors, 1 and 71.

6.4 Enrichment and Extension

1. 5 and 7   2. 2 and 11

3. 4 and 6   4. 6 and 9

5. *Sample answer:* 3 and 20

6. *Sample answer:* 3 and 26

7. 1, 3, and 7   8. 10, 14, 35, and 70

6.5 Daily Skills Practice

1. 4,304

6.5 Vocabulary Practice

1. *Sample answer:* a number greater than 1 with exactly two factors, 1 and itself; 7

6.5 Prerequisite Skills Practice

1. composite; 21 has more than two factors, 1, 3, 7, 21.

2. prime; 17 has only two factors, 1 and 17.

6.5 Extra Practice

1. 15, 21, 27, 33, 39, 45; *Sample answer:* The numbers are multiples of 3.

2. 1,458, 486, 162, 54, 18, 6; *Sample answer:* The numbers are multiples of 3.

3. 80, 76, 72, 68, 64, 60; *Sample answer:* The numbers are multiples of 4.

4. 2, 12, 72, 432, 2,592, 15,552; *Sample answer:* The ones digits are all 2.

Answers

5. 4,096, 1,024, 256, 64, 16, 4; *Sample answer:* The numbers are multiples of 4.

6. 100, 91, 82, 73, 64, 55; *Sample answer:* The numbers show an even odd pattern.

7. 4, 12, 36, 108, 324, 972; *Sample answer:* The numbers are multiples of 4.

8. 25, 35, 45, 55, 65, 75; *Sample answer:* The numbers are multiples of 5.

9. 70, 63, 56, 49, 42, 35; *Sample answer:* The numbers are multiples of 7.

10. 6, 12, 24, 48, 96, 192; *Sample answer:* The numbers are multiples of 6.

11. *Sample answer:* 1, 7, 49, 343

12. *Sample answer:* 100, 90, 80, 70

13. *Sample answer:* 10, 15, 20, 25

14. *Sample answer:* 200, 100, 50, 25

15. *Sample answer:* 3, 12, 48, 192

16. *Sample answer:* 9, 18, 27, 36

17. 5, 10, 15, 20, 25, 30, 35, 40, 45, 50; *Sample answer:* The digits in the ones place are either 0 or 5; The digits in the tens place are the same two times, then increase by 1; yes

18. 10 times

19. 385 students

6.5 Reteach

1. 8, 12, 16, 20, 24, 28; *Sample answer:* The numbers are multiples of 4.

2. 100, 90, 80, 70, 60, 50; *Sample answer:* The ones digits are all 0.

6.5 Enrichment and Extension

1. Divide by 3, then add 3.

2. Multiply by 2, then add 1.

3. Multiply by 2, then subtract 5.

4. Subtract 3, then multiply by 3.

5. Add 5, then multiply by 2.

6. Divide by 2, then add 2.

6.6 Daily Skills Practice

1. 9 R 1

6.6 Vocabulary Practice

1. *Sample answer:* a whole number greater than 1 with more than two factors; 24

6.6 Prerequisite Skills Practice

1. 14, 21, 28, 35, 42, 49; *Sample answer:* The numbers are multiples of 7.

2. 2, 6, 18, 54, 162, 486; *Sample answer:* The numbers are even.

6.6 Extra Practice

1. ; triangle

2. ; circle

3. ; add

4. ; circle

5. The dot pattern is adding 3 to each figure; 360 dots

6. The dot pattern is adding 5 to each figure; 250 dots

7. no; You use 4 shapes (2 are the stars), so 50 stars. Your friend uses 5 shapes (2 are the stars), so 40 stars.

8.

The number of squares in the bottom row is 2 times the figure number.

9. 10 fish   10. 11 times

6.6 Reteach

1. ; triangle

2. The dot pattern is adding 5 to each figure; 200 dots.

6.6 Enrichment and Extension

1. Newton is correct but Descartes is not; *Sample answer:* $75 \div 4 = 18$ R 3, so the 75th shape is a triangle. $80 \div 4 = 20$, so the 80th shape is a trapezoid.

2. Both are correct; *Sample answer:* $100 \div 5 = 20$, so the 100th shape is a heart. $112 \div 5 = 22$ R 2, so the 112th shape is a star.

3. Neither is correct. *Sample answer:* $82 \div 5 = 16$ R 2, so the 82nd shape is an oval. $135 \div 5 = 27$, so the 135th shape is a parallelogram.

4. *Sample answer:* heart, triangle, star, circle

5. *Sample answer:* oval, star, heart

Answers

Chapter 7

7.1 Daily Skills Practice
1. 5,742

7.1 Vocabulary Practice
1. *Sample answer:* tells how numbers or shapes in a pattern are related; Rule: Add 5; 5, 10, 15, 20…

7.1 Prerequisite Skills Practice
1. $\frac{1}{3}$ 2. $\frac{4}{8}$

7.1 Extra Practice
1. *Sample answer:* $\frac{4}{12}$

2. *Sample answer:* $\frac{6}{8}$

3. *Sample answer:* $\frac{4}{6}$

4. *Sample answer:* $\frac{2}{4}$

5. *Sample answer:* $\frac{3}{4}$

6. *Sample answer:* $\frac{1}{3}$

7. *Sample answer:* $\frac{4}{10}$

8. *Sample answer:* $\frac{2}{8}$

9. 4   10. 3   11. 6   12. 3

13. the second circle representing $\frac{1}{2}$; $\frac{3}{4} = \frac{9}{12} = \frac{6}{8}$

14. yes

7.1 Reteach
1. *Sample answer:* $\frac{4}{6}$ 2. $\frac{2}{8}$

7.1 Enrichment and Extension
1. yes; $\frac{4}{6} = \frac{2}{3} = \frac{8}{12}$

2. no; $\frac{5}{10} = \frac{1}{2}$, but does not equal $\frac{3}{5}$.

7.2 Daily Skills Practice
1. yes

7.2 Vocabulary Practice
1. *Sample answer:* having the same value; $1 = \frac{4}{4}$

7.2 Prerequisite Skills Practice
1. *Sample answer:* $\frac{8}{10}$

2. *Sample answer:* $\frac{4}{6}$

7.2 Extra Practice
1. *Sample answer:* $\frac{2}{2}$; $\frac{2}{8}$

2. *Sample answer:* $\frac{2}{2}$; $\frac{12}{10}$

3. 4   4. 8

5. 10   6. 60

7. *Sample answer:* $\frac{4}{20}$ 8. *Sample answer:* $\frac{12}{6}$

9. *Sample answer:* $\frac{8}{16}$ 10. *Sample answer:* $\frac{4}{4}$, $\frac{6}{6}$

11. *Sample answer:* $\frac{18}{12}$, $\frac{27}{18}$

12. *Sample answer:* $\frac{6}{8}$, $\frac{9}{12}$

13. $\frac{8}{10}$ 14. yes; $\frac{3}{6} = \frac{4}{8}$

15. $\frac{4}{4}$ 16. $\frac{9}{12}$

7.2 Reteach
1. *Sample answer:* $\frac{2}{2}$; $\frac{2}{4}$

2. *Sample answer:* $\frac{2}{2}$; $\frac{8}{6}$

3. 2   4. 12

7.2 Enrichment and Extension
1. $\frac{6}{8}$ teaspoon of ginger; $\frac{4}{8}$ teaspoon of nutmeg; more ginger

2. $\frac{10}{12}$ of the cheese pizza; $\frac{8}{12}$ of the vegetarian pizza; you

3. $\frac{70}{100}$ of a dollar (Newton); $\frac{80}{100}$ of a dollar (Descartes); Descartes

7.3 Daily Skills Practice
1. a. and d.

Answers

7.3 Vocabulary Practice

1. *Sample answer:* two or more fractions that name the same part of a whole; $\frac{2}{3} = \frac{4}{6}$

7.3 Prerequisite Skills Practice

1. *Sample answer:* $\frac{2}{2}$; $\frac{4}{6}$

2. *Sample answer:* $\frac{2}{2}$; $\frac{18}{8}$

7.3 Extra Practice

1. *Sample answer:* $\frac{2}{2}$; $\frac{2}{3}$

2. *Sample answer:* $\frac{3}{3}$; $\frac{4}{3}$

3. 4   4. 3   5. 7   6. 6

7. *Sample answer:* $\frac{2}{5}$ 8. *Sample answer:* $\frac{3}{4}$

9. *Sample answer:* $\frac{4}{6}$ 10. *Sample answer:* $\frac{4}{4}$

11. *Sample answer:* $\frac{10}{2}$

12. *Sample answer:* $\frac{3}{6}$, $\frac{1}{2}$

13. *Sample answer:* $\frac{6}{3}$, $\frac{2}{1}$

14. *Sample answer:* $\frac{10}{8}$, $\frac{5}{4}$

15. *Sample answer:* You can find an equivalent fraction by dividing the numerator and the denominator by a common factor.

16. Divide each numerator and denominator by 2; $\frac{600}{10}$, $\frac{300}{5}$

17. $\frac{8}{10}$ 18. $\frac{7}{8}$

7.3 Reteach

1. *Sample answer:* $\frac{2}{2}$; $\frac{2}{4}$

2. *Sample answer:* $\frac{2}{2}$; $\frac{5}{1}$

3. 6   4. 4   5. 3

7.3 Enrichment and Extension

1. $\frac{3}{10}$ 2. $\frac{12}{10}$ 3. $\frac{3}{5}$ 4. $\frac{7}{5}$

7.4 Daily Skills Practice

1. 8,232

7.4 Vocabulary Practice

1. *Sample answer:* a factor that is shared by two or more given numbers; 1 and 3 are common factors of 9 and 15.

7.4 Prerequisite Skills Practice

1. *Sample answer:* $\frac{2}{2}$; $\frac{2}{8}$

2. *Sample answer:* $\frac{5}{5}$; $\frac{3}{1}$

7.4 Extra Practice

1. >   2. <   3. <   4. <

5. <   6. =   7. >   8. >

9. >   10. >   11. >   12. =

13. tan kittens

14. *Sample answer:* $\frac{3}{3}$

15. *Sample answer:* $\frac{1}{3}$

16. *Sample answer:* $\frac{8}{10}$

17. $\frac{3}{4} < \frac{11}{12}$ and $\frac{1}{5} < \frac{5}{12}$

18. no; *Sample answer:* You have enough blueberries $\left(\frac{5}{6} > \frac{5}{8}\right)$ but not enough raspberries $\left(\frac{2}{3} > \frac{5}{4}\right)$.

19. Newton will pay $1. Descartes will pay $1.25.

7.4 Reteach

1. <   2. =   3. >

7.4 Enrichment and Extension

1. Newton will pay $1.25. Descartes will pay 75¢.

2. $1.50   3. $2.25

7.5 Daily Skills Practice

1. 9

7.5 Vocabulary Practice

1. *Sample answer:* a commonly used number that you can use to compare other numbers; $\frac{1}{2}$

Answers

7.5 Prerequisite Skills Practice
1. < **2.** >

7.5 Extra Practice
1. > **2.** < **3.** < **4.** <

5. < **6.** > **7.** > **8.** >

9. = **10.** < **11.** < **12.** >

13. = **14.** < **15.** >

16. *Sample answer:* like denominators: $\frac{4}{6} > \frac{1}{6}$; like numerators: $\frac{2}{3} > \frac{2}{12}$

17. $\frac{1}{3}$-inch cork stopper; *Sample answer:*

$\frac{1}{3} < \frac{5}{8}$ and $\frac{3}{4} > \frac{5}{8}$

18. $\frac{10}{12}, \frac{5}{8}, \frac{2}{4}$

7.5 Reteach
1. < **2.** > **3.** >

7.5 Enrichment and Extension
1. $\frac{2}{3}, \frac{5}{6}, \frac{4}{4}, \frac{6}{5}, \frac{3}{2}$

2. $\frac{6}{3}, \frac{3}{2}, \frac{3}{4}, \frac{7}{12}, \frac{1}{8}$